Palmyra and Its Empire

Palmyra and Its Empire

Zenobia's Revolt against Rome

RICHARD STONEMAN

Ann Arbor

THE UNIVERSITY OF MICHIGAN PRESS

First paperback edition 1994
Copyright © by the University of Michigan 1992
All rights reserved
Published in the United States of America by
The University of Michigan Press
Printed and bound by CPI Group (UK) Ltd, Croydon, CR0 4YY

2008   2007   2006   2005   8   7   6   5

A CIP catalogue record for this book is available from the British Library.

Library of Congress Cataloging-in-Publication Data

Stoneman, Richard.
    Palmyra and its empire : Zenobia's revolt against Rome / Richard
Stoneman.
        p.   cm.
    Includes bibliographical references (p. 225–238).
    ISBN 978-0-472-10387-4 - ISBN 978-0-472-08315-2 (pbk:
    alk. paper)
        1. Tadmur (Syria)—History. 2. Zenobia, Queen of Palmyra.
    3. Rome—History—Aurelian, 270–275.   I. Title.
    DS99.P17S86   1992
    939'.43—dc20   92-2915
                                                                          CIP

To Andrew Goodson

Preface

Ancient history is in danger of becoming a closed shop. The classical world is still with us, and the problems its inhabitants had to face are not irrelevant to our own. But the pressure of ancient history as an academic discipline drives its practitioners to the amassing of data and the publication of specialized studies that, on the whole, are read only by other professional historians. Sometimes, perhaps, the profession forgets the purpose it is there to serve, the enhancement of understanding among the wider public with an interest in the ancient world. This is the excuse that I, as a nonprofessional historian, offer for this attempt to present to a wider public an exciting and important episode in the decline of the Roman Empire.

The figure of Zenobia of Palmyra has a number of obvious resonances in our own world. Her story introduces the figure of an Arab, and a woman, pitted against the Western world. She and her city of Palmyra have frequently attracted the attention of lovers of the ancient world, from Gibbon onwards; yet she has generally been very badly served by her historians. The sources are exiguous and difficult, and many of those who have written about her, in antiquity and modern times, have not resisted the temptation to bolster fact with invention. Despite the importance and attraction of the subject, there has never been a good serious book about Zenobia and Palmyra.

It has been my purpose to avoid fiction and to describe as far as possible what, owing to the researches and labors of professional historians and archaeologists, can be known about the history and the fall of Palmyra. I have tried to be aware of all the relevant historical issues and to be judicious in interpretation, however much I climb upon the shoulders of others. And yet I have not altogether eschewed the fictional. Because our world is the heir of the Roman world, the reception of Roman history through the centuries is part of Roman history. Every age makes its own interpretation, which not only illuminates its own concerns but draws a veil of distortion across the facts. In order to lighten the density of that veil, I have tried to shed some light behind it by drawing attention to the particularities of the interpretations that earlier students laid upon it. Those students range from the author of the *Historia Augusta*, and later Roman and Greek chroniclers, through poets like Chaucer and historians like Edward Gibbon, to nineteenth- and twentieth-century novelists. While quotations from such writers have their own justification as local color, there is also a serious historical purpose in my inclusion of their bizarreries and foibles. They not only deepen the resonance of the historical Palmyra and Zenobia but remind us of the relative nature of the interpretations we ourselves lay upon the past.

My fascination with Palmyra began with those haunting funerary portraits, first met in the museums of London and Vienna, and pursued through museums in Copenhagen, Toronto, New Haven, and eventually Damascus and Palmyra itself. I have tried to envisage a context in which those proud and magnificent people could have acted out their head-on collision with the Roman Empire and gone down defeated but unchastened.

This book has been researched and written in the short periods left free by a busy job in publishing. Memorable weekends of sustained concentration took place in locations as diverse as a hotel in Vancouver and a hall of residence in St. Andrews, in addition to longer stints in the peace of Devon or the comforts of home. I owe thanks to my wife and my children for forbearance over the long hours I spent in my study.

I am especially grateful to the following individuals and organizations.

The London Library and the Institute of Classical Studies, whose liberal allowances in borrowing enabled nearly all the necessary reading to be done at home out of hours

The Ashmolean and Bodleian Libraries in Oxford for their unrivaled resources

Dr. Afif Bahnassi of the Damascus Museum, for supporting my visa application at a time of political tension between Britain and Syria

Jasmin Tours of Cookham, Berks for allowing me to divert the course of a two-week coach tour in March 1988 to visit, in addition to its excellent regular itinerary, the site of Zenobia/ Halabiyye

Harvard University Press for permission to reproduce extracts from the Historia Augusta, Pliny, Strabo, and Herodian

Byzantina Australiensia for permission to reproduce extracts from R. T. Ridley's translation of Zosimus

Andrew Goodson for coming too, for speaking fluent Arabic, and for ensuring that the guide kept the map the right way up

History Today for publishing an exploratory article on some themes from the book in December 1988

Professor David Graf for generous and plentiful help with bibliography and offprints and for support over a period of years

Several anonymous readers of the manuscript for improving accuracy of detail and interpretation

Ellen Bauerle for including the book in a classical list growing with impressive speed and distinction

You who read it

Contents

Abbreviations XIII

Introduction: Approaching Zenobia   1

1.   The Syrian Scene   15

2.   Of Spices, Silk, and Camels   31

3.   Of Temples, Tribes, and Taxes   51

4.   Between Persia and Rome   81

5.   Zenobia: The Warrior Queen   111

6.   Of Philosophers, Oracles, and Bishops   129

7.   Revolt in the Desert   155

8.   A Villa in Tivoli   181

Appendix: Zenobia in Modern Times   197

Chronology   201

Notes   207

Bibliography   225

Index   239

Plates   247

Abbreviations

AAS	*Annales Archéologiques de Syrie*
ADAJ	*Annual Department of Antiquities of Jordan*
AJA	*American Journal of Archaeology*
ANRW	*Aufstieg und Niedergang der römischen Welt.* Ed. H. Temporini and W. Haase. Berlin.
AntClass	*Antiquité Classique*
BASOR	*Bulletin of the American Schools of Oriental Research*
BASP	*Bulletin of the American Society of Papyrologists*
CAH	*Cambridge Ancient History*
CQ	*Classical Quarterly*
ChrEg	*Chronique d'Egypte*
ClPhil	*Classical Philology*
DOP	*Dumbarton Oaks Papers*
HSCP	*Harvard Studies in Classical Philology*
JJS	*Journal of Jewish Studies*
JNES	*Journal of Near Eastern Studies*
JRS	*Journal of Roman Studies*
JRAS	*Journal of the Royal Asiatic Society*
JThS	*Journal of Theological Studies*
MEFR	*Mélanges d'Archéologie et d'Histoire de l'Ecole Française à Rome*
NumChron	*Numismatic Chronicle*
POxy	*Papyri Oxyrhynchienses*
SVF	*Stoicomm Vetemm Fragmenta*
TAPA	*Transactions of the American Philological Association*
YCS	*Yale Classical Studies*
ZDMG	*Zeitschrift der deutschen morgenländischen Gesellschaft*
ZPE	*Zeitschrift für Papyrologie und Epigraphik*

Introduction: Approaching Zenobia

'Tis great Zenobia, Tadmor's glorious queen.
Beauty hath oft put War's dread helmet on,
Since her who ruled earth-conquering Babylon;
Yet not Semiramis, who boasts her bays
Nor Gaul's bold maid, who graced these later days,
Swayed the rough hearts of men with wilder power,
Or met more bravely battle's dreadful hour,
Than she on whom pleased fame and fortune smiled,
The dark-haired mistress of the Syrian wild.[1]

These lines of the Cornish poet Nicholas Michell (1807–80) encapsulate a century's response to Zenobia, queen of Palmyra, who rose in A.D. 272 against the Roman Empire and nearly split it in two. Her failure is no disgrace, for the attempt is inseparable from the remarkable reconstruction of the Roman central power under her opponent Aurelian. The period is not much studied nowadays, and Zenobia is perhaps hardly a household name. Yet her story has much to commend it to modern attention. It is the story of a woman who rose to supreme power among a people—the Arabs—with whom one would now hardly associate ready opportunities for women to feature in public life. It is the story of a powerful but limited realm, whose wealth was based on just one resource—the silk trade—and which found itself squeezed between, and perhaps overtaxed by the effort to hold the balance between, the two superpowers of the empires of Persia and Rome. The story is entwined with the religious ferment of the third century, when the old gods of Rome seemed to be waning in their appeal to the educated and the powerful, who cast about in the East for a more powerful faith to unite the hearts of an empire. (The Persian emperor was contemporaneously engaged on a precisely similar task.) This episode, rightly understood, takes us to the heart of the crisis of the Roman Empire in the third century A.D. and is crucial to the change of the Roman Empire from a pagan dominion with its hub in the city of Rome to a Christian world state.

Zenobia was born in Palmyra, probably about A.D. 241, the daughter of Julius Aurelius Zenobios, or Zabdilas, who was one of the two duoviri or strategoi (generals) of the city of Palmyra in 242/3.[2] Though Palmyra had been a part of the Roman Empire for some two centuries or more, its people were of mixed Aramaic and Arabic stock, and the languages they used were Palmyrene, a form of the universal Aramaic of the Middle East, and Greek. Zenobia is the form of the name used by Latin and Greek historians; the Aramaic form is Bat-Zabbai, daughter of Zabba, and to Arabic writers she is known as al-Zabba'. Despite these clear signs of Semitic descent, Zenobia claimed descent from Antiochus IV Epiphanes, king of Syria in 175–164 B.C., and son-in-law of Ptolemy VI of Egypt.

Her rise to political importance was a result of her marriage to the senator and self-proclaimed king of Palmyra, the widower Septimius Odenathus, 'Udainat in the Arabic form. Odenathus had proved himself a valuable ally of the Roman emperor by suppressing the revolt of two pretenders in the reign of Gallienus, and he was regarded as savior of the East when in the 260s he repulsed the Persian invaders of Syria and pursued them as far as their own capital of Ctesiphon. Soon after this (267) he was murdered, along with his son by his first marriage, probably in a dynastic quarrel. His son by Zenobia, Vaballathus (Aramaic Wahballath), who was probably still in his teens, became king of Palmyra.

Gallienus seems to have been less than keen to renew the titles and honors of Odenathus arrogated by the new young king. As regent the king's mother, Zenobia, most certainly stood behind him. In late 269 she launched an invasion of Egypt, the northern part of the Arab peninsula, and Palestine, and she also penetrated into Asia Minor as far as Ancyra. Gallienus had been murdered in 268, and his successor Claudius was quick to launch a counterattack against Egypt under his general Tenagino Probus. But in the course of these months Claudius died, and after a short interregnum he was succeeded by Aurelian. Simultaneously the captured mints of Alexandria and Antioch began to produce coins honoring Wahballath and Aurelian as equal emperors of east and west, and in 271 Zenobia herself appears on the coins with Wahballath, while Aurelian is left off.

Coinage was the traditional way for a claimant to imperial power to state and legitimate his claim. There could be no clearer statement that Zenobia had set herself up in direct opposition to Rome, with far greater forces and wider support than any previous ruler of an eastern principality. Squeezed between Rome and Persia, the Levantine provinces could see advantages in a ruler from their own peoples, based in their own lands, who could protect them more effectively than the emperor of distant Rome, who as often as not was engaged on the Rhine and Danube in wars against the northern barbarians. Aurelian however was not to be trifled with. He was a tough Illyrian soldier, and lost no time in crushing Zenobia's revolt, reclaiming Asia Minor with hardly a struggle and besieging Palmyra until the city succumbed.

The conflict of Zenobia and Aurelian brings two of the most vivid personalities of the age face-to-face, locked in a combat that had to end either in the destruction of Palmyra or in a split down the middle of the Roman Empire. Palmyra, though not large, was one of the richest cities of the empire as a result of its control of the caravan trade in silk from the distant East. Over the centuries it had been adorned with some of the finest Roman Imperial architecture to be seen anywhere, as well as developing a distinctive style of portrait sculpture in its funerary memorials, which present to us today a vivid gallery of fine-featured, haughty, sometimes otherworldly faces of people who, one feels, would have no qualms about entertaining imperial claims. Zenobia had established her power base with the Palmyrene armies and perhaps with some disaffected Roman soldiers from the legions attached by Gallienus to Odenathus. She had surrounded herself with intellectuals, notably the orator Longinus, to give glamour and resonance to her court, and she had played on the religious affiliations of the peoples of Syria to unite them on her side.

Third-century Syria was a melting pot of religions (see chapter 6). The traditional pagan cults continued side by side with monotheistic religions, perhaps the most widespread of which was the worship of the sun. Jews could be found everywhere in the Near East, and they were established at Palmyra as well as at the frontier post of Dura-Europus on the Euphrates (destroyed by the Persians in 256). Zenobia's revolt coincided with the retirement of St. Antony to the Egyptian desert (another form of rejection of Roman secular power), and in Syria too the Christian communities and the settlements of anchorites were on the increase. Christian doctrine was hotly debated, and the factions were numerous and deeply divided. Unreliable suggestions that Zenobia was a Jewish proselyte, or a crypto-Christian, also underline the importance of religious support for her rule.

Aurelian by contrast had no intellectual claims. He was a soldier, with a reputation for keeping regimental discipline by acts of remarkable cruelty. He reimposed an iron hand on the disaffected provinces—not only Syria but the Gallic Empire too—and imposed his authority by dramatically changing the self-representation of the imperial person, anticipating the jeweled and haughty remoteness of Diocletian. One important element of his reforms was the introduction of the religion of the sun to Rome. He celebrated his conquest of Palmyra by bringing back its statues of the sun-god and placing them in a new temple in Rome. Solar imagery had been important to earlier emperors too, and in his early years Constantine was also a devotee of the sun. Aurelian's introduction of sun-cult can be seen as an anticipation of Constantine's later and more successful attempt to unite the empire under a single head by giving it a single god.

Sources that add a possible love interest to Zenobia's correspondence with Aurelian go beyond the evidence, indeed beyond what is likely, but the confrontation of these two powerful rulers is bound to evoke memories of the plans of Antony and Cleopatra to create a single empire between them. Zenobia is credited with having said to Aurelian on their first meeting, "I desired to become a partner in the royal power, should the supply of lands permit,"[3] and with having compared herself to Cleopatra in a letter she wrote to him during the siege of Palmyra.[4] If such plans, if they existed, had been realized, the development of the Roman Empire would have been utterly different, and so would our own history. Therein lies the importance of the revolt of Zenobia, a critical moment in the history of the Western world. Its importance was dramatized in ancient and later writers by the glamour they attributed to the queen herself, a beautiful but ferocious warrior queen, whose oriental ways could both fascinate and cause the West to tremble.

We have been taught by recent studies of Orientalism to be suspicious of our own romanticization of the gorgeous East, which we inherit from our Victorian forebears and from those who, like T. E. Lawrence, made the desert a conspicuous stage for their own glory. Yet modern novelistic writers have found in Zenobia a theme as rich as any that graced Hollywood. The heroine of Alexander Baron's novel *Queen of the East*, Zenobia, a sensual and cunning oriental beauty pitted against the hard and ruthless Emperor Aurelian, is a match for Cleopatra on any terms. Whether she bears any relation to the historical Zenobia is another question. The temptation to fill the gaps in our historical knowledge with fiction is one that has not always been resisted.

The limitations of our sources add an extra spice to the study. The history of Zenobia neatly exemplifies Edward Gibbon's dictum,

> Every man of genius who writes history infuses into it, perhaps unconsciously, the character of his own spirit. His characters, despite their extensive variety of passion and situation, seem to have only one manner of thinking and feeling, and that is the manner of the author.

Perhaps this trait is not confined to geniuses. The image of Zenobia varies extravagantly according to the hand that writes of her—from a shameless virago to a paragon of beauty and valor, from a model of chastity to a tyrant, from a Christian (nearly) to a debauchee. Part of Zenobia's history is the history of her reception by later writers. Thus the romantic, the fanciful, and even the absurd will not be excluded from the delineation of our composite portrait—though I have no doubt that my own vision will emerge from the pages that follow, as unconsciously as that of Gibbon's genius.

Dazzled by Zenobia's reputation, Gibbon wrote, fairly enough, "Palmyra for a while stood forth the rival of Rome: but the competition was fatal, and ages of prosperity were sacrificed to a moment of glory." For him, the clash was a military one and the occasion for Aurelian's restoration of the might of empire. In his impetus toward the true moment (as he saw it) of the decline of Rome through the impact of Christianity, he neglected the dramatic changes in the emperor's role, which later researchers have enabled us to lay firmly at the door of Aurelian as much as at that of his successor Diocletian.

Gibbon's paean to the queen is a famous purple passage of his history,

> If we except the doubtful achievements of Semiramis, Zenobia is perhaps the only female whose superior genius broke through the servile indolence imposed on her sex by the climate and manners of Asia. She claimed her descent from the Macedonian kings of Egypt, equalled in beauty her ancestor Cleopatra, and far surpassed that princess in chastity and valour. Zenobia was esteemed the most lovely as well as the most heroic of her sex. She was of dark complexion (for in speaking of a lady these trifles become important). Her teeth were of a pearly whiteness, and her large black eyes sparkled with uncommon fire, tempered by the most attractive

sweetness. Her voice was strong and harmonious. Her manly under-standing was strengthened and adorned by study. She was not ignorant of the Latin tongue, but possessed in equal perfection the Greek, the Syriac, and the Egyptian languages. She had drawn up for her own use an epitome of oriental history, and familiarly compared the beauties of Homer and Plato under the tuition of the sublime Longinus.

This accomplished woman gave her hand to Odaenathus, who from a private station raised himself to the dominion of the East. She soon became the friend and companion of a hero. In the inter-vals of war, Odaenathus passionately delighted in the exercise of hunting; he pursued with ardour the wild beasts of the desert, lions, panthers, and bears; and the ardour of Zenobia in that dangerous amusement was not inferior to his own. She had inured her con-stitution to fatigue, disdained the use of a covered carriage, gen-erally appeared on horseback in a military habit, and sometimes marched several miles on foot at the head of the troops.[5]

The details of this glamorous and hardy bluestocking are taken one and all from the fullest antique source, the *Historia Augusta*. But the author of the section therein on the *Thirty Pretenders*, or *Thirty Tyrants*, makes no such favorable construction of the whole. In fact he begins,

> Now all shame is exhausted, for in the weakened state of the com-monwealth things came to such a pass that, while Gallienus con-ducted himself in the most evil fashion, even women ruled most excellently.... She held the imperial power in the name of her sons Herennianus and Timolaus, ruling longer than could be endured from one of the female sex.[6]

A loyal Roman writer could hardly regard Zenobia as other than an ogress, however much he acknowledged her virtues. It was reserved for the age of Victoria in Britain to extend her fame. In fact it is only in the reign of Britain's own empress queen that Zenobia of Palmyra became an object of literary veneration. Perhaps there was a piquancy to be found in the memory of that queen on whose oriental empire the sun had set all too rapidly, as well as a muted parallel between the chaste queen and the virtuous Victoria.

It was in the age of Byron rather than that of Victoria that the reputation of Zenobia received its most startling modern instantiation.

On 20 March 1813, Lady Hester Stanhope, the niece of William Pitt, having forsaken hopes of love and marriage at home and repaired to the exotic East, set forth from Damascus to Palmyra, was received there with astonishing pageantry laid on by the Emir, and was actually hailed as the queen of the Arabs by the assembled crowd. No longer a female emperor, the queen of Palmyra had become a female Byron.

Though Lady Hester was the first European woman to visit Palmyra, visiting Palmyra was not in itself a new thing. Pietro della Valle the Italian traveler (1616–25) had been there, as had Jean-Baptiste Tavernier on the way to Persia in 1638. Swedish and German explorers had also noted its ruins. The city had been discovered for the English-speaking world by a group of merchants of the Aleppo Company in 1678. The first scholarly treatment of Palmyra, Abednego Seller's book of 1705, was illustrated by engravings of views prepared by those English merchants. But the climactic moment of discovery was the expedition of Robert Wood and James Dawkins in 1751, which resulted in the publication of their magnificent folio volume of architectural details, templates for a new classicism in architecture as important as the Athenian books of James Stuart and Nicholas Revett.[7]

Wood and Dawkins had exhibited no interest in the figure of the queen or in any historical circumstances. It was characteristic of the last decades of the nineteenth century to travel to distant places seeking confirmation of the great traditions of history, whether biblical or classical. William Wright, who published a fine study, *Palmyra and Zenobia*, in 1895, was quite clear about what he went for.

> An important item in my Palmyra programme was to find the statue of Zenobia. I set about the work with earnest deliberation, first going up on a ladder to the bracket on which the statue had been placed, and reading carefully the inscription in Greek and Palmyrene. Then we began to overturn the accumulation of sand at the base of the column where the statue must have fallen. To encourage the workers, I offered a *beshlik* for the discovery of a head. The head of Zenobia for five piasters, equal to one franc! And how the descendants of the proud Tadmorenes delved in the debris of the beautiful city for the head of the illustrious queen that once ruled the East, and set at defiance the Romans![8]

Naturally enough it was not long before a head was found. In fact, within a few minutes, two heads were found. "There are circumstances,"

Wright reflects in a chastened mood, "under which one may have too much of a good thing. The second discovery rendered the identification of the first with Zenobia doubtful."

Of course there was absolutely no evidence to support the identification of either head with the queen. The quest for history in stones was a worthy one, but not to be fulfilled in this manner.

The Sources

Responsible reconstruction begins from the sources. They are of two main kinds: literary (which have been known to all ages) and archaeological (which have largely become available only in the last two centuries). By its nature interpretation goes beyond the sources; but in this case the sources need to be approached with particular circumspection. We have no continuous and detailed source, such as those Thucydides or Tacitus, with all their hidden biases, offer for their own periods. Two historians who wrote the history of their own times in the second half of the third century, Ephorus and Dexippus, are lost.[9] The latter, from the fragments that are preserved, seems to have come closest to the Thucydidean approach.

The most reliable of the ancient accounts is the Greek history of Zosimus, who wrote a history of the Roman Empire from Augustus to A.D. 410. It was completed in the early sixth century. We know almost nothing of his life. The history concentrated very heavily on the later centuries. The first three centuries are summarized in book 1 only a few chapters of which deal with our decade. His interpretative line is clear: he regards the fall of the Roman Empire as the result of the abandonment of the pagan gods in favor of Christianity—not an uncommon view even a century earlier, for Augustine devotes many books of his *City of God* to combating this view. The fifth-century Christian writer Orosius, who devotes a few useful paragraphs to our subject, takes an exactly opposite line: all the disasters of the third century were the result of the emperors' refusal to embrace Christianity.

Zosimus' brief outline usually corroborates the sequence of events in the *Historia Augusta*, with a few exceptions (the Battle of Immae and the death of Zenobia). This extensive work poses particular problems. It purports to be a collection of brief accounts of the reigns of every emperor of Rome from Hadrian to Numerian, written by the hands of six historians whose names are otherwise unknown to history. The method is Suetonius', narrative combined with character assessment. These are lives not history, by the author's explicit avowal. Biography allowed the gathering of odd details, unlike the stern annalism or political concern of history: *curiositas nil recusat*.[10]

The exhaustive labors of Sir Ronald Syme have conclusively demonstrated that the work is all by a single hand and was written in the reign of Theodosius, after A.D. 395.[11] The proofs of "imposture" (as Syme calls it) are manifold: forged documents, bogus persons, along with the predilection of unique invented names and curious fables. A joke in the preface to the *Life of Aurelian* gives the game away. The setting is a carnival, during which mumming and masked personae were abundant; the pretended author of this *Life*, Flavius Vopiscus, is encouraged in his task by the prefect of the city with the remark "Write as you please. You will have for companions in mendacity those whom we admire as paragons of historical eloquence."

The proofs of single authorship are equally clear. The "authors" refer to each other's already completed works, and one, in an unguarded moment, refers to his own earlier researches in a section that appears under the name of another. The interests and quirks of the single author—his love of pageantry and of catalogs of curiosities—are consistent. His range of literary reference is constant. He shares with his contemporary, the cookery writer Apicius, a curious obsession with ostriches as articles of diet.[12] Verisimilitude is carried to an extreme in the preamble to the *Life of Aurelian*, but it is ruined by the writer's inadequate research on the date of the festival he refers to.[13]

It is curious why the author chose to write in this way. An argument put forward by Norman Baynes was that, writing in the fifth century, the author could not afford to utter openly the kind of criticism of Christianity that may be found in the *Historia Augusta*. The senatorial pagan opinions of the author were concealed by this multiple pseudonymity. A more recent approach, that of Syme,[14] draws attention to the similar fraudulent works of the fourth and fifth centuries: scholiasts whose erudition is bogus, the *Origo Gentis Romanae*, the correspondence of St. Paul and Seneca, and Dictys the Cretan's diaries of the Trojan War. Our author plays with history, scholarship, Christianity, and all sorts of miscellaneous data. In Syme's words he is "clever, but sly and silly . . . a collector with an untidy mind."[15]

All that is true, and the description betrays the modern historian's passion for truth and caution. His ideal is not however one that would have been recognized by ancient historians, even Thucydides.[16] If an ancient author set out to write an account of a subject, he did not stop at the limits of his data but tried to produce a rounded treatment. When Hesiod offered an account of the genealogy of the gods, he did so neither (obviously) as a careful researcher of objective fact nor in the spirit of a forger or impostor. His aim was to construct a system from an assortment of scattered, fragmentary, conflicting, and uncheckable data.[17] The ancient historian, like nature, abhors a vacuum. He is not content to shore fragments against his ruin, a very modern thought. From the wreckage of learning around him, he tried, more or less ineptly, to piece together a story.

When Thucydides inserted speeches in his history, he wrote not what was said, for this he could not know, but what in the circumstances ought to have been said. This, in his immeasurably feebler way, is what the author of the *Historia Augusta* does. This explains the fictional letters of Zenobia to Aurelian, for example, which modern scholars castigate so heavily. His failure is not one of method but of sources and his own incapacity for penetrating thought (though he does have one or two ideas). We must not believe his inventions or even take them seriously as insight. But where he fleshes out a known narrative, there is no real need to doubt his fuller detail. When he had a source, he may have abbreviated that source as often as he added local color.

Two further Latin works deserve mention here: the brief surveys of Roman history by Eutropius (ca. 360) and by Aurelius Victor (after 360). These surveys are so brief that they are unable to offer more than cursory corroboration of the main sources. By their coincidence, however, they do attest the existence of a previous, now unknown, work, which was postulated and dubbed the *Kaisergeschichte* by the German scholar Alex Enmann.[18]

More notable is the work of the twelfth-century Byzantine historian Zonaras, who compiled a history of the world from the creation to his own time. He is important for historians because he preserves in abbreviated form much of the historian Cassius Dio. Dio's history ended in 229, and the source of Zonaras' work on the later third century is uncertain. But he gives important details of chronology and action that are not recorded elsewhere (Odenathus' two campaigns against Persia and the motive of Odenathus' murderer).

Illumination is also gained from that curious work of a Judaeo-Hellenic milieu, the *Sibylline Oracles*. The fourteen books of oracles are of widely differing date, from the early Roman Empire onwards, and reproduce in Greek hexameter verse the characteristic allusive and generalized historical despair that is found in the prophetic books of the Old Testament. There is much unusable material. But in book 8 there is a fairly continuous history of the Roman Empire, composed (ex post facto, naturally) in the form of prophecy. Proper names are studiously avoided—they would spoil the generality of Hebrew prophecy—but in most cases the designations are clear, and several passages add detail to the bare outlines, which, interpreted with caution, can fill out the complexities of the story (see chapters 4 and 7).[19]

A few incidental details are contained in an extraordinary farrago of the sixth century, the *Chronicle* of John Malalas, a citizen of Antioch who wrote a history of the world and of his city, with excursions, which contains a great deal of undifferentiated material of legend and history.[20] Emperors rub shoulders with demons and talismans, and where Malalas adds new detail his chronicle is highly suspect; but his name will crop up from time to time in the following chapters.

The Arabs too have their traditions about Queen Zenobia, assembled in the universal history of al-Tabari (A.D. 839–923) as well as in other sources.[21] These legends are generally irreconcilable with the Latin and Greek accounts. For example, in the Arab account, she dies in the siege of the city of Zenobia by Arab foes, not under Roman arms. It may be that she has become conflated with another queen of similar name. Arab traditions share with Hebrew literature a certain indifference to historical specificity. But they do hint interestingly at what is hidden from our Latin and Greek sources—the political context Zenobia's bid for supremacy met among her Arab neighbors. Recently, inscriptions in the language of the neighboring Nabataeans (an Arab people) have shed further light on the history of the region and on Zenobia's links with her neighbors.[22]

There is, in short, so much that we cannot know. We have no Palmyrene literature—nothing to help us get inside the minds of those who masterminded the revolt against Rome or of those who followed them, those who lived, worked, loved and worshiped among the proud columns of Palmyra. Such fluidity is of the essence of fame. But historians in this century have what the ancients, and even Gibbon, did not—the important data assembled by the patient labors of archaeologists; the columns, the stones, and the inscriptions that have been forced out of their dumbness into speech. A few of these inscriptions were known even to Abednego Seller. But critical method was insufficiently developed to enable them to be used effectively. He was unable, for example, to read Palmyrene.

Many of the inscriptions of Palmyra are bilingual in Greek and

Palmyrene, which is a form of Aramaic and written in an alphabet similar to that of cursive modern Hebrew. Frequently the text in one language will supplement gaps in the other, and since many are dated, they are important to the construction of a chronology of Palmyrene history. They also reveal, occasionally, political affiliations that might not otherwise have been suspected, and cast interesting, if glancing, light on questions of motive.[23]

The coinage is also important. Seller's use of this evidence is wildly patchy and uncritical and shows more vividly than anything with what hard and patient labor the history of this period has been pieced together since coins were properly cataloged and studied, an enterprise that again belongs entirely to this century.

Archaeological Excavations

Palmyra was first excavated by the German and Austrian archaeologist Otto Puchstein in May 1902. In 1912 the Czech Orientalist Alois Musil made an exhaustive study of the region of Palmyra, though his detailed maps were stolen in an attack by bandits. Puchstein's associate Theodor Wiegand resumed work in April 1917 in the thick of the First World War. Wiegand was accompanied by his resonantly named Denkmal-schutzkommandos or Commandos for the Protection of Monuments. At the same time the French Academy of Sciences began the work of compiling the *Corpus of Semitic Inscriptions*, a work that has continued up to the publication of volume 12 in 1975. During the French Mandate, work continued under Henri Seyrig, director of the Service of Antiquities for the French High Commission. The village of Palmyra was moved from the ruins to its present site between 1929 and 1932, thus facilitating fuller excavation of the site. A guide book was produced in 1941, in the midst of war and soon after some intensive fighting in the area.

After Independence in 1946, archaeological work slowly resumed. A Swiss expedition organized by UNESCO was active at Palmyra from 1954 to 1956, concentrating on the Temple of Baalshamin. Since 1959 the Polish, directed by Kazimierz Michalowski and since 1980 by Michal Gawlikowski, have been making the running, with reports appearing regularly from 1960 to 1984.[24] Most of the work has been concentrated on the Camp of Diocletian (and the Valley of Tombs), though some of the reports contain syntheses on more general aspects. Valuable work has also been done by the Syrian archaeologists A. Bounni, N. Saliby,

O. Taha and Kh. As'ad. The excellent care and information provided by the Syrian Directorate of Antiquities and the Archaeological Excavation Service make Palmyra a very rewarding site to work on or to visit.

Every year new discoveries add detail to our picture of Palmyrene society.[25] Much is accessible even to the untrained visitor: the architecture of Palmyra is magnificent, and its portrait art is unique and haunting.[26] The buildings and the tombs bring us close to this proud people, even without their words. The stones help us understand the brief and glorious blaze of Palmyra's empire, even while they chasten us with the inescapable thoughts of decline and fall. If Gibbon had visited Palmyra, might he have found, as he sat among the golden anemones and the thorn bushes, musing under the columns of the tetrapylon while the barefoot mullahs were chanting the call to prayer beside the Temple of Bel, that here was a theme for his pen as great, if inescapably elusive, as the Decline and Fall of Rome?

In fact, even as the last volumes of the last great historical work written before the French Revolution were appearing, Count C. F. C. de Volney was traveling in Syria. Two year after the Revolution, Volney's own great work, *The Ruins, or Meditations on the Revolutions of Empires* (1791), appeared. It was explicitly inspired by his visit to the ruins of Palmyra. The tone of the opening meditation is nearly Gibbonian, though the thirty-four-year-old Volney is a Romantic: the destructive effects of time play for him the role that Gibbon attributed to human belief and political behavior.

> After a walk of three quarters of an hour along these ruins, I entered the enclosure of a vast edifice, which had formerly been a temple dedicated to the sun: and I accepted the hospitality of some poor Arabian peasants, who had established their huts in the very area of the temple. Here I resolved for some days to remain, that I might contemplate, at leisure, the beauty of so many stupendous works. . . . Here, said I to myself, an opulent city once flourished; this was the seat of a powerful empire. . . . And now a mournful skeleton is all that subsists of this opulent city, and nothing remains of its powerful government but a vain and obscure remembrance! To the tumultuous throng which crowded under these porticoes, the solitude of death has succeeded. The silence of the tomb is substituted for the hum of polite places. The opulence of a commerical city is changed into hideous poverty. The palaces of kings

are become the receptacle of deer, and unclean reptiles inhabit the sanctuary of the gods. What glory is here eclipsed, and how many labors are annihilated! Thus perish the works of men, and thus do nations and empires vanish away![27]

The stones of Palmyra have their own meanings, besides the tale of their almost legendary queen. We shall not find the statue of Zenobia. But William Wright's intuition was this far correct. The stones bring the past to life for us; from them we begin, and with them we will end.

1

The Syrian Scene

When, after a wearisome day of marching across the Syrian desert, the long caravans descry, in the pale clarity of the stars, the uniform horizon become a serrated line of uneven colonnades, of broken walls, of half collapsed palace facades; when the sand seems at last to disappear, not beneath the verdure of an oasis but beneath an accumulation of marbles and worked stones, silence falls among the travellers, even the calling cameleers cease from their marching songs, and there is nothing to be heard but the sand which cries beneath our feet, and the wind which moans afar among the ruins, and the lugubrious plaint of a hungry jackal; it is then that a man, even the least civilised, feels himself to be small and, despite himself, meditates on the presence of that mighty ruin as on a mighty sorrow.[1]

So L. Double began his book, now over a hundred years old, on the caesars of Palmyra. The overloaded prose conveys the flavor of many such responses to the massive and extensive ruins of the caravan city of Palmyra, the brief seat of an empire, since its discovery in 1678. The learned response of the architect and the archaeologist was often inclined to be overlaid by a more romantic response. In 1895 Dr. William Wright found arrival by daylight just as moving as Double's nighttime journey: "After the bare mountainous desert, we come gradually on a scene of enchantment, and though we have come expressly to see the scene, it breaks upon us as a surprise."[2]

Even the modern traveler, who arrives by bus rather than after the fatiguing rigors of a camel journey (much of it, no doubt, on foot, owing to the discomfort of the camel saddle), can feel that sense of astonishment as the dun-colored ruins lend a sudden relief to the barren undulations of the equally dun-colored plain. A shimmering surface in the distance, at first taken for a mirage, solidifies itself into the salt pans and briny lake of Tadmor,[3] and the feathered palms that give the

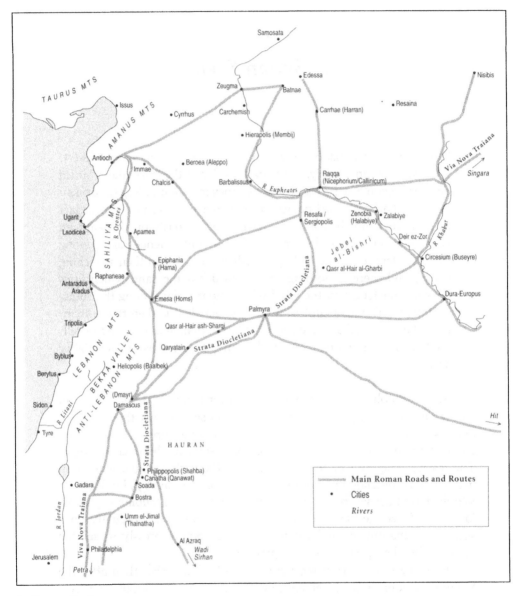

1. Roman Syria

city its classical name darken the ground and focus the eye on those miraculous ruins.

It is little wonder that the legends of the Bedouin have accreted so many wonders around the city. We have it on the authority of the Bible that the city was built by Solomon,[4] though some commentators make that city Tamar, unknown to us but different from Palmyra. Muslim embroidery is only too pleased to make this another of the wondrous achievements of Solomon, while the Antiochene chronicler Malalas even tells us why he chose this site—because it was here that David had killed Goliath. Malalas adds that the Jewish soldiers dwelt there until the city was taken and burned by "Nebuchadnezzar, King of Persia."[5] Other fabulous buildings of Solomon in Near Eastern tradition, besides the legendary Temple at Jerusalem, included his "throne" in far Iran, at Takht-e-Suleiman; the Temple of Jupiter at Baalbek;[6] and his baths, which may still be seen on a mountain ten miles north of Qaryatein.[7] With the aid of jinn who could always be summoned by the power of his magic ring, he built this city as a pleasure palace in the desert for the delectation of the queen of Sheba. The legend perhaps reflects conditions in the eighth-century A.D., when the Umayyads built such pleasure palaces in equally desert places—notably the two to the east and west of Palmyra at Qasr-al-Hair-ash-Sharqi and Qasr-al-Hair-al-Gharbi. The queen of Sheba is not, indeed, irrelevant to our story, but she had little to do with the foundation of Palmyra or the purposes of its first inhabitants.

The ruins of our story were a puzzle to those who lived around them. How much more they mystified the first Western discoverers of this great assemblage of Roman architecture at its artistic crest, so far from Rome and indeed from anywhere at all. Those who had read their Roman history knew the outline of the story that is the subject of this book—the brief florescence of an empire in rebellion against that of Rome, under the sole leadership of the almost legendary Queen Zenobia, and the crushing of the city and the demolishing of its walls by the cruel Emperor Aurelian, whose magnanimity yet allowed its queen to live.

> The Sun of Syria's power went down in might,
> On Freedom's tree there rained a withering blight,
> Glory to proud Palmyra sighed adieu
> And o'er her shrines Destruction's angel flew.
>
> (Nicholas Michell)[8]

The ancient evidence is sparse enough to allow interpretations of all colors, and even scholarly authors have not resisted the temptation to pad out their narratives with fiction. What were Zenobia's aims? To teach Rome a lesson? To rule and become wealthy? To emulate great queens like Semiramis, Nitocris, and Cleopatra, presaging female emancipation? To shift the center of the Roman Empire itself away from Rome, as Elagabalus had done before? To advance the cause of Judaism? All these have at one time or another been seriously advanced as explanations, or partial explanations, for the ambitious conquests of Zenobia. Some of them must inevitably seem less plausible today, but none is without foundation. Our interpretation of the events must begin from the geography, the setting of all human activity. To understand Zenobia, we must start with the hushed plains of the desert across which endless trains of richly burdened camels silently plod with swinging motion.

Roman Syria

Palmyra lies on the eastern margin of the Roman province of Syria. The region has preserved its boundaries with remarkably little alteration until the present day because like the boundaries of Britain or Italy they are firmly determined by geographical factors. This can be a point in its favor for a conquering power; Napoleon described Italy as "simply a geographical expression." But it also means that the region can preserve its most salient characteristics over the passing of centuries, the ebb and flow of population, urbanization, and nomad use.[9] For this reason modern accounts of the Syrian desert and its political and social structures can often illuminate the ancient scene.[10] This is particularly valuable since much of our ancient information on Syria is so scrappy[11] and is often imbued with prejudice and distortion.

Geographically, Syria is bounded to the north by the Taurus and Amanus mountains, which separate it from modern Turkey and the ancient province of Asia. (The Amanus range, with Antioch, is in fact in modern Turkey, but the Syrians have geography on their side in their claim to the area.) The minor barrier of the Jabal al-Sahiliyah (ancient Bargylus) ensures that Syria, despite its important ports at Latakia and Tartus, essentially looks away from the Mediterranean, which in ancient times was Phoenician territory. (The main Phoenician port was Ugarit, modern Ras Shamra, Fennel Cape.) Phoenician influence extended from the coastline into modern Lebanon, which is decisively separated from

Syria by the formidable ranges of the Lebanon and Anti-Lebanon mountains. South of this the Jordan valley forms a barrier to the west, and to the south the volcanic basalt desert of the Hauran merges without sharp distinction into the modern state of Jordan. Less than eighty kilometers from the coast the desert begins. The Hellenistic foundations of Homs (Emesa) and Hama (Epiphania), with the ancient site of Damascus, mark the eastern limit of urbanization. To the southeast the desert extends, wadi and steppe, directly into Arabia. But to the west and northwest Syria is bounded by the third great natural frontier, the river Euphrates, which rises in Turkish Armenia and flows to the Persian Gulf. Beyond is Mesopotamia, the Land between the Rivers. The river now separates Syria from Iraq, and in the first two and a half centuries A.D. it separated Rome from its eastern neighbor, the Parthian Empire, which in the course of our period was supplanted by the empire of the Sassanid Persians.

The Euphrates is one of the great unavoidable facts of Middle Eastern geography. But like many great frontiers, it is also an important means of communication. It offered direct access—by boat or as a route-marker for camel caravans—to the Persian Gulf and the sea routes to the Far East. Because of this a route from the Euphrates to the Mediterranean had to be developed. In the first three centuries of our era, the key to the route across the desert was Palmyra. The caravans would have left the river at Hit or at Dura, crossing the desert to Palmyra and thence to Emesa and the coast, or Antioch. Palmyra itself seems to have been the site of an annual fair, which after its destruction was relocated further north at Batnae.[12]

To the variety of Syria's frontiers correspond a variety of geographical conditions. In the west the mountains are terraced and fertile with olives and even (especially in Lebanon) vines. A springtime carpet of poppies, anemones, and other flowers reminds one that this is essentially a Mediterranean region. East of the Orontes the water runs out. The soil is rich but unwatered. Where irrigation can be achieved crops spring up with speed and in profusion. Though there is good reason to believe that Palmyra and the region around it were more fertile in antiquity than they are now, the region belongs essentially to the desert, which is characterized by a pastoralist economy operated by nomads in a constant interplay with the sedentarized villages and small towns. This is the essential pattern of life in all of Syria east of a line drawn through Homs, Hama, and Aleppo. Because of its distance from these cities, Palmyra still looks more to the East, and in Roman times its importance as a trading station gave it a character different again from the rest of the region to which it geographically belongs.

When Rome conquered Syria in 64 B.C., it acquired a region that, though it had been under Hellenic rule since Alexander's conquest in 332 B.C., and especially since the reorganization by Seleucus Nicator (from 301 B.C.), remained essentially oriental. The foundation of such cities as Apamea, Laodicea, Seleuceia, and Antioch had had a slow, though decisive, impact on the prosperity of the region, their cosmopolitan Greek settlers providing new markets for the rural peasantry's surplus. But the region as a whole was not Greek. The cities had grown and become glamorous and cosmopolitan Greek cities. Besides these, the more southerly cities of Gerasa, Gadara, Berytus, Tyre, Heliopolis-Baalbek, and even Jerusalem boasted such Greek institutions as gymnasia, athletic festivals, and temples of the gods. To the northeast, Edessa, though an independent kingdom, had many of the characteristics of a Greek polis. On the easternmost fringe, one of Seleucus' generals had founded the city of Europus on the site of native Dura, which was largely a garrison post and had acquired no identity as a city when the Romans took over.

The same was true of Palmyra. Though Pompey the Great had annexed the region of Syria to Rome in 64 B.C., it is clear that Palmyra was not in any sense a city at this time. In 41 B.C., when Mark Antony marched through the region to subjugate it more effectively, Palmyra was a village inhabited by the Cedri, who seem to be identifiable with the Kedar of Ezekiel, or the people the Assyrians called Kidri.[13] In the face of attack the citizens retreated in Bedouin fashion, that is, with all their possessions, to the left bank of the Euphrates, leaving nothing to sack.[14] They had not even needed to burn the city; it was no more than a camp. Present-day Kurds behave in just the same way, retreating in the face of invaders to their mountain fastnesses, so that the invaders have to return empty-handed.[15]

Pompey's annexation of Syria established the administrative framework that subsisted until the end of the empire. Judaea was left as a subject (or "client") principality. Such Arab dynasts as Sampsigeramus of Emesa and the Abgars of Edessa were restricted to their localities and left alone on condition of their support for Rome. The major Greek cities (Antioch and Seleuceia) were given autonomy under the supervision of the provincial governor.[16] The province as a whole was liable for land tax and poll tax, which together made up its stipend.

This arrangement continued through the predations of Mark Antony and Crassus and the period of the civil wars. When the provinces were divided in 27 B.C. between princeps and senate, Syria came under the control of a legate of the emperor. For the next hundred years Syria became an increasingly important part of the empire, as the base for such important campaigns as Corbulo's Parthian War (A.D. 55) to secure the position of Armenia. In A.D. 66 the military concentration in Syria was increased with Vespasian's expedition against the insurgents in Judaea. This was the first occasion when the Syrian legions raised a claimant to the imperial throne, and the tough general became emperor, thus reinforcing the truth newly perceived, according to Tacitus, that "an emperor could be made elsewhere than at Rome"[17]— a lesson to be exemplified with terrifying frequency in the third century. In 104 Trajan extended Roman rule south of Arabia into the kingdom of Nabataea, which he annexed, and he subsequently pressed even as far as Ctesiphon in Mesopotamia, though the latter gain, unlike the former, was only temporary.

In western Syria, as in Asia Minor, the culture of the great Greek cities adapted itself comfortably to Roman rule. The governmental structure of the Greek polis adapted itself subtly to its Roman overlords. As a prelude to our investigation of the unique example of Palmyra, it is worth emphasizing the difference between the cities of western Syria and the culture of the East.

Western Syria boasted some of the most distinguished cities of the Greek East. Gadara prided itself as the Athens of the East and had been the home of the poets Philodemus and Antipater in the first century B.C. and Meleager in the first century A.D. Berytus had been founded as a colony of Roman veterans by Agrippa in 15 or 14 B.C. and had developed by the early third century into one of the most important Roman cities of the East, boasting a noted law school that drew pupils from all over the empire; it flourished until well into the sixth century, its distinction only fleetingly marred by scandals involving black magic among the students. Gerasa and the other cities of the Decapolis represented one of the most brilliant concentrations of Roman culture— preserved for us in its architecture—in the Roman East. Gerasa drew its wealth from the transit of caravans from the south. This traffic had formerly gone through the Nabataean capital of Petra, and the latest archaeological discoveries indicate that Petra too preserved its importance throughout the first three centuries of our era. It was another city that acquired a remarkable and beautiful concentration of buildings in the High Roman style.

Different already from these highly westernized cities were the religious centers, such as Jerusalem, where the god of the Jews had his temple (until its destruction in A.D. 70); Heliopolis-Baalbek, where the worship of the sun was important; and Hierapolis-Membij, which was the focus of the ecstatic cult of the Syrian goddess described by Lucian. To disapproving Romans, the ecstatic rites of this and similar cults seemed to typify the excesses of Syrian religion. Not far from Hierapolis was the small city of Harran, from which Abraham had set out for Canaan, and which had housed since at least the thirteenth century B.C. the temple of the moon-god Sin. It was known to the Romans as Carrhae and dreaded by them as the scene of one of their worst defeats, where Crassus had been killed and his legion wiped out.

Finally there were the independent principalities. Of these, Emesa lay within the bounds of the province and was ruled by a family of priest kings of the sun-god Elagabal. This family was in due course to produce one of the most extraordinary emperors the Roman people had yet experienced—Marcus Aurelius Antoninus Bassianus, known as Elagabalus (A.D. 218–22). The kingdom of Edessa lay beyond the Euphrates but had close links with the West. One of its kings (all of whom were called Abgar) was even said to have maintained a written correspondence with Jesus, which was preserved. So Christianity had established a foothold here quite early and adapted to its own uses the healing pools containing the sacred fish so common in the paganism of this region.

But the pearl of all the cities of the eastern empire was Antioch. Ernest Renan, in his book *Les Apôtres*, richly evoked the cosmopolitan flavor of Hellenistic Antioch, its narrow streets and bazaars thronged with charlatans, thaumaturges, magicians, sorcerers, and false priests; its people absorbed in races, games, dances, processions, festivals, and bacchanals—"all the follies of the Orient," even down to superstition and orgies.[18] Antiochus, in founding the city, imitated the buildings and porticoes of Athens, and an Arab legend that describes him as "Antiochus of Rome" records the assistance of the demons in erecting its buildings and the talismans that drive away all noxious influences.[19]

Its splendor continued in Roman times. Apollonius of Tyana found it a decadent and idle place,[20] no doubt continuing the very practices that in the second century B.C. had made Posidonius from neighboring Apamea loud in its praises.

The people of these cities are relieved by the fertility of their soil from a laborious struggle for existence. Life is a continuous series of social festivities. Their gymnasiums they use as baths, where they anoint themselves with costly oils and myrrhs. In the grammateia (such is the name they give the public eating halls) they practically live, filling themselves there for the better part of the day with rich foods and wine; much that they cannot eat they carry away home. They feast to the prevailing music of strings. The cities are filled from end to end with the noise of harp playing.[21]

Antioch was perhaps too pleasant to become a major cultural or intellectual center, though by the third century it had acquired philosophical schools, which were never as prestigious as those of Berytus and Apamea. Its most pleasant suburb was Daphne,

> the famous shrine that marked the spot where the nymph baffled the desire of the god, the House of the Waters as it is called in Arabic. . . . No trace remains of the temples that adorned this fairest of all sanctuaries. Earthquake and mountain torrents have swept them down the ravine, but the beauty of the site has not diminished since the days when the citizens of the most luxurious capital of the East dallied there with the girls who served the god. The torrent does not burst noisily from the mountain side; it is born in a deep still pool that lies, swathed in a robe of maidenhair fern, in thickets annihilating all that's made to a green thought in a green shade.[22]

Such boscage would have seemed as alien as the dinner parties and the street lighting (another first for the city) to a nomad of the Euphrates borderlands—which only makes it more remarkable that a city to vie with any we have mentioned should spring up in the center of those nomad lands. The Romans, however, felt at home with the urban amenities of Antioch. Less familiar to them was the desert and steppe of eastern Syria, the land of nomads and peasants that they had somehow to control, to whose world we now turn.

Like their Hellenistic predecessors, the Romans used the urban administrative centers to organize and tax the peoples of the countryside as much as they could. We know little detail about the political administration of Alexander's Syria, and it seems that by and large the administrative structure of its previous, Persian rulers was left in place. Cities in northern Syria were the administrative centers of extensive toparchies, while at least some villages further south had independent status in what was obviously a more fluid arrangement.[23]

Roman taxation made paupers of many. Ironically, it may have increased the Romans' problem in controlling the region, by driving those on the borders of sedentarized lands into brigandage.[24] Brigandage and rebellion were never rare in the empire, and there are several signs of increasing insecurity in the Euphrates region in the third century A.D. (see chapter 3). Diocletian's solution to the crisis turned the dispossessed in a different direction: taxed to the loss of all their property, the peasants paid by tying their persons to their estates and their lords in a bond that initiated the feudal relations of the Middle Ages. Diocletian's law tied peasants to their land. Their only escape was recruitment into the army, which landowners did their best to prevent. The empire could afford no loss of production or taxes—what matter if the peasantry could pay only by their own starvation?

We know that in modern Syria, until recent times, city buildings alone counted as private property.[25] The rest of the country belonged to the community of Muslims (or to a prince, a miri). This seems to reflect the ancient position, where land in the cities was private while all land outside belonged, at least vaguely, to the king, and was therefore free for the use of all. The ruling elements of the villages were the headmen, komarchs, perhaps assited by a council of elders, whose names vary from village to village; syndikoi, bouleutai, pistoi, pragmateutai, epimeletai.[26] The countryside was given over to the nomads or parceled out under local agreements into strip-farming. The vagueness of such arrangements under imperial rule made it vital for the villagers to have patrons in the cities to protect their interests in the fair assessment of tithes and taxes.[27] Those who had none would suffer severely; and in one of his speeches the fourth-century orator Libanius makes clear that the patron's position was open to abuse, for he could extract ruinous bribes as the price of preventing ruinous taxation.[28] Soldiers might assume this role of patron or protector as their own commanders in turn exploited and pauperized them.[29] The need for patrons, though it protected the peasants, circumscribed, if it did not annihilate, their freedom.[30]

The cities stood in little real economic relation to the surrounding country.[31] Even today the cities are situated for their own convenience and not for that of their hinterlands. They take from the country but give little.[32] Libanius makes a philosophical point about the preeminence of the country, but in fact it serves to emphasize the economic dominance of the cities: "One can assert that cities are founded on the country and that this is their firm footing, providing them with wheat, barley, grapes, wine, oil and the nourishment of man and other living beings."[33]

Today, as then, markets are held in villages, and the cities are administrative centers. Market taxes, property taxes, and poll taxes are evidenced in Roman Syria, and they displaced the meagre wealth of the villages to the coffers of the towns. In addition the villages had to provide border troops and to endure the billeting of soldiers. Later, in the fourth century, peasants could even be coerced into providing forced labor for the rubbish disposal of Antioch.[34]

We have nothing like the Greek accounts of their sufferings under the Ottoman Empire to bring these scraps of information to life—but it must have felt much the same. Roman taxes, the legions, and urban consumption were all imposed on the rural population at once. In the end the cities fell apart by their own dead weight. Having become purely machines for processing the taxes of the poor, and ruled by aristocrats who could no longer support the traditional financial burdens of the rich, they declined both culturally and politically. Max Weber concludes, "Their main function was to obtain money for the State bureaucracy, while about them the land was transformed into a network of manorial estates."[35] The Middle Ages were beginning.

The nomads too suffered from the Romans. In particular, they faced a good share of Greco-Roman prejudice. From Herodotus onwards, the dwellers in mountain and plain were regarded as no better than bandits. Gibbon shared the prejudice found even in Homer's account of the Cyclopes[36] that the mark of civilization is the growing of corn (or rice) and that the "eaters of flesh and drinkers of milk" are beyond that pale: they define by their otherness the nature of civilization. Brent Shaw has drawn attention to a more sophisticated analysis in Ibn Khaldun that emphasizes the interconnectedness of nomad and sedentary: the one develops from the other.[37] The researches of J. T. Luke and P. Briant have suggested that in this region there is no such radical opposition between nomad and sedentary peoples. Rather a dimorphic structure prevails, in which the shepherds constantly tend to sedentarism and have tender roots in the villages as well as the open plains.[38] This structure was already well described by T. E. Lawrence in the early pages of *Seven Pillars of Wisdom*.

The economic life of the desert was based on the supply of camels, which were best bred on the rigorous upland pastures with their strong nutritive thorns. By this industry the Bedouins lived. . . . The camel markets in Syria, Mesopotamia, and Egypt determined the population which the deserts could support, and regulated strictly their standard of living. So the desert likewise over-peopled itself upon occasion; and then there were heavings and thrustings of the crowded tribes as they elbowed themselves by natural courses towards the light. . . .

The inexorable trend northward continued. The tribes found themselves driven to the very edge of cultivation in Syria or Mesopotamia. Opportunity and their bellies persuaded them of the advantages of possessing goats, and then of possessing sheep; and lastly they began to sow, if only a little barley for their animals. They were now no longer Bedouin, and began to suffer like the villagers from the ravages of the nomads behind. Insensibly, they made common cause with the peasants already on the soil, and found out that they, too, were peasantry. So we see clans, born in the highlands of Yemen, thrust by stronger clans into the desert, where, unwillingly, they became nomad to keep themselves alive. We see them wandering, every year moving a little further north or a little further east as chance has sent them down one or other of the well-roads of the wilderness, till finally this pasture drives them from the desert again into the sown, with the like unwillingness of their first shrinking experiment in nomad life. This was the circulation which kept vigour in the Semitic body.[39]

Sheikhs might dwell permanently in villages or even in towns. The caravan trade diversified their way of life and brought wealth to an otherwise meager and marginal existence.

What the Romans really objected to in the nomad Arabs was that it was almost impossible to control them sufficiently to exact tribute. There were rich pickings to be had because of the part played by the nomad cameleers in the spice trade. Most imperial powers have felt the same need, from the Assyrian rulers in the eighth century B.C. to the Russian imperial control of the Caucasus in the nineteenth century and the attempts of Reza Shah to obliterate nomadism in Iran. Tolstoy wrote in *The Raid:*

If it were not for this war (against the mountain tribes) what would secure the neighbouring rich and cultured Russian territories from robbery, murder, and raids by wild and warlike tribes?[40]

As for Reza Shah, he went even to the lengths of poisoning wells to deter nomadism.[41] Rulers find it even harder than scholars to accept the interplay of nomad and settled.

The affinities of the subject of our story, Palmyra, were all with this third group, the nomads, rather less so with the peasants, and scarcely at all with the Greek cities. A desert city like Petra and Dura-Europos, it marked the borderlands of Roma and Parthia. Its culture was unique (as we shall see) and blended Syrian and Persian essentials onto Roman forms. Greek was spoken there (Zenobia claimed Greek descent), but its character takes us away from the Greco-Roman forms of city life (there is no hippodrome, though there is a small theater) toward the desert. Rome's approach, however, was essentially the same: to dominate and exploit.

As early as the reign of Tiberius, we find increasing signs of prosperity in Palmyra, which made Roman domination a more pressing need for greedy Rome. But what form did that domination take? What was the constitutional position of this remote city in the first two centuries of the Roman control of Syria?

The earliest of the surviving public buildings at Palmyra is the Temple of Bel, which was begun in A.D. 17 or 19 (the year Germanicus was sent on a mission to Syria and visited the tenth legion at Carrhae) and was dedicated in A.D. 32. Mommsen took this as decisive proof that Palmyra was at this time formally part of the Roman Empire and that it had become so perhaps as early as the reign of Augustus (d. A.D. 14).[42]

A date for the annexation of Palmyra before A.D. 75 is assured by a single piece of evidence. A milestone of Trajan's father, who is thus proved to have built a road from Palmyra to Sura on the Euphrates in the reign of Vespasian, makes clear that Roman territory at this time stretched well to the east of Palmyra. The picture is confused by the statement of Pliny the Elder (23/24–79) that Palmyra was still an autonomous buffer state between Rome and Parthia in his own day, "having a destiny of its own between the two mighty empires of Rome and Parthia."[43] Against this, E. Will proposes, surely rightly, that Pliny was simply ignorant about the region and its politics in general, and may safely be ignored.[44]

At the opposite extreme, Février thought that Palmyra only entered the empire in 114, after Trajan's annexation of Nabataea.[45] It was only two years after this that Trajan formed the first Palmyrene army unit, the *ala dromedariorum Palmyrenorum,* for the execution of his campaign against Persia. Hadrian certainly honored the city on his visit in 129, and in the early third century it became a colony, probably under Caracalla in 211—along with the cities of Tyre, Laodicea, Emesa, and Heliopolis—or in 212, when all inhabitants of the empire acquired the *ius italicum* (a set of legal privileges originally allowed only to the cities of Italy).[46]

In fact none of these dates prior to the creation of the colony is susceptible of proof. My preference is for a Tiberian date: this would best explain the strongly Roman character the city developed from this time on. It may be a mistake, however, to explain Roman relations with her subjects in the legalistic terms appropriate to modern states. Rome had many ways of controlling cities and peoples besides signing documents of their legal status within or without the empire. The institution of the "client king" or "friendly king" is one of the best known. By this means Rome could ensure the assistance of a frontier realm without having to garrison it thoroughly; the implied threat in the friendship was enough. Similarly, as Benjamin Isaac has argued,[47] Roman control of any region was simply a function of what its military might could enforce or coerce, and territorial limits may sometimes be irrelevant. *Provincia* in origin has no territorial meaning but the sense of the modern abstract use of the word province, a field of competence or authority. Rome, especially in the early days of the empire, preferred to exercise hegemony without the added responsibilities of annexation.[48]

It is therefore not surprising that Roman control of Palmyra is clear long before the end of the first century. Government will have been carried out at least in part by edict from the Roman military governor of the region as early as Corbulo (A.D. 60).[49] Little can be deduced from the enlistment of 8000 Palmyrene archers among the auxiliary troops of Vespasian—as these need not have been Roman citizens—except that the Roman presence here was powerful and even seductive.[50] More telling is the milestone of Trajan's father mentioned above, proving that Rome effectively controlled the region at this period. There are even signs of a Roman garrison at this time in the remains of burials found north of the city, in the area under the modern village.[51] The first written record of a garrison dates from 167, in the reign of Lucius Verus.[52]

The cumulative evidence, while making clear that Rome exercised hegemony over Palmyra from the reign of Tiberius on, seems to favor positive annexation at an early date. The city will then have become a tributary city, with a garrison, from A.D. 19. It then followed the pattern of other Syrian cities, becoming a metropolis under Hadrian and a colony in 211. Interestingly it preserved its own forms of government and was apparently not impeded by Rome even in the very extraordinary, and quite undocumented, rise of a regal dynasty in the course of the third century. It would appear that it was so remote from Rome that the rulers and people of Rome for the most part preferred to forget about it—out of sight, out of mind. In that, Palmyra shared the fate of most of Syria in the minds of the citizens of Rome, even the literate classes, whose ideas of Syria were partial and prejudiced. Their information was limited and their preconceptions about the Syrian race can be illustrated easily.

Emperor Julian, who was on the whole well disposed to Syrians because of their prevalent devotion to solar religion, seems to sum up a common complex of attitudes: "The Syrian people are unwarlike and effeminate, but at the same time intelligent, hot-tempered, vain and quick to learn."[53] The contemporary philosopher Eunapius referred to the "charm and sweetness of intercourse of all Syro-Phoenicians."[54] But for many Romans the most notable feature of Syrian culture was the ecstatic cults that they brought, alongside the quieter devotions tendered in the temple of the Syrian gods on the Janiculum, to the capital city itself. Juvenal snarled,

> Long since the stream that wanton Syria laves
> Has disembogued its filth in Tiber's waves,
> Its language, arts; o'erwhelm'd us with the scum
> Of Antioch's streets, its minstrels, harp and drum.[55]

In another poet's work, a Syrian female innkeeper danced even in her tavern, "her head crowned with a Greek fillet, moving her wiggling flanks to the sound of the castanet."[56] Minstrels and drums accompanied the ceremonies of the sun-god in his shrine at Emesa, which, not long after Juvenal, Rome was to see with horror in her very streets, when the amazing Emperor Elagabalus brought his cult to Rome. Minstrels and drums beat and shrilled at the ceremonies of the Syrian goddess, the Great Mother, at Hierapolis (Membij), where devotees castrated themselves and hurled the severed parts into the crowds of observing women and even through their windows. Minstrels and drums sounded too at the great Temple of Baal at Heliopolis-Baalbek, and at many other native shrines where the Greek overlay was the thinnest. But as we shall see, such rites were altogether alien to the religious life of Palmyra.

More significant than such oddities, and apparently a constant throughout the history of the empire, is the role of Syrians (in the broadest geographical sense) as merchants. The Syrians were one of the most mercantile peoples in the Roman Empire, and records of them span the centuries and the whole breadth of the empire. The temple of the Syrian gods on the Janiculum, founded in the mid-second century, indicates the importance of the Syrian presence in the capital.[57] Several Syrian merchants are known from the northern empire, including one Aurelius Sabinus of Porolissus in Moesia, who dedicated a temple to Jupiter Dolichenus, and two merchants named Julianus from Lyon.[58] Interesting here is that "the merchant who operated a large general store in that city,"[59] Thaimus Julianus, was also a councillor of his home city of Canatha in the Hauran. Although most citizens of Rome looked down on trade, in Syria it was a respectable pursuit, even for those in the higher levels of society. This suggests that fortunes might be made from trade and lead to status, while in the other parts of the empire status came from land and trade was merely an inescapable by-product of the productivity of one's fields.

Much later the fifth-century author Salvian wrote that "crowds of Syrian merchants occupied the greater part of nearly all cities."[60] One senses, perhaps, a touch of the prejudice that was attached to the usurious and mercantile Jews in the Middle Ages (though Jews in antiquity were not traders). In Syria the importance of traders, and of trade, provided one of the keystones of Roman interest in the East. The military aspect of Syria's importance is discussed in chapter 4. Here it is appropriate to narrow our focus onto Palmyra, looking in more detail at the role, routines, and routes of trade of which Palmyra stood at the hub.

2

Of Spices, Silk, and Camels

The desert of Syria never made anyone rich with its characteristic products of salt, saltpeter, charcoal, terebinth, truffles, and the skins of abandoned carcasses. The importance of the desert to its inhabitants was like that of the Aegean Sea, which the Greeks called "unharvested": it was a means of communication, not a resource in its own right. The traffic across the desert made its cities wealthy. The importance of the Palmyrenes was as merchants, and it is as merchants that they become known to us in our earliest Roman reference.

> Being merchants, they bring the products of India and Arabia from Persia, and dispose of them in the Roman territory.[1]

In his brevity Appian includes in his expression all goods that came from India and Arabia, even though they might not have originated there. In fact the luxury trade in Rome brought goods even from Indonesia and China, though they first entered westerners' consciousness as they were loaded on ships at the Indus ports.

Syria (which for the Romans geographically included the land of Judaea) was of special significance to Rome because of its connection with the luxury trade of spices and silks. Montesquieu, the model for much of Gibbon's analysis of Roman history, traced Rome's decline from the beginning of its attachment to luxury. In doing this he only echoed such Roman moralists as Sallust and Emperor Augustus himself. Almost any age looks back to the one before as a better age, with sterner ("Victorian") moral values and a more rigorous approach to life. Sallust traced the decline from the abandonment of military rigors as the result of increasing wealth. Augustus saw the decline of traditional religion as resulting from the same cause. And the encyclopedist Pliny was able to fill out the detail of Rome's increasing greed for luxury items from the Orient.

Spices

First and above all were spices and aromatics. Aromatics were used for religious purposes, in offering incense to the gods and for carrying in Roman triumphs. Frankincense and myrrh came from what is now Yemen in South Arabia, and also from northern Somalia and Oman. South Arabia was an important producer of pearls (not as good as Indian ones according to Pliny), bdellium, ladanum gum, and four types of cardamom. Other luxury goods, such as ivory, tortoiseshell, and various aromatics, came from Somalia.[2]

Balsam (pistacia lentiscus) grew near Jericho and was farmed by Herod.

> The balsam tree is now a subject of Rome, and pays tribute together with the race to which it belongs. . . . The Jews vented their wrath upon this plant as they also did upon their own lives, but the Romans protected it against them, and there have been pitiful battles in defence of a shrub. It is now cultivated by the Treasury authorities, and was never before more plentiful; but its height has not advanced beyond three feet.[3]

The balsam is extracted from the trees as resin, with cuttings like those in a rubber tree.

> When Alexander the Great was campaigning in that country, it was considered a fair whole day's work in summer to fill a single shell, and for the entire produce of a rather large garden to be six congii and of a smaller one one congius [about six pints], at a time moreover when its price was twice its weight in silver: whereas at the present day even a single tree produces a larger flow.[4]

One pound of wood balsam cost 6 denarii (a year's wages, or the price of 600 pounds of bread), but a pint of the resin could fetch more than 300 denarii, and on occasions even up to 1000 denarii.

Balsam was regarded as far inferior to the rarer products of the Arabian coast. The trade in these from Sabaea (Sheba) to the north can be traced back to the tenth century B.C. and was very likely the occasion of the legendary journey of the queen of Sheba, who crossed 1400 miles of desert to visit King Solomon in Jerusalem. As early as the time of Ptolemaic rule in Syria, that country's wealth could be attributed to the fragrances produced by the Sabaei and Gerrhaei.[5]

These people have not got cinnamon or cassia, and nevertheless Arabia is styled "Happy"—a country with a false and ungrateful appellation, as she puts her happiness to the credit of the powers above, although she owes more of it to the power below. Her good fortune has been caused by the luxury of mankind even in the hour of death, when they burn over the departed the products which they had originally understood to have been created for the gods. Good authorities declare that Arabia does not produce so large a quantity of perfume in a year's output as was burned by the Emperor Nero in a day at the obsequies of his consort Poppaea.[6]

But these aromatics were only a fraction, though the most costly, of the items Rome imported from the East to feed its sybaritic tastes. The aromatics were used not only for the gods and for the dead but in the creation of perfumes. One may picture the perfumer's bazaar at Capua, the Seplasia, evoked by Varro,[7] as an extravagant version of the spiciest of Levantine souks, where scents of aromatic gums mingle with those of hartshorn, lupin, fleur de lys, and roses, to delight the nose and eye and intoxicate—ever so slightly—the unseasoned brain.

For spices as opposed to aromatics, Rome was dependent on the even more distant traffic with India and the East Indies. Of those used in cookery, the most important were pepper and ginger. The latest historian of the ancient spice trade goes so far as to aver that Rome's oriental politics were entirely determined by their need for these piquant substances.[8] One can still visit the remains of Trajan's market, where the Via Piperatica displayed, in heaps of red, purple, yellow, and black, the costly purchases from the East—cumin, allspice, ginger, saffron, pepper, cloves, and cinnamon. Saffron was the costliest of all, and when the price was fixed by Diocletian's edict of A.D. 301 its price was 2000 denarii per pound. The Roman gastronomic writer Apicius gives a full list of all the "condiments which should be in the house so that seasoning may not be absent":

saffron, pepper, ginger, laser [silphium ferula tingitana], bayleaf, myrtle berry, costmary, cloves, Indian spikenard, cardamum, and spikenard;
seeds: poppy, rue seed, rue berry, laurel berry, aniseed, celery seed,

fennel seed, lovage seed, colewort seed, coriander seed, cumin, parsley, dill, caraway, and sesame;

dry seasonings: laser roots, mint, Italian catmint, sage, cypress, oregano, juniper, onion, gentian roots, thyme, coriander, pellitory, citrus leaves, parsnip, shallots, rush roots, pennyroyal, cyperus, garlic, pulse, marjoram, elecampane, silphium, and cardamum;

and dried fruits and roots.[9]

Apart from the seeds and herbs, many of the items in all these categories came from the distant East. Even the keenest devotee of Elizabeth David might be hard put to find all these items in his or her kitchen, but this was basic housekeeping for a man like the author, who would take a ship from Campania to Libya at a rumor of prawns of exceptional size and, on finding they were no bigger than those of Campania, turn straight round again without even landing.[10]

The total cost to Rome of all these imports was estimated by Pliny as 100 million sesterces per annum.[11] The meaning of this statement has been much debated: does Pliny mean that this was their book cost or that this was the difference in the balance of payments between Rome and the East?[12] The number is so suspiciously neat that it is not worth the trouble to calculate more precisely. Pliny is saying—and it may be only a moralist's point anyway—that Rome spent an enormous amount on, and laid great store by, these Eastern luxuries. So much, we would hardly wish to dispute. Tiberius grumbled that "the ladies and their baubles are transferring our money to foreigners."[13]

The spices came from all parts of the East. Cinnamon came from Indonesia via Madagascar; ginger and cloves from China; bdellium, costum, spikenard, and galbanum from Bactra via Charax on the Persian Gulf; sesame, long pepper, and sandalwood from northern India; black and white pepper, as well as cardamom, cyperus, sweet flag, and turmeric, from southern India; nutmeg and mace from Ceylon; and cassia ("cinnamon"), as well as aromatics, from South Arabia.[14]

Though Appian attributes the wealth of Palmyra to the trade in spices and aromatics as well as to that in silks, in fact the trade in aromatics from South Arabia had been in the control of the Nabataeans since Ptolemaic times (312 B.C.). When we first hear of this intriguing people, they are a completely nomadic race based in the region between the northern tip of the Red Sea and the southern border of modern

Syria. According to Diodorus Siculus, who was describing conditions in the fourth century B.C., they held an annual trade fair but were otherwise seldom long in one place.[15] They seem however to have been completely sedentarized by Strabo's time (first century A.D.).[16] By A.D. 100 they were masters of a kingdom whose capital and central mart was at Petra, and they also controlled the important city of Bostra. Their rise to riches was the result of their specialization in the caravan trade of the aromatics from Arabia, though for a time in the first century B.C. they also managed to take a hand in the trade in spices from the more distant East. The route along which the aromatics were brought to the Roman Empire followed the east coast of the Red Sea as far as Aelana and then continued overland to Petra, which as a result developed into a magnificent city in the third and second centuries B.C.

After the late second century B.C. discovery of the monsoon, the trading expeditions with the parts of northwest India from which the spices came could be carried out in less than a year; before it had taken up to three years to make the journey.[17] One could leave Egypt in July with a following northerly wind down the Red Sea and be carried by the southwest monsoon to the northwest coast of India by early September. Departure was in December or early January, though it was possible to leave as early as November, reaching one of the Red Sea ports by February at the latest.[18] One added advantage of this route was that the ships could cross the open sea, avoiding dangers from pirates that attended a coastal voyage.

It is possible that the Nabataeans were able to profit from the development of the new sea route. Their construction of a port at Aelana shows their interest in it. Freshly harvested frankincense and myrrh might suffer evaporation in the long hot summer journey along the overland route.[19] If they could be consolidated at the lower end of the Red Sea, they could follow a cooler, sea route at least as far as the Nabataean port of Leuke Kome, where there was "a way up to Petra,"[20] or perhaps as far as Aelana and thence via the overland route to Gaza. From Leuke Kome to Aelana, caravans "as big as armies"[21] transported both spices and aromatics into the lands of the empire.

An alternative view is that the discovery of the monsoon enabled traders with India to bypass Petra altogether by going directly up the Red Sea.[22] The effect this may have had on the Nabataean trade depends on the date of the discovery. Much here is uncertain, but we can be sure that the Nabataeans were still actively involved in trade when

Rome first became interested in the region. The case for detriment to the goods via the overland route may be exaggerated, and it is certain that the Gaza-Petra route remained in use in Pliny's time.

The advent of Roman power altered the pattern of trade, first by reducing banditry and piracy in the Nabataean lands. The increase of seaborne trade could be seen as a result of growing Roman domination of the region. In 63 B.C. Pompey turned Nabataea into a client kingdom. We know of a "centurion" (the term used is the Greek *hekatontarches*) stationed at Leuke Kome to levy tax on the trade through Nabataea, but it is disputed whether this refers to a Roman official extracting Roman dues or to a Nabataean official with a Roman name. In a recent discussion, S. T. Parker supports the former, which seems the most likely view.[23] Roman control of Leuke Kome may have been established as early as 24 B.C.

In 25 B.C. Augustus sent an expedition of 10,000 men, including Nabataeans and Jews from Herod's kingdom, commanded by Aelius Gallus, the governor of Egypt, to secure the east coast of the Red Sea as far as Aden. But because his troops were not used to the harsh desert conditions, and perhaps because the Nabataeans were not as helpful as had been hoped or were even actively disloyal, the expedition was a failure.

> He did not proceed without difficulty; for the desert, the sun, and the water (which had some peculiar nature) all caused his men great distress, so that the larger part of the army perished. The malady proved to be unlike any of the common complaints, but attacked the head and caused it to become parched, killing forthwith most of those who were attacked, but in the case of those who survived this stage it descended to the legs, skipping all the intervening parts of the body, and caused dire injury to them. . . . In the midst of this trouble the barbarians also fell upon them. . . . These were the first of the Romans, and, I believe, the only ones, to traverse so much of this part of Arabia for the purpose of making war.[24]

This was not an auspicious start to Roman relations with their eastern neighbors. Nevertheless Rome did make an effort to direct the trade from the Leuke Kome route to the Egyptian ports on the Red Sea. By the time of Augustus most of the Red Sea commerce was coming through Myos Hormos and Berenice.[25] Excavations by the University of Delaware at Abu Sha'ar, probably to be identified with Myos Hormos, indicate a squalid port with roofless mudbrick buildings, perhaps inhabited for only part of the year. For Berenice, an inscription from Coptos of A.D. 90 records the transit charges for caravans from that port.

Trade also increased substantially in this period.

> In earlier times, not as many as twenty vessels would dare to traverse the Arabian Gulf far enough to get a peep outside the straits, but at the present time even large fleets are despatched as far as India and the extremities of Ethiopia, from which the most valuable cargoes are brought to Egypt, and thence sent forth again to the other regions; so that double duties are collected, on both imports and exports; and on goods that cost heavily the duty is also heavy.[26]

Presumably it was advantageous to bring goods as far as possible by sea before transferring to the land route, which, though quicker, was more expensive and subject to tolls.

> Fixed portions of the frankincense are . . . given to the priests and the king's secretaries, but beside these the guards and their attendants and the gate-keepers and servants also have their pickings: indeed all along the route they keep paying, at one place for water, at another for fodder, or the charges for lodging at the halts, and the various octrois; so that expenses mount up to 688 denarii per camel before the Mediterranean coast is reached; and then again payment is made to the customs officers of our empire.[27]

This was the situation at the time of the composition of the *Periplus Maris Erythraei*, a sailor's or shipmaster's (not a merchant's) handbook of the first century A.D. All the trading then was with the west coast of the Red Sea. The Nabataeans were being edged out of the spice trade with the East, though they continued to specialize in aromatics.[28] It has recently been argued that Petra was in decline by the time of Augustus and that the Via Nova Traiana bypassed Petra. But the latest investigations suggest that this was not the case and that Petra retained its importance at least into the Byzantine period.[29] Thus we should picture a continued specialization by Petra in the aromatics trade.

Arab alternatives to the Nabataean route continued to emerge. Palmyrene merchants were established at Coptos in the early empire.[30] Perhaps connected with the misfortunes of Petra is the rise of the Central

Arabian entrepôt of Qaryat al-Fau,[31] where finds from the first to the fifth centuries A.D. include Roman and even Hellenistic coins, as well as grain, textiles, perfumes, gems, gold, silver, copper, and lead. The rise of Qaryat al-Fau suggests a constant effort by the Arab peoples to circumvent Roman domination of their commercial activities.

Roman control of the trade involved a substantial ad valorem tax of 25–50 percent. This should be viewed in conjunction with Pliny's suggestion that merchants sell their oriental goods at one hundred times the cost:[32] it was still worth their while to continue trading.

With the decline of Petra in question, how much of Trajan's annexation of Nabataea in A.D. 106 should be seen as having an economic motive? It could be simply the regularization of a situation in which Nabataea was already unimportant. It seems clear that any importance Petra retained was very firmly harnessed by Rome. But if it was not economic imperialism, Trajan's policy certainly had an economic dimension. His and Hadrian's construction of the Via Nova Traiana from Aqaba to Bostra via Petra facilitated the trade that was controlled by Rome's men. It increased the prosperity of Gerasa, Philadelphia, and Gadara.

Other motives may also have been important in the annexation, not least frontier security and the control of external nomads and internal brigands.[33] Rome always moved its frontier forward to monitor the people who remained outside it—so the Stanegate in Britain was paralleled by a wall, built by Hadrian, a mile or so to the north. It is sometimes suggested that the decline of Petra after the annexation of Nabataea resulted in the transference of much of the Arabian and Indian trade to Palmyra, whose heyday is thus set in the second century A.D. But as we shall see in the next chapter, Palmyrene prosperity was already well advanced in the first century A.D. Furthermore, there is an increasing amount of evidence that Petra did not suffer any real decline in importance even after the transference of the capital to Bostra by Trajan. The habitual versatility of merchants would suggest that all possible routes continued in use at any particular time, and that we are looking at fluctuations rather than at dramatic and complete alterations of trading patterns.

That Palmyra had a role to play in the Indian trade is clear from Appian,[34] as well as from the presence of Palmyrene merchants on the Arabian Gulf ports. But the most important source of Palmyra's wealth was not spices but silk.

Silk

If the trade in spices and aromatics was important to Rome, that in silk was of perhaps even greater significance. Ammianus specifies the two luxury trades in his analysis of the alleged corruption and decline of Rome: "The lavish use of silk and of the textile arts increased, and more anxious attention to the kitchen."[35] It was a conspicuous part of the wealth of Rome. When Alaric captured the city in the fourth century, he extorted from its citizens as booty, among other items, four thousand robes of silk.[36]

> Virgil is the most ancient writer who expressly mentions the soft wool which was combed from the trees of the Seres or Chinese; and this natural error, less marvellous than the truth, was slowly corrected by the knowledge of a valuable insect, the first artificer of the luxury of nations. That rare and elegant luxury was censured, in the reign of Tiberius, by the gravest of the Romans; and Pliny, in affected though forcible language, has condemned the thirst of gain, which explored the last confines of the earth for the pernicious purpose of exposing to the public eye naked draperies and trans-parent matrons. A dress which showed the turn of the limbs and colour of the skin might gratify vanity or provoke desire; the silks which had been closely woven in China were sometimes unravelled by the Phoenician women, and the precious materials were mul-tiplied by a looser texture and the intermixture of linen threads. Two hundred years after the age of Pliny, the use of pure or even mixed silks was confined to the female sex, till the opulent citizens of Rome and the provinces were insensibly familiarized with the example of Elagabalus, the first who, by this effeminate habit, had sullied the dignity of an Emperor and a man. Aurelian complained that a pound of silk was sold at Rome for twelve ounces of gold; but the supply increased with the demand, and the price diminished with the supply.[37]

The way silk was produced was one of the most cherished secrets of the Chinese emperors.[38] According to tradition it was discovered accidentally by a princess of the imperial house named Hsi-Ling-Shih, who lived in the reign of Emperor Huang-ti, about 2460 B.C. She observed a large and ugly caterpillar feeding on the leaves of a mulberry

tree in the palace garden. Amazed at its voracity, she took it indoors
to observe more closely. With perplexity she watched how it soon began
to swathe itself in a cocoon of fibre; and to her even greater amazement,
a few days later, from this apparently defunct creature, a moth emerged
like a soul released from its prison. At this point chance intervened as
she knocked the now empty cocoon into a bath she had prepared for
herself and was amazed to find the cocoon unwind again into a fine
and very strong thread.

The legend is a charming one, but in fact the means of silk production was certainly known to the Chinese in at least 3000 B.C. It
pleased them, however, to keep it a close secret, since the silk moth
was unknown in other parts of the world (even the Coan silk of Hellenistic Greece was only from an inferior type of fibre).[39] Even the close
neighbors of the Chinese were not privy to the secret. In about 200
B.C. a prince of Khotan sought, successfully, to marry the daughter of
the emperor of China for the sole purpose of getting her to reveal the
secret. She smuggled some silkworms out of the palace in her hat on
her wedding day, and the Khotanese became wealthy too.

The earliest archaeological evidence of the export of silk to western
lands dates from the sixth century B.C. It has been suggested that the
legend of the Golden Fleece may be concerned with the silk trade route
through south Russia.[40] But the route with which we are concerned lay
further south. Nowadays holiday package tours are organized along the
Silk Road, but in antiquity and throughout the Middle Ages it was a
gruelling journey over mountain and steppe.[41] Like the northern route,
it began at Ch'ang-an, whence the caravans proceeded to Tunhuang on
the edge of the Taklamakan desert, then either north or south of the
desert itself to Kashgar. Thence they made for the Stone Tower and
continued as far as Bactra, where a silent trade was conducted at a
mart where the traders were mutually unintelligible.

> Chinese merchants faced Persian traders with bales of silk between
> their two parties. With both hands buried under the folds of their
> robes, and with only fingers showing, bargaining was accomplished
> by signs. The Chinese merchants had good reasons for remaining
> silent, for an uncautious word might have revealed the secrets of
> where silk came from and thus destroy the source of their
> livelihood.[42]

Through Persia the silk of the Far East became known to the Greeks

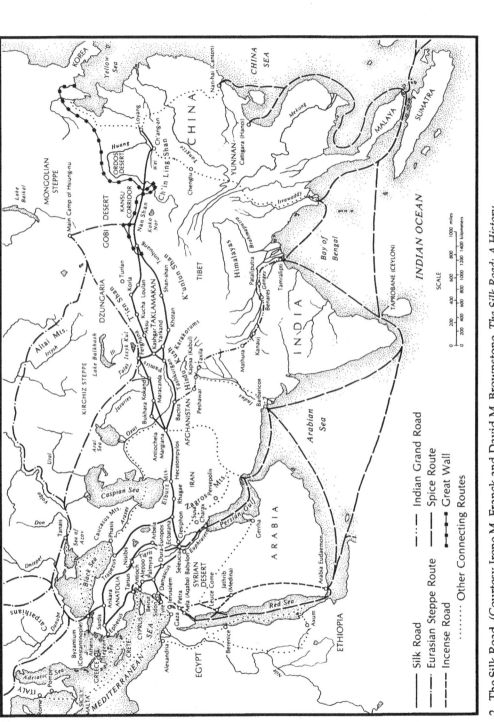

2. The Silk Road. (Courtesy Irene M. Franck and David M. Brownstone, *The Silk Road: A History*. [New York and Oxford: Facts on File Publications, 1986]. Cartographer: Dale Adams.)

after the expedition of Alexander the Great. And by Roman times it was a common luxury, if one may use such a phrase. Silk was worn mainly by women, and the increasing use of it by men was disapproved of by Seneca as not modest or philosophic.[43] From the time at least of Marcus Aurelius, traders from the Roman world itself were participating in those distant silent marts, as is made clear in a passage from the *Annals of the Han Dynasty* that shows that Chinese knowledge of the Roman West was at least as hazy as the Roman knowledge of China, where, as Gibbon remarks, it was believed that silk grew on trees and was removed with a special comb.

> The country [the Roman Empire] contains much gold, silver, and rare precious stones, especially "the jewel that shines at night," "the moonshine pearl," the hseih-chi-hsi, corals, amber, glass, lang-kan [a kind of coral], chu-tan [cinnabar?], green jadestone [ching-pi], gold-embroidered rugs and thin silk-cloth of various colours. They make gold-coloured cloth and asbestos cloth. They further have "fine cloth", also called Shui-yang-ts'ui [i.e., down of the water-sheep]; it is made from the cocoons of wild silk-worms. They collect all kinds of fragrant substances, the juice of which they boil into su-ho [storax]. All the rare gems of other foreign countries come from there. They make coins of gold and silver. Ten units of silver are worth one of gold. They traffic by sea with An-hsi [Parthia] and T'ien-chu [India], the profit of which trade is tenfold. They are honest in their transactions, and there are no double prices. Cereals are always cheap. The budget is based on a well-filled treasury. When the embassies of neighbouring countries come to their frontier, they are driven by post to the capital, and, on arrival, are presented with golden money. Their kings always desired to send embassies to China, but the An-hsi wished to carry on trade with them in Chinese silks, and it is for this reason that they were cut off from communication. This lasted till the ninth year of the Yen-hsi period during the Emperor Huan-ti's reign [A.D. 166] when the king of Ta-ts'in, An-tun [Antoninus] sent an embassy who, from the frontier of Jih-nan [Annam] offered ivory, rhinoceros horns and tortoise shell. From that time dated the direct intercourse with this country.[44]

The meeting place at this time seems to have been the Stone Tower. Here the caravans halted, the Chinese loaded up with Roman products (glass, amber, asbestos, cut gems and cameos, henna, and even ostriches),[45] and the central Asian caravaneers proceeded with the Chinese silk, ginger, spices, steel, and ink, via the Hindu Kush, on dromedary, yak, horse, mule, ox, or human porter, to Iran and Mesopotamia. From here the caravan could join the familiar Seleucid trade route from Persia via Mosul, Diyarbakir, and Aleppo to the Mediterranean coast at Antioch, where the silk would be conveyed to Rome. Fragments of the bales in which silk was brought from China to Rome were found in the wastes of the Gobi Desert by Sir Aurel Stein.[46]

Around 100 B.C., after the Parthian conquest of Merv (Alexandria Margiana), the route was altered. It is described in detail in the survey by Isidore of Charax, the *Parthian Stations*, which he wrote in about 25 B.C., very probably for the information of Emperor Augustus. It began like the previous route, but separated from it at Bactra; thence it came via Herat and Merv to Seleucia (Baghdad) and thence up the Euphrates, an easier and less rugged route, the last part of it by water. This will always have been the route of first choice for merchants, but it had its problems.

Most obviously this route depended on political conditions in the intervening territories. The Kushans controlled the Tarim Basin in the central Taklamakan Desert (where China's nuclear testing stations now are), and it was not until 73 A.D. that the Chinese general Pan Ch'ao brought this territory firmly under Chinese control.

Further west, robber barons in the High Zagros Mountains were a danger. Canadian excavations at a site called Qaleh-e-Yazdegerd in northwest Iran have uncovered the remains of such a raider's stronghold, dating from the second century A.D., and lying a little to the northeast of the route from Parthia. Its remarkable decorations, which include such classical details as a column with a Pan as well as such Sassanian types as the griffin and senmurv, demonstrate the level of culture obtainable by simple banditry.[47]

> To escape the Tartar robbers and the tyrants of Persia, the silk caravans explored a more southern road. They traversed the mountains of Thibet, descended the streams of the Ganges or the Indus, and patiently expected, in the ports of Guzerat and Malabar, the annual fleets of the West."[48]

Thence the silk and its purveyors, augmented now with such local products as turquoise, lapis, and perhaps cotton and carnelian,[49] could take ships to the mouth of the Euphrates and to Seleuceia-Ctesiphon. But the journey from Peking to the Indus could take nine months and was never attractive: "The dangers of the desert were found less intolerable than toil, hunger, and the loss of time."[50]

A puzzling piece of evidence is the account in the Han annals of the journey of the Chinese envoy Kan Ying, who in A.D. 97 accompanied the Parthian merchants to the West in the hope of making direct contact with the end-purchasers of the silk. He followed the normal route through An-hsi (Parthia) to Aman (Ecbatana) and Ssu-pin (Ctesiphon); thence his route went "south across a river and again southwest to the country of Yü-lo [perhaps Hira or Charax], 960 li to the extreme western frontier of An-hsi; from here you travel south by sea, and so reach Ta-ts'in [the lands of Rome].[51] But the next stage of his journey is a puzzle. Kan Ying "arrived in T'iao-chih [Mesopotamia], on the coast of the great sea." When about to take his passage across the sea, the sailors of the western frontier of An-hsi told Kan Ying:

"The sea is vast and great; with favourable winds it is possible to cross within three months; but if you meet slow winds, it may also take you two years. It is for this reason that those who go to sea take on board a supply of three years' provisions. There is something in the sea which is apt to make men homesick, and several have thus lost their lives." When Kan Ying heard this, he stopped.[52]

Franck and Brownstone, like G. F. Hudson and F. Hirth, argue that this was simply a piece of scaremongering by the Parthian merchants: they did not want Kan Ying to meet the Roman consumers and perhaps find a way to bypass the Parthian middlemen.[53] (Certainly the Romans would have liked to do this, for example in the mission under Marcus Aurelius Antoninus mentioned above.) So they described the route from the Persian Gulf to the Red Sea as impossibly long and dangerous. This is in fact an arduous journey outside the monsoon season, with hostile shores and contrary winds, and might take an extremely long time (though scarcely two years). But this argument does not seem very plausible. If the Parthians did not want the Chinese to discover their trade secrets, why did they humor Kan Ying for the first three thousand miles of his arduous journey? Furthermore, why did he go down the Euphrates to the Persian Gulf when the regular route was from the mouth of the Euphrates up the river to Syria? It would appear that what was described to Kan Ying was the eastward journey from Spasinou Charax to India, or even to China—not the route to the lands of Rome. The timings correspond to the journey before the monsoon (three months) or against it (two years).

J. I. Miller argued, against the other authorities, that both the sea route and the Euphrates route coexisted.[54] The disposition of the Parthian stations suggests that they surely did. The Hellenistic city of Seleuceia (founded ca. 312 B.C.) seems to have been the normal headquarters for the silk merchants as early as A.D. 19.[55] There transport would be exchanged once more for the camels necessary for the desert crossing.

After Marcus Aurelius destroyed Seleuceia, the headquarters was moved to Spasinou Charax, the capital of Mesene. Charax, a foundation of Alexander the Great, had declared its independence under its first king, Hyspaosines, in 126 B.C., and had thus become known as Spasinou Charax after its liberator.[56] It came under direct Parthian control at the end of the first century A.D. This is the city described in the "Hymn of the Soul": "I passed through the borders of Maishan [Mesene], the meetingplace of the merchants of the East,... which sits on the shore of the sea."[57] The earliest record of a Palmyrene at Charax in fact dates from A.D. 50 or A.D. 70.[58] One may imagine an imposing commercial quarter, like Corporation Square at Ostia, the port of Rome, with offices of all the merchants surrounding a courtyard where cameleers, retailers, armed escorts, and the gaudy-robed merchants themselves would jostle and bargain among their bales of raw, dyed, and woven wares. The Palmyrenes were important enough at Charax for one to become established as satrap of Characene in A.D. 131.[59] Colonies of Palmyrene merchants established themselves also at Vologesias on the Euphrates;[60] this was a foundation of Vologaeses I, king of Parthia (A.D. 51–80), and the first Palmyrene record dates from A.D. 108. The Parthian ports of Phorath (Basra), Teredon, and Apologos were also used.[61] There were also Palmyrene merchants at Babylon,[62] despite its supercession by Seleuceia and eventual destruction some time before A.D. 115; their successors were established at Seleuceia.[63]

Palmyrene inscriptions have been found also at Merv (in 1958), at the mouth of the Indus (dating from 157 A.D.), and in Coptos.[64] Clearly they kept outposts at every likely entrepôt of the silk trade. Their involvement in seaborne commerce in addition to the camel caravan routes is emphasized by the occasional appearance of ships—rather than camels—on the funerary reliefs of Palmyra.[65]

The route north up the Euphrates had its own problems. Chinese and Roman sources concur interestingly on this point. The *Hou Han Shu* tells us:

> The country is densely populated; every ten li are marked by a t'ing [shed?]; thirty li by a chih [beacon tower?]. One is not alarmed by robbers, but the road becomes unsafe by fierce lions and tigers who will attack passengers, and unless these be travelling in caravans of a' hundred men or more, or be protected by military equipment, they may be devoured by these beasts.[66]

Both the locale referred to and the date are uncertain. But Strabo, writing around the turn of the era, has even more circumstantial detail about the hazards of the route up the Euphrates.

> And on that road are camel drivers who keep halting places, which sometimes are well equipped with reservoirs, generally cisterns, though sometimes the camel-drivers use water brought in from other places. The Scenitae [tent-men, as the Arab Bedouin were known] are peaceful, and moderate towards travellers in the exaction of tribute, and on this account merchants avoid the land along the river and risk a journey through the desert, leaving the river on their right for approximately three days' journey. For the chieftains who live along the river on both sides occupy country which though not rich in resources, is less resourceless than that of others, and are each invested with their own domains and exact a tribute of no moderate amount. For it is hard among so many peoples, and that too among peoples that are self-willed, for a common standard of tribute to be set that is advantageous to the merchant.[67]

The Barbaricon-Euphrates-Palmyra route became even more important when the Kushans under their king Wima Kadphises reconquered the Tarim Basin and northern India about A.D. 100.[68] The land route being again broken, the long circuit from China to Burma via Yunnan—and thence by sea—or via Sikkim direct to the mouth of the Ganges, came into its own again. Here goods could travel either across country to the mouth of the Indus at Barygaza and neighboring ports or round Ceylon via Arikamedu (where Roman pottery and other goods have been found) to the Indus again. From here the natural course was to coast to the mouth of the Euphrates, and from here the merchants might equally continue to the Red Sea, where Roman tolls and taxes would amount to as much as 25 percent of the value of their goods, or go to Palmyra, where a similar tax applied.[69]

Trajan's conquests in this area, presented by contemporaries as bids for glory and acts worthy of a successor to Alexander the Great, undoubtedly benefited Roman trade. The first act was the conquest of Nabataea. After that, Trajan's armies pushed forward across the Euphrates (113–17) to the Parthian capital at Seleuceia. With the Euphrates thus in Roman hands, it seemed possible to open up the Parthian route again. The route through Parthia had certainly become very unfamiliar by this time, as we can tell from the expedition to explore it once more that Maes Titianus undertook in the reign of Trajan.[70] Trajan is known to have longed to conquer India itself. As usual, this was presented as a desire to emulate Alexander the Great, but since he also received embassies from Kadphises, we may suppose he was aware of the advantages to be gained from controlling the ports of northern India.

On balance, the Kushans must have discovered that it profited them to control rather than to bar the precious convoys from China. But the Persian Gulf traffic, once opened, remained important. In the period we are concerned with, then, the silk came either via the Indus or through Northern Iran, to Seleuceia-Ctesiphon and the mouth of the Euphrates, and thence no longer by sea to Petra but up river to Palmyra.

As a natural consequence the spices for Rome's delectation now also came this way, and Palmyra was the linchpin of the route. Goods could transfer from ship to camel at three points on the Euphrates according to provenance. They could travel overland from Hit, north of Baghdad, across 295 miles of road of Roman construction, protected with wells every twenty-four miles and frequent fortifications—the road now known to the Arabs as Darb el-Kufri, road of the unbelievers. By ship the goods could go north to Circesium (Buseyre) and then due west to Palmyra and Damascus, while the land route had its Euphrates stage at Raqqa, from which it, like the others, descended to Palmyra. In the time of Ammianus, the caravans arrived in late September each year and provided the occasion for a great fair at Batnae that coincided with important religious festivals.[71] This fair belongs to a period when the route had been moved north from the now destroyed Palmyra, but its timing is likely to have been unchanged. Ammianus remarks that the goods exchanged there arrived both by land and sea (i.e., both by the overland Silk Road, via Nisibis, and by the Euphrates road). One should perhaps envisage the colorful scene that characterized fourth-century Batnae as the great annual event of Palmyra in the preceding centuries.

The Camel

To fill out the picture of that last stage of the journey, it is worth pausing for a moment on the indispensable vehicle of the caravan trade, the camel. Both camels and ships appear as attributes of the prosperous dead on Palmyrene tombstones, indicating the means by which they had gained their wealth. Ships are relatively rare. But it is not uncommon to see camels peering with a gaze of conscious importance over the shoulders of the mortals fast evaporating into the Palmyrene afterlife. Important gods at Palmyra, Arsu and Azizu, were the protectors of camels, and at least one relief from Dura-Europos shows the god Arsu riding on a camel.

If it is legitimate to compare the desert, as a means of communication, with the "unharvested sea" of Homer, then the sobriquet "ship of the desert" comes into focus with full significance. Indeed, this simile, which is current in Arabic, has been used to suggest that the original place of domestication of the camel was in South Arabia on the Arabian Gulf, since in no other area did Arabs ever have any acquaintance with ships and the sea.[72] The camel is central to the economy of the desert peoples. Our earliest references to the use of the camel come from the Book of Genesis, where they are mentioned as among the valued possessions of Abraham, who may have lived at any time between about 1900 and 1600 B.C. Despite arguments that these references are anachronistic, later insertions to the text, it seems more than plausible that camels were domesticated in the Middle East by the beginning of the second millennium B.C.

The camel is often regarded by westerners as a somewhat comic animal, and myths about it abound: that it can store water in its hump and travel for many days without eating or drinking; that it has four stomachs; and that its stupidity is equaled only by its bad temper. One exhaustive camel-management handbook from the nineteenth century lists the camel's numerous moral failings, including obstinacy, vengefulness, want of discrimination, and moroseness, concluding that the camel is above all a fatalist, though not positively suicidal.[73] One senses in this assessment a touch of the Orientalism that is often used to discredit the Arab or Muslim, here applied to his most indispensable animal. In fact the camel is a creature unusually well-adapted to desert conditions by its ability to eat almost anything, even the ferocious camel thorn, and to let its body temperature rise by as much as ten degrees Fahrenheit before it begins to perspire, thus conserving (rather than storing) water. Its placability made the camel a much more economical mode of transport for desert regions (or indeed for most dry regions before the construction of roads) than any other, including the wagon and the horse. When Burke and Wills set out to cross Australia from south to north in 1860, their wagons had to be abandoned after very few days, but the camels kept going without trouble as long as the going remained dry, only succumbing when the expedition reached the marshes around the creeks of the center.[74] Without camels, Palmyra would have had no trade. A measure of the importance Palmyra attached to the camel, and of the jealousy with which the cameleers guarded their primacy, is the punitive tax that was charged on the entry of carts into the city compared with that on camels. The duty on a cartload was four times that on a camel load, though a cart, it seems, could only carry twice as much as a camel.[75] Until the Romans began to build roads in Syria, there was little competition between the camel and the wheel.

The new power of Roman arms deterred the bandits, and even the wild beasts, yet the sheikhs remained the rulers of the desert, and they knew how to profit by the luxury of the Romans. We have seen why Rome cultivated Syria, and we will see more of how Rome controlled it. It is time to turn our attention to the city that is our subject, and to see just what the trade meant to Palmyra.

3

Of Temples, Tribes, and Taxes

On the nodal point of the silk route arose a city that could boast itself a new Athens, a city of rhetors and bankers, of merchants and warriors, of fine gentlemen and ladies in flowing embroidered gowns, of cameleers and small traders and farmers. For a little over a hundred and fifty years, the city exploded into a profusion of architectural splendor. Then it was emptied, like a shell, of all its life. Only the colonnades and temples remained, like an uncertain vision in the dun expanse of the desert. And that efflorescence of glory is indissolubly linked with the family and the name of Queen Zenobia.

The colorful scene of Zenobia's Palmyra has not been better re-created than by William Ware in his novel about the last days of Palmyra. His hero, Piso, describes the exotic scene:

> Everything wears a newer, fresher look than in Rome. The buildings of the Republic, which many are so desirous to preserve, and whole streets, even, of ante-Augustan architecture, tend to spread around here and there in Rome a gloom—to me, full of beauty and poetry—but, still gloom. Here, all is bright and gay. The buildings of marble, the streets paved and clean, frequent fountains of water, throwing up their foaming jets, and shedding a delicious coolness; temples, and palaces of the nobles, or of wealthy Palmyrene merchants, altogether present a more brilliant assemblage of objects than, I suppose, any other city can boast. Then conceive, poured through these long lines of beautiful edifices, a population drawn from every country of the Far East, arrayed in every variety of the most showy and fanciful costume, with the singular animals, rarely seen in our streets, but here met at every turn,—elephants, camels, and drome-daries, to say nothing of the Arabian horses, with their jewelled housings, with every now and then a troop of the queen's cavalry moving along to the sound of their clanging trumpets.[1]

The city of which Zenobia became queen in A.D. 267 had risen to prosperity as suddenly as Calcutta grew out of the little villages occupied by the English in the 1690s into a major port and capital of British India eighty years later. Palmyra's raison d'être, and the site of its first dwellings, was the spring Efqa—an oasis in the desert, which is so precious to a nomad people. Throughout Seleucid times it had been no more than a trading station, though there had been a temple on the site of the present Temple of Bel, and some of the merchant families' tower tombs already stood along the valley in the second century B.C. One sheikh of Palmyra, Zabdibel, is known to have fought in the Seleucid army at the battle of Raphia in 217 B.C.[2] The tombs of the Bene Yedi'bel, on the site of the present temple of Baalshamin, date from the mid-second century B.C. By A.D. 67 the tombs of the Bene-Ma'ziyan on the same site had become a porticoed courtyard; the classical formulary of architecture had taken over.

The friction generated by Rome's increasing economic, political, and military interest in the Euphrates region generated the energy that created the magnificent city whose remains we see today. Palmyra was important to Rome in two spheres, economic and military. We have seen in chapter 1 the reasons for its economic importance, which did not survive its fall. For Procopius, however, writing in the sixth century, its military function was the primary reason Rome had supported its growth. By his time it was in fact a purely military site, and he knew nothing of its former commercial splendor; in the sixth century the silk mart was further north, at Nisibis. Procopius' picture is not an inaccurate one: Palmyra's position alone gave it military importance as a pivot of two great empires.

Its incorporation in the ambit of the empire made it a Roman city in appearance. The earliest surviving public building is the Temple of Bel, begun in A.D. 17 or 19 and dedicated in A.D. 32. It may be that the building of the Temple of Bel was paid for by the Emperor Tiberius to signal his acquisition of Palmyra.[3] Late in the reign of Tiberius, the emperor's nephew Germanicus was sent on a long diplomatic mission to the East, in the course of which he visited Palmyra. His name is mentioned in connection with the erection in A.D. 18 of the first version of the tariff inscription (*CISem* 2.3913), which is an important source of information on the Palmyrene economy, and which is clear evidence of Roman control even of the local trading of the city. Germanicus was also associated with the dispatch of an ambassador, one Alexander of Palmyra, to Characene. From that date on, the Romanization of the city of Palmyra gained in momentum, though it always remained an

overlay. Roman elements start to be attached to the Semitic names of
the inhabitants in the second century. Hadrian was entertained in 129
by Sheikh Male Agrippa and honored the city with the title of Hadriane.
It became a colony under Septimius Severus or Caracalla in 211 or 212.
Its citizens were thus freed from the duty of paying the land tax and
probably the poll tax as well,[4] a privilege that could be construed as a
reward for service to the Roman state in the wars of Septimius. One
result of this was that Septimius and Aurelius (Caracalla's real name
was Marcus Aurelius Antoninus) became common elements in Palmyrene names. If Roman propaganda in the third century saw Zenobia
as an invader not a rebel, that is a testimony only to the distance and
strangeness of a city that was now largely Roman in name and outward
appearance.

As a Greek polis, Palmyra had controlled a chora (territory) that
extended seventy-five kilometers to the northwest to Kheurbet el-Bilas,
and sixty-five kilometers to the southwest to Qasr el-Hair, which formed
its boundary with the territory of Emesa. To the east and northeast its
boundary ran along the Euphrates. The western limits seem to have
been fixed as early as A.D. 2–17 by the Roman governor of Syria, Creticus
Silanus. The eastern limit is implied by the description in Appian of
the Palmyrenes retreating from Antony to the left bank of the
Euphrates.[5] A recent estimate of the population of Palmyra in the heyday
of the empire is 150,000 to 200,000 people, probably two or three times
the size of the Hellenistic city.[6]

The institutions of the city included a council or senate and an
assembly of the people.[7] A dedication of A.D. 114 mentions also the
argurotamiai or public treasurers, and by A.D. 52 we hear of archontes,
or archons, translated into Latin as duumviri: their meeting place, the
arche, has become the loanword 'rk' in Palmyrene.[8] Numerous other
titles of officials are also known, including the president and secretary
(of the boule), the dekaprotoi or top ten magistrates, the syndikoi, or
syndics, who regulated financial matters, and the strategoi, or military
commanders, the eponymous officers of the city's calendar.[9] Most of
these titles, and many others, reappear in other cities and villages of
Roman Syria, probably with slightly varying connotations.[10] In the third
century the symposiarchs, or chief priests, of the Temple of Bel were
generally men of considerable political importance.[11] Overall we gain
an impression of local institutions continuing to flourish under Rome's
general supervision, with local variations and, probably, such ad hoc
appointments as building committees. A garrison commander seems

once, probably in Hadrian's time, to have been appointed umpire in a dispute of toll collectors,[12] perhaps suggesting a more general supervisory authority over the transactions of the marketplace.

The most conspicuous expression of the Roman character of the city is its magnificent architecture. In most cities of the Roman Empire the decurions, or local councillors, involved themselves in conspicuous expenditure on taking office: wealthy men had a duty to use their wealth publicly. How are we to imagine the funding of the immense building program at Palmyra that began in A.D. 32 and did not end for nearly two hundred years? The period of construction closely parallels that of other cities, for example in north Africa, where it typically took a city from 120 to 160 years to acquire a complete set of public buildings as recommended by Vitruvius.[13] Where did the skilled labor come from— the architects, the master masons, the ornament designers, and the monumental sculptors? We do not know, though there are many hints of Greek training in the detail of Palmyra's monuments. The architect of the Temple of Bel was most probably a Greek, and we know the names of three Greeks who worked on that temple.[14] We do know that Hadrian made generous donations to Palmyra—as he did to most other cities of the Roman East—on the occasion of his visit in 129; but the building began long before that.

We know of a number of specialist crafts carried on in the city. Gold- and silversmiths are referred to in an inscription of 258. There must have been leatherworkers (referred to in the tax law). And the elaborate and distinctive brocades of Palmyrène costume are surely a local product. The demand for workers in stone was perhaps also sufficiently continuous to allow the establishment of local ateliers of size and skill adequate to carry out the immense public works of the city.

Where did the wealth come from? A city of the size of Palmyra needed to control a sizeable hinterland simply to feed itself if it was not to import basic foodstuffs. There is little doubt that Palmyrena was more fertile in classical times that it is now. In the early second century Appian refers to the sand "stretching from Palmyra to the Euphates,"[15] but the remains of ancient habitations in now barren spots suggest a greater plenitude of water, though there is little evidence of irrigation. Pliny describes Palmyra as "a city noble in its situation, in the richness of its soil and the pleasantness of its waters, (whose) fields are surrounded by a vast encircling area of sand,"[16] Olives were produced here, as a tessera of Bel Protector of Olives attests.[17] The cultivation of the olive was common generally in northern Syria in antiquity,[18] though it

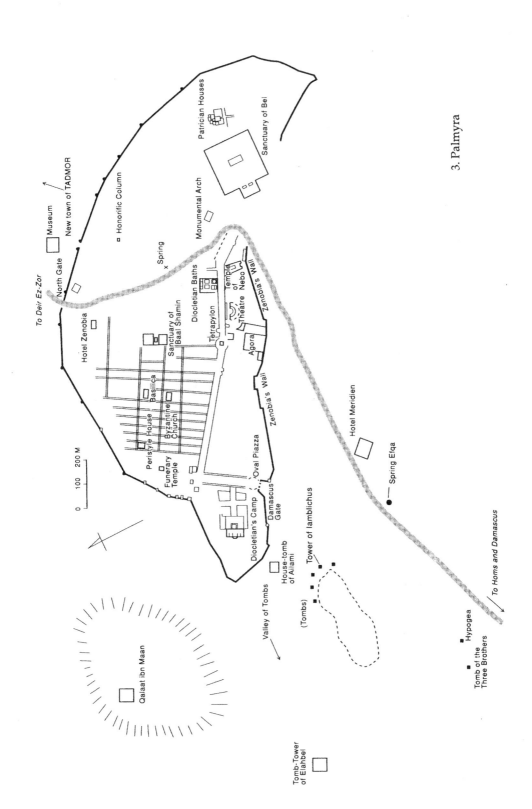

3. Palmyra

To Deir Ez-Zor

Museum

New town of TADMOR

Honorific Column

North Gate

Spring

Hotel Zenobia

Sanctuary of Baal Shamin

Diocletian Baths

Tetrapylon

Theâtre

Temple of Nebo

Zenobia's Wall

Agora

Basilica

Byzantine Church

Peristyle House

Funerary Temple

Oval Piazza

Zenobia's Wall

Diocletian's Camp

Damascus Gate

Tower of Iamblichus

House-tomb of Ailami

Valley of Tombs

(Tombs)

Patrician Houses

Monumental Arch

Sanctuary of Bel

Hotel Meridien

Spring Efqa

To Homs and Damascus

Hypogea

Tomb of the Three Brothers

Qalaat ibn Maan

Tomb-Tower of Elahbel

0   100   200 M

is scarcely found now. The salt flats east of Palmyra must have supported life before their waters seeped away, turning Palmyra into an oasis on the modern pattern. The typical vegetation of an oasis culture—palms and figs—was what travelers saw in 1691, though fifty odd years later Robert Wood saw only one palm tree. William Wright remarks on the extent of land cultivable as late as 1895:

> The plain, which runs between mountains, like the level bed of a narrow sea, from near Karyatein to Palmyra, varies in breadth from four to ten miles, and consists of good soil, which might be cultivated. On my first return trip from Palmyra, I found it carpeted with grass and flowers to the fetlocks of the horses. One nowhere meets the desert sands of tradition till almost at the entrance to Palmyra.[19]

Pliny emphasizes the sands, as a contrast to the locality of Palmyra itself; but he does not specify the size of the fertile chora. An inscription at Qa'ara, two hundred kilometers to the southeast, refers to "reapers here at the boundaries,"[20] on which Matthews builds a picture of traders touring the desert in search of wadis where the seed has managed to grow in a particular year. If this is so, we must see the city as drawing on the economic resources of a very extensive area, sucking the wealth of the sown desert into its greedy buildings. For produce, the tax law lists—besides sheep (nomad produce), dry goods (such as nuts and dates), and the easily obtainable salt—olive oil, corn, and fodder (hay?).

In 1920 Mark Sykes remarked on the new prosperity of northern Syria in terms that recall the situation of Palmyra in the first and second centuries A.D.

> On the way from Haleb to Meskene, as far as the eye can see, there stretches a glorious tract of corn-bearing land, spotted with brown mud villages, containing a mixed race of people who reply equally readily in Turkish, Kurdish or Arabic [Syriac, Palmyrene, and Greek?] to the questions put by a passing traveller. Many of these villages are the property of wealthy citizens of Haleb [Palmyra?] whose influence is sufficient to obtain protection of their tenants from the Government. The cultivation is not elaborate, but the ground is fairly tilled.[21]

But even if we can envisage a toiling peasantry supporting the luxuries of city life in the desert, the simple staples of the fields are not suffcient to explain Palmyra's wealth. Are we to assume cheap purchase accompanied by a steady income from the letting of lands for pasturage and agriculture—landowners draining the income as well as the produce of the hinterland? The wealth of the Roman Empire was concentrated in the hands of a very small proportion of the population and largely took the form of land. Liquidity might come from rents, though these could often be paid in kind, or possibly from mortgages. The sale of the produce of the fields, while it would ensure that the landowner did not make a loss on the extensive tracts that enhanced his status in the city, would not of itself make a Palmyrene a wealthy man.[22] In any case most of the market for the goods would be in the city itself. The growth of extra markets would enhance productivity and thence profits. An example in this region would be the two villas of Qasr al-Hair under the Umayyads, where a rulers' playground in the desert attracted a surrounding population and made it an important agricultural center. Roman camps had a rather similar effect on their surrounding countryside, as can be seen in the growth of vici at, for example, Vindolanda on Hadrian's Wall. But there is little evidence of this kind available for Syria, and in any case Palmyra was home only to a garrison, not to a legion.

One should not ignore the economic impact of a Roman garrison or nearby army station. The hard cash so plentiful among legionaries as among few of the other inhabitants of the empire attracted a plentiful civilian population, who by the late empire established themselves in vici around the military base. The Syrian troops would have had need of the services of craftsmen, who in this case were most likely to be situated in the city itself. But many cities had soldiers nearby—Antioch for one, but also minor towns like Zeugma and Samosata—and they did not prosper as Palmyra did. Army wealth will not explain Palmyra's wealth.

In early twentieth-century Syria, the urban elite of priests and officials built their wealth from two main sources, landownership and the farming of taxes.[23] It is important to consider the possible role of taxation in the wealth of Palmyra. For this reason considerable stress has often been laid on a very important inscription known as the Tariff of Palmyra,[24] discovered in the agora of Palmyra by prince Abamalek Lazarew in 1881.

This document is a combination of two successive edicts, the first datable to some time before A.D. 67, perhaps in part to the visit of

Germanicus in A.D. 18, and the second to A.D. 137. It is an unrivaled source of information on the economic life of Palmyra, but it may prove less than has been thought. It has often been interpreted as if it reflected the goods in transit through Palmyra from the Far East, and as if the proceeds of the taxes explained the wealth of Palmyra. A. H. M. Jones actually remarks that such local control of a frontier traffic is "unusual."[25] But when one looks at the commodities taxed, it is clear that the reference of the inscription is to local market traffic. They include dried goods, olive oil, lard, and dried fish, as well as myrrh, slaves, and prostitutes. The latter are in a sense "luxury" items; but as regards the rest, the city hardly became rich on the proceeds of wool and camel-fodder. The only exotic commodity is the myrrh. There is no mention of the other aromatics, or of any spices, and above all no reference to the silk that was Palmyra's reason for existence.

The inscription represents both an old and a revised or clarified text of the tax decree. The second version provides for the supervision of the publicans by the senate's functionaries and is designed to reduce the possibilities of friction between publicans and traders. It thus illustrates Roman control of Palmyra's internal and local trade.

In Cicero's day Roman control was mainly exercised through tax farmers,[26] but by the imperial period this system of tax farming had been much reduced. Only indirect taxes were collected this way. Even more significant, the only named tax farmer from Palmyra known to us is not a Palmyrene but a foreigner, L. Spedius Chrysanthus. This inscription of A.D. 58 shows that even at this early date Rome controlled the levying of taxes in Palmyra.

The first category of goods in the Palmyra tariff inscription is slaves, each of whom will be taxed at 22 d (denarii). There is a tax of 3 d per camel load of dry goods (2 d per donkey load), 8 d on each fleece dyed with purples, and 25 d on aromatic oil brought in. Then there was a tax for use of the water of Palmyra: 800 d, though the period covered is not specified. Agricultural produce, salt, and fats were taxed—salt at 1 as per modius. Bronze statues were taxed at the same rate as bullion. Though these were not local goods, equally they did not come from the East, and in most cases they were being bought by city residents—no doubt with the very wealth whose origins we are trying to explain. Perfumes were taxed in bulk and perfumiers paid a further tax; these were not transit goods but imported luxuries, again drains on wealth rather than its source.

Prostitutes paid a monthly tax equivalent to their charge for a single transaction (8 *asses* for one who charges 8 *asses*, 6 for 6, and so on). Novelistic writers have let their imagination run riot with these prostitutes: Alexander Baron envisages thousands of them in their silk-lined boudoirs or under every street lamp, in quantities practically equal to the entire female population of the city. For him, no doubt, the entire city might have been built on the immoral earnings of a few weeks in the caravan season. Agnes Carr Vaughan puts supposedly falling revenues from the prostitutes' tax (insidious, creeping morality among the local girls?) prominently among the motives for Zenobia's decision to seize Egypt. It is all grossly exaggerated. Furthermore, it does not explain our problem; again, the prostitutes are not transit goods. One gets the impression that the tariff is not a systematic document but a regulation of a variety of taxes collected for convenience in a single place.

Though some of the goods in the tariff are luxury items, most are basic necessities, and there is no mention of the most important item of trade through Palmyra, the silk from the East. This would indeed have been a seasonal trade. More importantly, the taxes of the silk trade would have constituted an imperial revenue and not a local one. The Romans would have exacted taxes on goods in transit just as they did at such known entrepôts as Alexandria—or at Leuke Kome, where Rome levied an import duty on all goods of 25 percent.[27] It is clear that the tariff on the whole is designed to cover regular items of exchange, many of them in the context of either the local monthly market or the day-to-day business of the souq. Such taxes do not make a city wealthy.

There is no doubt that the wealth of Palmyra was the direct rather than the indirect result of the trade and traffic coming through the city. But who were the merchants whose wealth enriched the city? And was it the investment of the merchants themselves that enriched it?

Rostovtzeff, in a type of analysis common to many earlier economic historians of antiquity, saw Palmyrene wealth as the product of the activities of a trading aristocracy.[28] It is a vexed question whether any aristocracy in the ancient world can properly be described as engaging in trade, as the aristocrats of medieval Italy and Flanders certainly did; though M. I. Finley accepted the view in the unique case of Palmyra.[29] Aristocrats in the ancient world were essentially landed gentry. They disposed of the surplus produce of their estates through commercial agents, not directly; and they did not aim to make money, in the sense of maximizing profits, through such commerce. If a notable kept grain in his storehouses to release it only in times of shortage, it was not in order to sell dear but in order to increase his standing and the gratitude of the citizens.[30]

An interesting hint comes from another part of the ancient Semitic world: "Who has planned this against Tyre, the bestower of crowns, whose merchants were princes, whose traders were the honoured of the earth?"[31] The implication of this passage is that trade could produce wealth that would be a source of honor to its possessor, that commerce could make an aristocrat. Is this how we should picture the ruling classes of Palmyra? As we have seen in chapter 1, the Syrians were merchants par excellence, precisely because they made a living by trade rather than by rents. Those Palmyrene merchants with their offices in Vologesias, Seleuceia, Coptos, and even Merv eventually brought their wealth back to their home towns. But did they rule it?

Crucial evidence is found in the dedicatory inscriptions of Palmyra. In the first place, the dedications of the great buildings and temples of Palmyra are all made in the name of the tribes. The tribes existed in parallel with any commercial organization at Palmyra and reflected, not the interest groups of different trades (as they might have done, like medieval guilds) but a social structure belonging to the nomad origins of the peoples, the quasi-feudal troops of Bedouin under a leading sheikh. The association of the wealth of the city with the tribes and their leaders, rather than the merchants as such, is likewise reflected in the dedicatory inscriptions erected to benefactors of the caravans at Palmyra. These do not commemorate the merchants; rather the merchants set them up. The bronze statues are now all lost, but the consoles survive along the main thoroughfare of Palmyra and before the chief buildings.

The dedications form a series running from A.D. 132 to 266. One of the most honored of the protectors of the caravans is Soados:

> The council and people honored Soados the son of Boliades the son of Soados the son of Thaimisamsos, the pious man who loved his native land, who on many and important occasions protected in a noble and generous way the interests of traders and caravans and of his co-citizens established at Vologesias, and in addition was commended by a letter from the god Hadrian and from the most divine Emperor Antoninus his son, as well as by the decree of Publicius Marcellus and by his letter and that of the succeeding consulars, and was honored with decrees and statues by the council and people and by those who traveled with him at any time and

by all the citizens individually; and now, alone of all citizens ever, he has been honored by his country for his continual and mutual beneficence by four statues erected at public expense on columns in the city square, as well as three other statues in Spasinou Charax and in Vologesias and in Gennaes, at the expense of those who traveled with him and the council and people. He also established and dedicated in Vologesias a temple of the Augusti; and for his great generosity, his exceptionally beneficent dynasty . . . [32]

Further dedications for Soados date from the years 140 to 161: he seems to have devoted much of an adult lifetime to this service. The same service is recorded also for Ogelos in 199,[33] and T. Aelius Ogeilas got four statues and an equestrian statue.[34] The dedicators thank the gods munificently for their assistance, with the implicit hope that they will help again. *Do ut des, da ut dem*, is the constant interplay of the oriental bargain with the gods.

In the series there is a gap between 161 (the end of the Persian War) and 193, when Taimarsu paid 300 gold denarii for the protection of the caravan.[35] This is the first reference to a synodiarch's paying for the protection of the caravan. Previously there is no mention of expenditure, only of assistance. From this point on the expenditure by the synodiarchs is almost invariably mentioned. The increasing number of such inscriptions in the later period may suggest the greater risks of caravan traffic in an ungoverned zone preparing itself for a further war in 216/8. In 198/9 we hear of more extreme measures: the creation of a *strategia kata ton nomadon* (generalship against the nomads) and a *strategos epi tes eirenes* (general to keep the peace). The keeping of peace in the desert borderlands seems to have become a formal magistracy. It appears that the Romans had enlisted the aid of the city notables and their tribesmen, who were in a quasi-feudal relation to them, to carry out the formal task—which was called a liturgy—of policing the desert borderlands between the empires. Such a liturgy would, as elsewhere in the empire, be undertaken by the notable at his own expense, and this would explain why the inscriptions begin to refer to the synodiarch's paying for the service he provided.

Typical of the inscriptions of this period are those for Yaddai of A.D. 211, Julius Aurelius Zebeida (date uncertain), and Julius Aurelius Shalamallath of 257/8:

The council and people honored Julius Aurelius Shalamallath Males the chief merchant, who escorted the caravan at his own expense.[36]

Most interesting is the long inscription of A.D. 266 for Septimius Vorod who had become one of the most important citizens in Palmyra:

> The council and the people [honor] Septimius Vorodes the mighty steward of Augustus, with the rank of ducenarius, lawgiver of the mother colony, who escorted the caravans at his own expense and was commemorated by the chief merchants, who led the troops magnificently, who was market surveyor of the mother colony and spent a great deal of his own funds and was pleasing to the council and people and now is glorious symposiarch of the god Zeus Bel because of his holiness and glory.[37]

The language of these decrees is not that in which merchants are usually addressed. One must observe here the distinction between the emporoi and archemporoi, the merchants and chief merchants, and the synodiarchs, which may be translated as "chief accompaniers" of the expedition.[38]

More likely the synodiarch was a town-dwelling sheikh, who would recruit a body of troops from his tribesmen in the desert to guarantee the camel train's safe-conduct in its slow progress through 250 kilometers of Bedouin territory.[39] The desert dwellers provided this crucial service for the merchants. It was very probably paid for by the merchants in the earlier period under consideration; emphasis on the synodiarch providing this service at his own expense only occurs after 193 and may suggest a notable change in practice. However, despite the rhetoric of beneficence, the protection still might have been paid for ultimately by the merchants or chief merchants. It was commonplace throughout the empire for notables to receive bribes or "sweeteners" for carrying out their statutory duties, when these would benefit a particular interest group.

An intriguing parallel to the honorable duty of protecting caravans can be found in Isabel Burton's description of the "blackmail" paid to a leading sheikh of Damascus in the last century to afford protection for the caravan of the pilgrimage to Mecca: "He receives the annual sum of 200,000 piastres, nominally to supply 650 camels and men for carrying barley, but really for permit to pass, a blackmail . . . politely called voluntary contributions."[40] The Palmyrene sheikh maintained a militia, with the support of Rome, to keep the nomads at bay. This police force, if one may call it that, was paid for from his own pocket, but it is not impossible that he received just such "voluntary contributions" from the merchants.

An alternative interpretation of these dedications by the merchants to the synodiarchs is suggested by the dedications from Coptos, where the emporoi, merchants, thank the naukleroi, the shipowners, for their investment in the trade.[41] Shipowning and shipping insurance are the most clearly identifiable forms of capitalism in the ancient world. It may then be legitimate to suppose that, while some synodiarchs were sheikhs whose wealth in the past had come from the characteristic brigandage of the nomad, others had made their way up as traders and capitalists and had become the top of the tree in the hierarchy of merchants in the city. Perhaps they owned the souq![42] Their expenditure on keeping the caravan trade going in safety, though it is represented by the traders as a piece of altruistic beneficence (*euergetism* in the technical parlance of antiquity) is in practice an investment in the protection of the sources of wealth of the city.

Euergetism, an important aspect of ancient social life, is comparatively unfamiliar today, though it would not have seemed strange to the great self-made industrialists of Victorian Britain. Many a textile manufacturer or mill owner from Yorkshire or Devonshire, after making his fortune from industry, would use his wealth not only to build a fine residence in parkland for himself but to endow educational institutions, libraries, or other civic amenities—this quite apart from the benefits offered to his workers themselves. A recent book by Paul Veyne, *Bread and Circuses,* has exhaustively discussed this important aspect of ancient civic life, the effects of which ranged from the building of temples and theaters to the organizing of gladiatorial games and the running of fire brigades.

The wealth of the sheikhs and of the tribes they commanded provided the resources that paid for the buildings of Palmyra. The cities of neighboring Persia and Arabia are built of brick or mud, but the public edifices of Palmyra are all of polished stone, of marble and porphyry. The Hellenistic city lay largely to the south of the later wall. The brick houses with flat roofs, enclosing narrow streets, remained a purely residential quarter, and the same characteristic belonged to the area around the spring (where the Meridien hotel now stands) and that around the Temple of Baalshamin. Between these—doubtless through the razing of much of the residential building—a monumental center inched skyward.

The Buildings of Palmyra

The prosperity of Palmyra is most vividly expressed in the continuous program of building that occupies much of the next two centuries. "Looking at separate plans of great cities certainly will not tell you about the form and order of the world," wrote Polybius;[43] but it could tell you a good deal about the Roman order. The Roman imperial might encouraged the construction of public buildings, and every self-respecting city had to have a complete set, which at its minimum would consist of a forum / agora, a senate house, a theater, baths, and perhaps a capitol as well as the temples of the gods—all situated in appropriate parts of the city (Mercury, god of traders, near the market; Venus, goddess of love, well away from the center, if not actually outside the walls, and so on).[44]

The conservative architect Vitruvius gave detailed instructions on the layout of a proper Roman city: the streets were to follow lines drawn between the main directions of the winds, to avoid unhealthy breezes blowing directly down the streets; theaters should normally face any way but south; statues in temples should normally face west; and so on. Such instructions were followed with a good deal of freedom, but it is remarkable how similar from side to side of the empire the architectural styles remain. The orders, derived from the Greeks, remain fundamental; and though some buildings might rise up on special plans, still the detail and ornamentation remained recognizably Roman and imperial from Palmyra to Gades, from Djemila to Colchester. The rhetor Aelius Aristides was quite explicit about the meaning of imperial civic architecture: it was a statement of Roman power quite as strident as the glory of arms, but one more appropriate to time of peace—one of the "arts of peace" that Rome claimed proudly to have brought to its happy subjects.[45]

Palmyra's architectural glory began with the building in A.D. 17–19 of the porticoes of the Temple of Bel.[46] Bel is one of the oldest gods of the variable Semitic pantheon, originating from Babylon where he is the lord of all the gods. Though it lies east of the city proper, this temple dominates Palmyra as surely in its present form as Wells Cathedral does its own little city. Roman in its detail—its columns, its architraves, and its elaborate floral-abstract mouldings—it is entirely Semitic in its general conception. Like the Temple of Solomon in Jerusalem, it consists of a large open courtyard with the house of the god placed noncentrally against one of the long sides, facing the long side in which the entrance to the sanctuary is situated. The house of the god itself is entered by a central monumental gateway. Within, to left and right, stand symmetrical roofed shrines, one perhaps for the permanent statue of the god, the other for its portative replica used in processions. Such a layout may be recognized throughout Syria. The central temple at Ebla, more than a thousand years older, is similar in ground plan, as are several of the temples at the Phoenician city of Ugarit. The temple of Baalshamin at Palmyra is also similar, but other temples at Palmyra, built somewhat later, conform instead to a Greek-classical ground plan.

The layout is in sharp contrast to the other traditional Syrian ground plan, which developed over the centuries into the apsidal church. A long nave with a god-niche at the end is found at Ebla and later sites and develops directly into the first churches of Syria and, for example, the temple of the Syrian gods at Rome. But no pre-Christian shrines on this model are found at Palmyra.

The Temple of Bel may have been built by imperial funds, but subsequent temples were built on Palmyrene wealth. Bel's dedication in A.D. 32 was soon followed by the building of the Temple of Baalshamin, the Lord of Heaven. This was dedicated in A.D. 89, and the Temple of Nebo (identified by the Greeks with Hermes) dates also from about this period. The altar before the Temple of Baalshamin is dated A.D. 115, and the present temple was dedicated in 130/1, the year after Hadrian's visit, by his host Male Agrippa. The suggestion that this new dedication, to the "Lord of Heaven," represents a spiritualization of cult over the earlier more personal deities is perhaps negated by the almost contemporaneous erection (ca. 103–164) of the Temple of Allat, which is very similar in style to that of Baalshamin. The goddess Allat, who enters the Qur'an as one of the daughters of Allah, is a strongly personal deity, sometimes pictured riding on a camel. On his visit Hadrian made sacrifice also to Aglibol and Malakbel[47] and must surely have made donations to their shrines too. Other building from this period includes the tetrapylon and the street to its west, and perhaps the nymphaeum.

The accession of the Syrian dynasty of the Severi at Rome saw further advances in building at Palmyra. The great monumental arch was built between 193 and 211 to link the main street and the Temple of Bel, and the busts of Septimius Severus and his wife Julia Domna that were erected in the agora prove that the construction of this marketplace also dates from Septimius' reign.

The theater, like other Syrian theaters, also belongs to the second century, though the first inscriptions found in it are from the Flavian period in the late first century. The theater was used perhaps less for dramatic performances than for public announcements, political meetings and speeches, and the displays of oratory of which the Roman Empire was so fond. Alexander Baron imagines the newly arrived refugee from Antioch, Bishop Paul, delivering one of his sermons here, surrounded by his retinue of choirgirls (see chapter 6, pp. 149–50).

By this time the roads to the Euphrates were also under construction. The father of Emperor Trajan was responsible for them, indicating a firm Roman grip on the city and its surroundings. No doubt the city streets were paved at this time, making them as splendid and secure as the famed streets of Antioch—though whether Palmyra also boasted street lighting we do not know. William Wright observed:

> Looking at the ruins of Tadmor, one wonders at the rage that must have existed for columns. Little houses had their tiers of little columns and great houses had their tiers of correspondingly great columns. Public edifices for civil and religious uses had their quota of lofty columns. Little streets and public squares all had their rows of columns; and wherever you move, columns without number block your path. . . . The columns mania found its fullest expression in the great colonnade of the main street.[48]

Colonnades were, indeed, an essential element of the Eastern Roman city. The origin of the colonnade is disputed—perhaps under Herod's rule in Antioch.[49] It began with the porticoed building or block and gradually grew to become the characteristic articulation of entire streets, a provider of grateful shade in the desert heat.

Equally characteristic of Roman splendor, though more private, were the mosaics. From Antioch to Bostra and east as far as Palmyra (though not it seems at Dura-Europos), the houses of the wealthy were adorned with mosaics—of exotic scenes, like the one of Nile life in the Terme Museum at Rome; of maps of the Orient, like the one at Madaba in Palestine; and of genre scenes and mythological tales. The Damascus museum exhibits mosaics from Antioch, among others the legend of Pelops and Hippodameia and a philosophical allegory of Justice and Virtue. The Museum at Apamea houses a collection—Virgilian scenes, Christian texts, mythological scenes, hunting tableaux, groups of philosophers in discussion—that bears comparison with the mosaics of Piazza Armerina. Relatively few have been found at Palmyra, though two fine ones show respectively the discovery of Achilles on Scyros

(Palmyra Museum) and the legend of Cassiopeia (Damascus Museum). Such adornments show more clearly than anything the way in which classical culture dominated the ideologies of the wealthy. Imperialism was at its most effective when it infiltrated the minds and the leisure, not the public face, of its subjects.

Yet in one respect Palmyra was not a typical Roman city. Unlike the cities of the Greek East it had no gymnasium; and unlike these, and even those in the desert regions of North Africa, it had no public baths and no amphitheater. This in itself speaks volumes about the distinctiveness of Palmyrene culture and its distance from the Hellenic ideals of the Roman world or from the amusements of Roman citizens elsewhere.

By the time that the dynasty of Odenathus became powerful, then, we may envisage a Palmyra already in more or less the state of splendor whose ruins survive today. All the main buildings were in place. The Baths of Diocletian, of 293–303, seem to stand on the remains of an earlier building that has lately been plausibly identified as the Palace of Zenobia.[50] Remarkable is the funerary temple, a fine classical structure of the third century containing the only tombs within the city walls. It is possible that this too should be associated with the family of Odenathus, whose newly established kingly power alone might receive the special honor of burial within the city perimeter.

Despite the Roman character of Palmyra's outward appearance— its temples, arches, agora, laws, and constitution—the structure of Palmyrene society remained essentially tribal. We know the names of at least thirty of the tribes of Palmyra, including seventeen major ones, many of which bear names clearly representing their dedication to a particular god, for example,

Bene (sons of) Gaddibol (Bol is my Fortune)
Bene Zabdibol (slave of Bol)
Bene Yedi'bel (known to Bel)
Bene Mattabol (gift of Bol)
Bene Penabol (Bol looks kindly)

and a few of other deities, such as the Bene Taymarsu (servant of Arsu). But many of these tribes are apparently subdivisions of major tribes— many appearing only in a single inscription. The tribal names indicate various racial origins: bene Ma'zin (goat-men) is an Arab name; Kohennadu and Zmr' are Amorite; the bulk (Gaddibol, Zabdibol, Yedi'bel,

Mattabol, Zbud, Komara) are Aramaic; and some are of uncertain derivation. Nabataeans also participated in the cosmopolitan mix of Palmyrene society.[51]

It seems that by the second century A.D. the population of Palmyra had been subdivided more neatly on a quasi-Roman system into four main tribes, each with responsibility for one of the four major cults of the city.[52] Increasing hierarchization of rule from above thus coincided with an increase of city cult as distinct from tribal cult; family loyalties were slowly submerged in the growing self-consciousness of the people as citizens of Palmyra. The bene Komare tended the shrine of Aglibol and Malakbel with its dining room; the bene Ma'zin and their branch the bene Yedi'bel were responsible for Baalshamin and the Arab gods; the Kohanim tended the Garden of the Gods; and the bene Matabol looked after Arsu and Atargatis.[53] One tribe with a Roman name, Claudia, is also referred to. It plainly dates from Corbulo's time in the East under the last of the Julio-Claudians, but its later history and its relation to the indigenous tribes are unclear. In general, it is far from easy to construct a tidy system of these tribes. We must assume fluctuations of power and alliance, varying perhaps with the dominance of one or another cult in the city.

We can scarcely doubt that these tribes engaged in rivalry, often of a far from friendly kind. In an inscription of A.D. 21, the Chomareni and Mattabolii praise a man who made peace between them.[54] Would that we knew more of the stories that grew out of the bitter feuds of these antique Montagues and Capulets. We can only imagine the jockeying for power and influence, the careful expenditure of wealth, and the ostentation of display in which the sheikhs engaged.

We have already seen that several cults were especially associated with particular tribes; and tombs, too, were often the property of one tribe or group of families. Generally they were reserved for the members of that family. But here as elsewhere in the Orient—and indeed throughout the empire—there were burial clubs to which individuals would pay a subscription in their lifetimes to ensure a fitting lodgment after their deaths; these would amount to advance reservations on a niche in one of the tower blocks of the hereafter. If we know nothing of the leasing of lands in Palmyrena, we can guess at least that the great tribal leaders might receive valuable mortgages on such little plots of eternity.

The tomb towers are, with the colonnades, one of the most striking features of Palmyra. They are not unique: such towers are found also at the old Parthian capital of Hatra, and at Qanawat. But here alone do they continue into the style of the Roman Empire. William Wright wrote:

> I shall never forget the consternation with which I first saw the tomb towers. There they towered up to heaven, more than one hundred feet high, most of them horribly cracked and toppling over; even the stones seemed rotten. . . . Around the base of the mountains, on all sides, these huge towers of death lifted their heads aloft, grim and inaccessible.[55]

His horror was compounded by his anxiety about climbing the towers. On the advice of Sir Richard Burton (who had been unable to explore them), he had come equipped with huge thirty-foot ladders, ropes, and grappling-irons, but the prospect of the actual climb was nearly as alarming as the thought of the view his local guides would consequently take of his sanity. Exploration eventually produced a loot of numerous skulls and "many pieces of broken statuary . . . so stiff and conventional that we could not much blame the barbarian iconoclasts."[56] I cannot share his artistic taste; but what Wright calls those "simpering ladies" did perhaps achieve their most characteristic instantiation in the frozen postures of immortality. Tribal life and custom does not change much faster than eternity.

With their rich contents the tower tombs are the most remarkable index of the prosperity of individual Palmyrenes. They spread over two centuries. Most contain sculptured portraits of the dead and their families, but a few, like the underground Tomb of the Three Brothers, are decorated with painted portraits whose colors, preserved in the dry dark penetralia of the desert, are as fresh and natural as the day they were painted. There is the tomb from 103 of the four sons of Wahballath: Elahbel, Manai, Shokadji, and Malikhu. They are surrounded by grooms and pages, and winged jinn who perhaps afford protection on their journey to the beyond.

They disturb one, these Palmyrene portraits. Male and female alike stare out at you with an unsettling self-assurance, indeed an arrogance, not with a gaze that betokens anger at the disturbance of their rest but with a gaze fixed with absolute confidence on a beyond of whose lineaments we have absolutely no idea. The faces are sharply individual, and yet it is argued that all cannot be portraits in our sense, for in a few cases the same features reappear with different names attached. Yet we feel we know something of these haughty people clad in rich garments and jewelry and often accompanied by symbols that tell us more of their profession: the priest in his hat or diadem, the cameleer with a camel peering over his shoulder. It is inconceivable to me that these effigies should not be intended for portraits. That would not preclude the occasional use of a standard design when a client was too poor to afford bespoke or in the case of an urgent commission. I am not convinced by the cases where the same individual is allegedly portrayed with different features in two separate monuments. After all, such portraits are bound to be idealized: the subject did not sit on his death bed for his portrait but commissioned it long before, so a man who died at seventy may well be represented by a portrait of a man of thirty-five.

Some, perhaps poorer rather than shyer, literally draw a veil over their features: their monument is a curtain inscribed with a name. The play is over; the light is out for this faceless soul. The Palmyrene word for these portraits is, in fact, the word for "soul," *naphsha* (cf., Hebrew *nephesh*). Perhaps two souls may look the same when their bodily counterparts differ. One text from Petra uses the term to refer to the representation and stele of a deceased person actually buried at distant Jerash.[57] Were the Palmyrenes all individuals in the sight of their gods, in the sight of Him who is blessed forever, in the sight of the All-Merciful? Or did they assert their individuality so ferociously at death as a defiant gesture against the shadowy interchangeability of souls that go into the dark?

The Gods of Palmyra

Though the connection of certain tribes with certain gods seems clear, it is far from easy, in the absence of any mythological or liturgical literature, to distinguish one of the numerous gods of Palmyra from another. We do not find, as we do in North Africa, Roman gods taking on local coloring. There is no equivalent of the Egyptian Pan, no Syrian Bacchus or Hercules of the desert. Roman beliefs made no impact here, despite the incidence of scenes from classical mythology on the beautiful mosaic pavements in some of the most sumptuous houses. The classical culture remains a topdressing.

Semitic gods tend to gather into triads: an example is the triad of Baal, Astarte, and Melqart at Tyre. Gods of essentially the same attributes will have different names in different places. Conversely, names may be an unreliable guide to function. The dominant Arab cult of the sun has overlaid many of the earlier characteristics of such gods as Yarhibol (whose name implies a moon-god, and who is shown on reliefs with a crescent crown like the moon-god Sin of Harran). The Babylonian god Bel has displaced the similarly named indigenous god Bol, whose name is preserved in the theophoric names of the tribes. Bel seems indeed to retain dominance, not least in the exceptional size of his sanctuary.

Outsider gods like Du-rahlun of Mt. Hermon seem to arrive with their tribes, in this case bene Maazin. Allat, another goddess tended by the bene Maazin, was a very important goddess among the Arabs, but at Palmyra she seems to have become almost indistinguishable from Atargatis, as Artemis and Athena alike merge in the Greek perception of this goddess. She is of special importance at Palmyra as the guardian of the city, in which form she is portrayed on a beautiful relief now in the Palmyra Museum.

Finally there is the Anonymous God, "He whose name is blessed forever." The first dedication in these terms dates from 132, the last from 236.[58] He has many altars at Efqa, the spring whose special care is Yarhibol's, but he is almost certainly to be identified with Baalshamin, the Lord of Heaven. One can imagine what St. Paul would have made of encountering such a dedication to an "unknown" or "unnamed" god; but we should resist the temptation to spiritualize the conception as betokening a move in the direction of an awed and humble monotheism. After all, the name of Yahweh was also not to be spoken aloud, and this designation may simply signify a particular respect for a still highly individualized god. The expression "He whose name is blessed forever" appears also in Jewish writings.[59] The designation of the Lord as "highest and ready to listen" may recall to us Psalm 118.5: "I called upon the Lord in distress: the Lord answered me and set me at liberty." Such "Judaizing language" has been seen as Jewish influence over Palmyra[60] but it can have no bearing on the supposed Jewish sympathies of Queen Zenobia. The inscriptions peter out before she could have been born; and as we shall see, in her generation another God attracted the honors of the dominant family of Palmyra.

Ultimately one can only note the diversity of Palmyra's august deities whom little distinguishes, and note, perhaps with relief, more characterful gods like Arsu and Azizu, mounted on camel and horse respectively, who guard the caravans as they cross the desert.

Conspicuous is the absence—characteristic of all Syria—of any cult of the Roman emperor. Were Palmyra's gods too otherworldly to find a place for the emperor among them, even though they themselves were generally clad in the military uniform of Rome? Or did some ideological objection resist such a form of cult, as the Jews resisted the placing of the emperor's image in the Temple of the Lord at Jerusalem?

The cult of these gods is easier to recapture than the theology. Most received their worship in sanctuaries made pleasant by groves or gardens. The "holy grove" is the chief place of cult for Aglibol and Malakbel. A temple seems to have been an extra, reserved for the most august gods—or perhaps for the richest tribes. Cult included both animal sacrifice and offerings of incense. Surviving cult apparatus—bowls, vases, braziers, and censers—bring to life the rich complexity of the liturgy.

A Palmyrene liturgy may be recognized in the fresco from the Temple of the Palmyrene Gods at Dura-Europos. A figure clad in priestly garb of white linen robes and a tall conical hat dips a branch into a vase of—perhaps—holy water, no doubt to asperge the celebrants. At the same time an assistant throws incense into a censer. Both men are carrying a ewer, a bowl, and two knives. The lustral water is important here as throughout Syria. Offerings were thrown into the spring Efqa every year, and perhaps oracles were sought here as at Aphaca.[61] At Hierapolis water was brought twice yearly from the "sea," to replenish a chasm before the temple.[62] The knives imply a following sacrifice, perhaps of a black bull as at Harran.

Though it is scarcely safe to generalize from one sanctuary to another in this far-flung desert of isolated cities, some sense of occasion may perhaps be gained from the description by a Christian writer of a spring festival at Edessa in the late fifth century:

> There came round again the time of that festival at which the heathen tales were sung; and the citizens took even more pains about it than usual. For seven days previously they were going up in crowds to the theatre at eventide, clad in linen garments, and wearing turbans with their loins ungirt. Lamps were lighted before them, and they were burning incense, and holding vigil the whole night, walking about the city and praising the dancer until morning, with singing and shouting and lewd behaviour.[63]

Burning incense and shedding the blood of cattle may often have been part of religious ritual at Palmyra; but equally often cult took the form of a sacred meal, usually eaten by no more than a dozen people. One thinks of the Essene rule reported by Josephus that if more than nine persons come to such a meal the presence of a priest was obligatory.[64] The tale of the Last Supper of Jesus also comes to mind. In Palmyra such gatherings were called *marzeah*, corresponding to the Greek word *thiasos*, "a sacred company"; at those of Baalshamin at least, wine was drunk in a kind of eucharist. Admission to these feasts was by ticket. Enormous numbers of these tickets, in the form of terracotta tesserae, have survived, and they bear the symbols of the gods to whose feasts they admit: for example, a horse for Elqonera (Poseidon) and two altars with an ox and a cypress tree for Aglibol and Malakbel.[65] There was also a bath for ritual washing before the meal.

Altogether one may imagine that a feast of one of the gods of Palmyra much resembled the more populous ones of the tomb reliefs—dignified and gracious men and ladies, clad in elaborately embroidered or brocaded robes, the women with heavy earrings and plentiful necklaces and bracelets, the men in the tall pillbox hats of priests or bareheaded, reclining on the couches in the temple dining room (perhaps one was left empty for the god), singing a hymn, perhaps, and decorously tasting of the meats and wine as the heavy fragrance of incense wafted around the room. The largest known such dining room holds forty-five, but most are much smaller. Apart from the splendor and the servants, the atmosphere cannot have been altogether unlike the communal piety of the early Christians in their upper rooms. It is all quite unlike the ecstatic cults of western Syria. The chief of the priests of Bel was known as the symposiarch, master of dining, which suggests the special importance of the ritual meal in the cult of Bel here, as at Babylon.[66]

Such a feast was at once a celebration of the ancestors and a worship of the god. Dining in temples goes back a long way in the Near East. The Temple of Bel in Babylon contained a couch and a golden table:[67] perhaps only the priests consumed the viands. A favored individual like Paulina, whose story is told by Josephus,[68] might sup alone with the god—in this case Anubis. In the Palmyrene case the clan as much as the priests were the celebrants: the event was more social than personal or mystical. As R. Wilken writes in an excellent characterization of ancient religion:

In the ancient world, religion was less a matter of individual choice than a social reality created by traditional institutions and patterns of life, with their accompanying social, cultural and moral values. These values were not "secular" in the modern sense. They were

intimately intertwined with religious traditions. . . . Religion served
to unite the past with the present, law with morality, education
with politics, the family with society, architecture with mythology,
the calendar with religious ritual.[69]

The Palmyrene grave-feast, like the temple-feast, was an expression
of clan cohesiveness and of the stability of the social order. It carried
on into Christian practice with feasts in graveyards. As one might
expect, St. Augustine inveighed against grave-feasts of this kind, calling
them "drunken revels in cemeteries and social orgies."[70] Perhaps he
divined that they not only were depraved but could be socially divisive,[71]
for a feast at the ancestral grave could also be seen as a statement of
social exclusiveness.

The cyclic element in the divine year was important, and the cult
at least of Aglibol and Malakbel was of special importance at New
Year. Tending the god by inviting him to dinner is known also, though
less well attested, among the Greeks. The attitude toward the gods is
in sharp contrast to that of, for example, the Egyptian religion, where
priests tend the image day in and day out, getting the god up, dressing
it, feeding it, and putting it to bed. In Palmyra the god is an honored
guest, not a pampered object of wonder. It is so hard to recapture the
diversity of feeling in the innumerable religions of antiquity. One has
the impression of a quiet, sober people, in character like the present-
day Bedouin, whose life is measured by the movements of the stars and
the slow growth of the desert plants—a people ideally suited to the
peace of Islam and the fatalism of *Mektoub*. I wish we could recapture
more of their daily life, but their concerns only become visible through
their gods.

Of particular importance from our point of view is the emergence
of a cult of the sun (Sams) as distinct from the radiate sun-god Yarhibol
of Bel's sanctuary. Sams is first found sharing a sanctuary with Allat.
But he acquired a sanctuary to the west of the transverse colonnade,
and some time between the death of Odenathus (267) and 272 a statue
was erected to him in his own right:

The Senate and people for [. . .] of the city of [Septimius Odena]
thus the King of Kings, when he erected the marble (statue) of
Helios the ancestral [god] of the Augusti and dedicated the [. . .]
and of the Emperor . . . for his honour and generosity.[72]

Another inscription shows us Helios and Sams identified.[73] The Augusti here are certainly Zenobia and Wahballath, so we may see here a dedication set up at their authority in the city still seen as the personal kingdom of Odenathus. Is it going too far to link the rise to power of Odenathus and Zenobia with the new prominence of the sun-god, perhaps the preserve of Odenathus' own tribe? Are theological interests again involved? Or is this the arrival of a new god with a new leader having strong connections with the desert Arabs?[74]

Besides the high gods there are the "helper" gods, the manifold djennaye and gadde—the latter identified with the Greek Tyche, or Fortune of the City, the former developing into the Judaeo-Christian guardian angels and the jinns of Islam who protect the Bedouin and their flocks. They are dressed in long-sleeved tunics, cloaks, and loincloths. The caravan gods Arsu and Azizu are mounted like their charges. Abgal, the god of the steppe, appears as a long-haired youth with a moustache. Allat, riding on a camel, is often accompanied by her Gad, the protector of village and garden.

Among these gods in the changeless garb of the desert, it is startling to find that the great gods like Yarhibol, Aglibol, and Malakbel generally dress, at least from the first century, in Roman military uniform. However, this is by no means uncommon in the East:[75] Jupiter Dolichenus, Mithras, and even the Dioscuri in Africa are similarly attired, and some of the most famous early representations of Christ likewise show him as a beardless soldier. The strength of the soldier implied the power of the god to protect his weak followers. In Palmyra at least military strength was to lead to hybris and to be put sorely to the test. The strength of the city's gods was not enough.

Easiest to envisage at Palmyra is the physical appearance of the people, with their notably gorgeous style of dress. Countless portraits and tomb reliefs display every detail of their attire.[76] Over a linen tunic in its natural color were worn woolen (and, occasionally, cotton) garments in a range of warm, vivid colors—reds and blues, browns and purples and gold—often in floral or geometric patterns. But the tiny surviving fragments of silken garments with their woven bands of flowers and beasts are the most evocative of all, for they at once testify to the basis of Palmyra's existence and instantiate the Palmyrenes' love of the soft, gorgeous, and intricate. Though women often went veiled, this did not prevent them from adorning themselves with jewelry.

A performance in the theater must have been a wonderful sight as the men and women in shimmering and ornate, brightly colored garments moved into place along the marble seats in the glaring sun. In the cool of the colonnaded main street, the traders squatted in their boxlike shops, the size of stalls in a modern souq, almost hidden behind piles of fabrics, nuts and dried fruits and other food stuffs, rare joints of meat, and the simple wooden and pottery artifacts of household use. Perhaps a few also sold glass, which was a major product—and export— of Syria as of Egypt.[77] Every year, in season, the great caravans would come from the Euphrates to hand on their goods to a relay of cameleers and would be taxed as they did so; and there was no doubt a weekly market, perhaps before the Temple of Bel, where the villagers brought their few grapes, apricots, or figs, or a pair of trussed and squawking chickens. Beyond the walls, the Roman camps housed the soldiers, who tramped occasionally along the frontier roads but spent more time in camp with dice and tankard—and no doubt with those famous prostitutes.

High above the crowds, along the consoles of the colonnade, stood the statues of famous men of all the tribes of Palmyra—merchants and synodiarchs, warriors of the desert, and officials of the city. These are the men in whose honor the dedications of gratitude for the protection of caravans were erected. These are also the men—and their wives— whose portraits stare out at us from the funerary sculptures that survive. They are the leading men of Palmyra. The statues of the colonnade— probably bronze—are lost, and only the inscriptions that stood beneath them survive.

As the centuries progressed, more and more power seems to have been concentrated in the hands of a few. Though the inscriptions continued to be erected in the name of the council and people, by the 250s one family had arrogated princely power to itself, and the might of arms had finally displaced the civic institutions of the city—just as happened in the last days of the Roman Republic. This was the family of Odenathus and his wife Zenobia.

The Emergence of Odenathus

The family of Odenathus emerges suddenly from the flitting penumbra of aristocratic clans. It may be that his family was one that had amassed wealth at a greater rate from landowning and the protection of caravans. Alternatively, it has been suggested that the rise of the dynast is the result of the arrival of bands of newcomers driven across the Euphrates by the aggressive new Persian dynasty of Shapur I.[78] The new elite bear names of varied linguistic origin. Odenathus is Arabic (Little Ear), but he is the grandson of Nasor and son of Hairan (both Aramaic names). His lieutenant Worod bears a Parthian name suggesting an Iranian origin, but his son Ogeilo bears an Arab one. They seem thus distinguished from the Aramaic race that makes up the bulk of Palmyra's population, and the linguistic argument provides slight further support for the supposition that Odenathus was one of the tribal sheikhs who was involved in the caravan escorts.

It is possible that the Roman love of a strong division of classes in the cities encouraged the narrowing of the elite, already reduced to four tribes by the second century, to a single princely family and its satellites. Even more important would have been the Roman support for the military leadership, in her own service, of one princely family. In this connection it is suggestive to note the revival of other local dynasties in the course of the third century. Rostovtzeff points to the examples of Emesa (see chapter 4) and Termessus, where

> a man with a good Roman name, Valerius Statilius Castus, appears with the strange title . . . *egregius socius Augustorum.* He is a commander of the local detachments of soldiers, no doubt a local militia, and he is praised for having established peace on land and sea.[79]

At the beginning of the third century, we observe already certain individuals amassing power in their hands. One such person was Julius Aurelius Zabdila,[80] who was strategos (general) when Alexander Severus came to the city in 229. He was in office when the prefect Crispinus arrived with his legions. He was also agoranomos and was noted for his expenditure on the city's behalf. One interesting point that emerges here is that *strategos* is now taken as an equivalent to *duumvir* (the local "consul"); the archon of Seleucid times has given way to a military position.

Zabdila's position clearly shows the linkage of wealth and political status in third-century Palmyra. By this time a number of the top people of Palmyra had acquired senatorial rank. Another such was Septimius Haddudan, symposiarch of the priests of Bel, whose father Ogeilu may have been the same Ogeilu who made a dedication in honor of Odenathus.[81] The family of Haddudan was perhaps in some sense the kingmaker of Odenathus.

Septimius Odenathus was born around A.D. 220, the son of Hairan, the son of Vaballath Nasor. His Arabic name, where his father's is

Aramaic, suggests a mixed Aramaic and Bedouin descent.[82] His Latin name shows that his family acquired citizenship, like Haddudan's, under the reign of the Severi. The first we hear of him is in a dedication of uncertain date, by Ogeilu (just mentioned), the son of Maqqai Haddudan Hadda. The dedication is in Palmyrene only and refers to Odenathus as *ras dy tadmwr*, "chief of Tadmor." It speaks of an offering of a throne, with a hearth, brazier, and holocaust. Two other inscriptions referring to him as *ras tadmor* date from 252.[83] The first of these, which like a fourth inscription[84] is in Greek as well as Palmyrene, attributes senatorial rank to Odenathus. The latter marks his building of a burial monument for himself and his descendents forever. Its date is uncertain: Odenathus may have acquired senatorial rank at any time between 222 and 254,[85] but it is hard to reconstruct his early career. His military successes on Rome's behalf in the 250s brought him to the rank of consularis by 258,[86] and from Gallienus he received the title of strategos of all the East, indicating an imperium held over all the Asiatic provinces and Egypt but subject to the imperium of the emperor.[87]

The family of Odenathus is difficult to disentangle.[88] An inscription that is a dedication to Septimius Hairanes, son of Odenathus, used to be taken to refer to an elder Odenathus, grandfather of the great king, whose father was known to be named Hairan.[89] But an inscription published in 1985 makes clear that Odenathus was in fact the grandson of one Vaballathus Nasor and son of Hairan.[90] Who then is this son Hairan? He must surely be identified with the one son mentioned in the *Historia Augusta*, Herodes, who was the child of Odenathus' first wife[91] and was murdered along with Odenathus in 267. Herodes is also found elsewhere as the Greek equivalent of Hairan.[92] Odenathus' other sons, by Zenobia, pose further problems (see pp. 114–15). But it does seem clear that Odenathus was the only ruler of that name. "Prince of the Saracens of the Euphrates banks" is Procopius' orotund term for him.[93] He acquired yet more from the Roman emperor, as we shall see.

We know nothing of the way in which Odenathus acquired his kingly power, which predates his repulse of the Persian forces in 253 (see chapter 4). On a posthumous inscription of 271 he is called King of Kings,[94] but there is no evidence that he used this title in his lifetime. (An inscription of either 261/2 or 266/7 calls him only "king," *mlk*.)[95] He did not receive the title of Augustus from Gallienus. At any rate his power was not, at least in form, absolute; several inscriptions of the 260s refer to one Septimius Vorodes (Worod), "procurator Augusti ducenarius" and "argapet" (a Parthian term meaning "commander of a fort"), who probably administered Palmyra for Odenathus while he was on campaign.[96] The fullest dedication, dating from April 266, has been quoted above (page 62, n. 37). Vorodes received a total of eight honorific statues in the grand colonnade, a number unequaled by any other Palmyrene. It has been suggested on the basis of his Iranian name that he may have had Persian sympathies and may have acquiesced in Odenathus' policy of conciliating his eastern neighbors rather than his western (see chapter 4).

Clearly Odenathus was able to place his own men in positions of power while he pursued his metier as military commander. Was the Senate of Palmyra more acquiescent than that of the late Roman Republic at the rise of a military dynast, or did they chafe at his supremacy? Civic life in the late third century was already beginning to lose some of its charm, and we see the beginnings of a tendency that became pronounced in the fourth century, in which the way to advancement was no longer through ostentatious service of your city but through entry into the imperial service (later the bureaucracy). No more than a hint of discord can be deduced from contemplation of the inscriptions (see chapter 5). He had his enemies—for he was in due course murdered. We must profoundly regret the lack of alternative, literary evidence on the mood of Palmyra at this time.

By the time we encounter Odenathus, his first wife has died leaving him a grown-up son, Herodes or Hairan. The latter, according to the *Historia Augusta* "was the most effeminate of men, wholly oriental and given over to Grecian luxury, for he had embroidered tents and pavilions made out of cloth of gold and everything in the manner of the Persians."[97] This description, if it is anything more than fiction, casts a light on the luxury of the Palmyrene court. But this Herodes is also honored for leading an army to victory against the Persians[98]—in which campaign is unknown. Perhaps he was not such an unworthy son to the tough and cautious Odenathus after all.

In sum, Odenathus was established as "king" in Palmyra before the Persian onslaughts of 252. When he married Zenobia is unknown. What brings him into the limelight is his part in the defeat of the Persians as they invaded the Roman Empire. We must therefore look next at the origin of that conflict in the resurgence of Persian power under the Sassanid dynasty, and at the way in which Odenathus made himself indispensable to Rome. Only then will we be in a position to discuss the ambition and achievements of his spouse and successor.

4

Between Persia and Rome

The Eastern frontier was Rome's most intractable problem. The Roman Republic had begun to acquire an empire more than 400 years earlier, and it had made empire a duty and a virtue, at least in the eyes of its rulers and their poets. There was no natural reason for empire to stop, though Augustus had, in a memorandum written shortly before his death, counseled against further expansion, favoring instead consolidation within established frontiers. But in the East, as generations of men since have discovered again and again, there are no natural frontiers. To the north and west the Rhine and Danube could be policed and linked with a palisade; even on the Northumberland fells a wall was sufficient for border control. But though the Euphrates marks a frontier of sorts, it runs through desert: and it is impossible to garrison a desert.

The north African frontier also bordered on desert. Here the arid equivalent of Hadrian's Wall, a simple ditch system known as the *fossatum*, marked the boundaries of empire. Interpretations of this, as of other borders, have varied. It is surely incorrect to see these simple frontiers as intended to keep out decisively those on the other side. A more plausible interpretation sees Hadrian's Wall as much more like a modern frontier, a means of controlling the traffic between one side and the other.[1] In a somewhat similar way, the north African *limes* may have been intended neither to keep the nomads out nor to control their activities, but to control and monitor native movement inside the border.

The Arabian *limes*, or frontier, has evoked analogous interpretation as an attempt to mark the borderline of the world of the nomads and the world of Rome. Rome itself may have seen it as a line demarcating the frightening world of "brigands" on the other side, and this attitude has seeped into modern popular consciousness in such formulations as that of Bruce Chatwin, who sees the Fall of the Roman Empire as "simply another episode in the conflict of nomad and settled peoples."[2]

But far more important than the Arab *limes*—the numerous forts of which have been excavated or surveyed over the last fifty years and

81

are now receiving a good deal of scholarly attention[3]—was the long and intractable border between Rome and Parthia,[4] which was formed by the northern courses of the river Euphrates as far south as the Syrian border. From here on, an uncertain no-man's-land divided the two empires. The roads and lines of military posts have been thoroughly plotted through Syria. They raise several questions. First, are these lines in any way sufficient defense against foreign invasion? The answer has to be no. Second, should they be interpreted as defensive at all or as a system of communications, a way of keeping the traffic going, though under control, between the empires? From the point of view of Palmyra and its caravans this was obviously an important function of the Roman presence in the area. A third, more extreme view is that all Rome's building in this region is essentially aggressive in purpose: Rome was never content with her borders but always seeking an opportunity to push across the border.[5] While this explains very well the wars of Trajan and Caracalla in the second century A.D., it seems doubtful whether Rome felt so aggressive in the third century. This view assumes that Rome's eastern neighbor was devoid of territorial ambitions, and while this may have been true of Parthia, it was certainly not true of the Persian Empire that succeeded Parthia in the third century. It is intriguing that no Parthian or Persian border forts have been discovered, suggesting that neither attack nor defense necessarily required the line of roads and military posts that Rome relied on everywhere. Mobile troops could be just as important.

Rome had always found her eastern neighbors particularly hard to come to terms with. The might of Parthia (and its successor, Sassanian Persia) was the most serious and most enduring opponent Rome had to face between the destruction of Carthage in 146 B.C. and the beginning of the barbarian invasions in the fourth century A.D. It is remarkable that Rome was, on the whole, so unsuccessful for so long in reaching a modus vivendi with the relatively placable Parthian kings. This may of course suggest that they wanted conquest, not accommodation. The Sassanians, however, were far from placable.

The youthful energy of blossoming empire dictated conquest. That was the policy of the great generals of the civil wars of the late first century B.C. Over them all, as they jockeyed for military supremacy, loomed the shadow of Alexander the Great. To emulate his conquest of the Eastern empire would be a genuine claim to military supremacy and the leadership of Rome. That shadow hung too over the Parthian king Mithridates, whose ambitions were as great, for he intended to be an Alexander in reverse—to restore the Achaemenid domains and to include in them, perhaps, the western lands of Rome.

Marcus Crassus was the last of that generation to attempt the conquest of Parthia. He died in the attempt, after suffering one of the most humiliating defeats ever known in Rome. The story as told by Plutarch is sufficiently harrowing and indicates the formidable dangers of the terrain even for the highly trained Roman army.[6]

It was spring 54 B.C. when Crassus marched out from winter quarters in Syria (we are not told where) to cross the Euphrates. He had, Plutarch writes, "spent his time in Syria more like an usurer than a general," so that the enemy had had time to prepare against him. Artabazes, the king of Armenia, invited Crassus to march through his kingdom,

> for not only would he be able there to supply his army with abundant provisions, which he would give him, but his passage would be more secure in the mountains and hills, with which the whole country was covered, making it almost impossible to horse, in which the main strength of the Parthians consisted.

Crassus however insisted on marching directly into Mesopotamia. A series of omens as they crossed the river at Zeugma did not deter him. Plutarch writes, "He marched his army along the river with seven legions, little less than four thousand horses, and as many light-armed soldiers." It was now that nemesis came in the form of an Arab chief named Ariamnes, who had been sent by the Parthian king to entice Crassus and his army from the river and hills into the open plain where they might be surrounded. He offered himself as guide to the Roman army. Leading them by a way entirely possible for the dry Bedouin and their hardy camels, he drew them into a region of deep sand without trees or water. Plutarch writes that there was "not a bough, not a stream, not a hillock, not a green herb, but in fact a sea of sand, which encompassed the army with its waves." We may suspect the sand, more typical of the Empty Quarter several hundred miles to the south, while fully accepting the barrenness and waterlessness of this land that suddenly was expected to support more than forty thousand men and the four thousand horses. "What, do you think you march through Campania," joked the Bedouin, "expecting everywhere to find springs, and shady trees, and baths, and inns of entertainment? Consider you now travel through the confines of Arabia and Assyria."

Suddenly, near Carrhae (Harran), the Parthian army was reported at hand. Crassus drew up his army into a square with twelve cohorts along each side, supported by a troop of horses. Before long they heard the sound of the kettle drums to which the Parthians march to war. Plutarch writes that this "dead hollow noise, like the bellowing of beasts, mixed with sounds resembling thunder," terrified the Romans. Then came the archers, wreaking destruction on the tightly massed legions without the need of close engagement. The famous testudo formation of the Roman legions did not protect the heads or feet of the Roman soldiers. (Eighteen years later, Antony responded more effectively to Parthian tactics: his soldiers knelt down behind their shields.)[7] If the Romans gave chase, the Parthians fled on their horses, shooting as they went (hence the "Parthian shot"). Before their quivers were exhausted, a troop of camels arrived with further supplies. The Romans had no way to turn, and the dust of the desert flew up and made it impossible to see and scarcely possible to breathe. The Gaulish cavalry took the heat and parching thirst the worst; and being unarmored, they had no defense against the arrows.

Only night brought an end to the destruction. To fly was as impossible as to fight because of the number of wounded, and the Romans made slow marching back to the Euphrates. They were split up in the darkness and entangled in the fens, and the Parthians caught up with them at dawn. The Parthian general Surena invited Crassus to a parley, but a scuffle broke out and the Roman was killed. Twenty thousand men were slain and ten thousand taken prisoner. The greatest disgrace of all was that legionary standards were captured. Crassus was beheaded and ended his career as a stage property at the Parthian court, in a hastily improvised recitation of the scene from Euripides' Bacchae where Agave recognizes the severed head of her son. The conjunction of high Greek literary culture and a bloodiness exceeding even the Roman provides an unforgettable image of the Parthian civilization that was to cause Rome anxiety for a quarter of a millenium still to come. The prisoners went as far as possible from their Roman home—even to Merv (Alexandria Margiana),[8] provoking Horace's anguished question: "Did Crassus' soldiers, men of the Marsi and Apulia, live under Median rule, linked in shameful marriage to barbarian wives?"[9]

Revenge for the disgrace was a long time coming, and it did little for the Crassan troops, some of whom in the meantime may have been displaced to the very borders of China, where they found service under a Hun chief with the unmellifluous name of Jzh-jzh and founded the new city of Li-kien (the Chinese name for Rome). This sequence of events, upheld by Homer H. Dubs in his book *A Roman City in Ancient China*,[10] has met with considerable scholarly skepticism: the linguistic problems are considerable, and the whole story is totally rejected by Raschke.[11]

From this disastrous episode, the Romans learned many lessons about desert warfare: the necessity of accurate information about the desert wastes, where one bare wrinkled hill is so much like another, and where the wastes of dune and scrub give no guidance except what can be gained at night from the clarity of the stars; the need and yet the untrustworthiness of local nomad guides; the importance of commissariat, above all the provision of water, since an army could not live off the local population as it advanced; the terrible effects of the heat on heavily armed Roman legionaries; the agonies of the iron-shafted arrows that could nail a man's arm to his shield or his foot to the ground; and the impossibility of defense against, or engagement with, archers. They also learned that, as a later military commander remarked,[12] the climate of the region was healthy apart from dysentery, malaria, typhoid, cholera, and plague.

All these factors would be borne in mind by the leaders of future expeditions to the East, and as we shall see, Aurelian excelled in circumventing the difficulties. But that lay far in the future. The humiliation of the loss of standards induced Rome to suspend ideas of Parthian conquest, and the Parthians had no wish to extend westward a realm in which they could already live comfortably and cultivate the arts of peace.

Rome never felt safe with an armed nation directly on its borders. Instead they produced what Freya Stark has called the policy of "the weak periphery," the "theory that only the sea or an unarmed nation must exist on her borders."[13] To achieve this, Rome had a policy of establishing client kingdoms, or in the now preferred terminology, "friendly kings."[14] Rather than garrison a volatile border, Rome relied on the use of buffer states under kings who could be relied on to favor Roman interests. Such support was fostered in many ways—for example, by providing education for the king's sons at Rome, the benefits of citizenship for his family, and political and military support in his country's internal affairs. There were a number of "friendly" kingdoms on the eastern edge of the Roman Empire. They included Commagene and the Bosporan kingdom. The most familiar now is Herod's kingdom of Judaea. And the most troublesome for Rome was, always, Armenia.

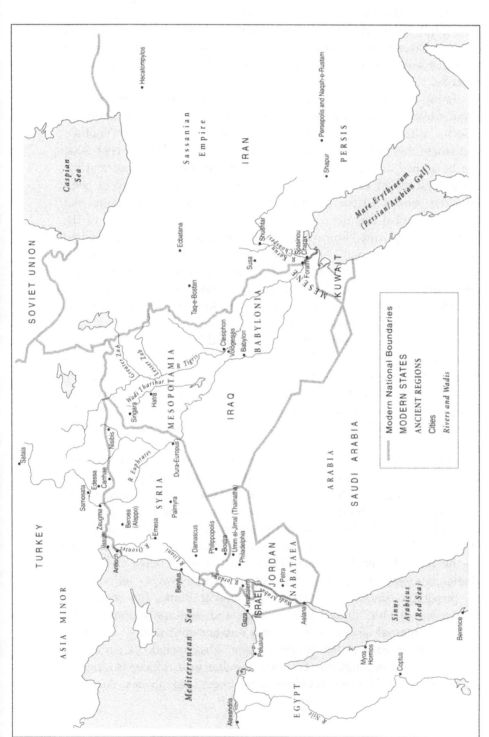

4. Rome's Eastern Frontiers and the Sassanian Empire

This kingdom, which bordered directly on Parthia, was equally volatile and was liable to return to allegiance with its eastern neighbors, with whom it perhaps had more affinities in terms of race, geography, and mode of life. The attempt to reach a settlement in Armenia lasted for generations. Augustus won back the standards Crassus had lost, and he sent several reconnaissances to the East to establish what else might be gained and firmly held. Much of Pliny's account of the contemporary known world is based on the reconnaissance made by Isidore of Charax for Augustus.

Corbulo, Nero's general, finally settled the Armenian question and brought Tiridates into fealty to Rome. Armenia, the Poland of antiquity, seemed securely in the Western camp. The empire felt like a unity— circumscribed by its great rivers, the Rhine, the Danube, and the Euphrates, and by the Sahara desert to the south; more distant parts could be regarded as beyond the pale. Only the Syrian frontier remained strategically unsound, for Rome could in no way control the comings and goings of the desert. This lay behind Vespasian's annexation of the client kingdoms of Commagene and Lesser Armenia as provinces. In Vespasian's reign, Ulpius Traianus, the father of Emperor Trajan, built the frontier road from Palmyra to Sura along the Euphrates. The Roman mind liked no loose ends: a nation that was not with Rome was against her. But that again brought Rome square against her military opponent.

It remains debatable to what extent Rome can be viewed as having a consistent and rational "Grand Strategy" throughout the period of its empire. Edward Luttwak's introduction of this term into the study of Roman history has, at the least, provided historians with a model for interpreting Roman actions or for showing that Roman actions cannot be interpreted in such pure terms.[15] In the "Grand-strategic" view, Trajan realized that to control the Euphrates he must hold Mesopotamia. As we have seen, there were certainly other factors at play in Trajan's desire to conquer the East: emulation of Alexander, desire for glory, and the protection of trade. But that does not exclude the additional desire for a "rational frontier," though the suspicion remains that the rational frontier is a construct placed on events by the modern mind (if it worked, it must have been meant to work). In these terms a rational frontier demanded a weak buffer region beyond. If the Euphrates was to work as a control over movement, Rome must also control access to it. So Trajan pushed Rome's holdings right to the Euphrates and led a new Roman expedition against the Parthians, taking even the capital, Ctesiphon, itself.

In 106 Trajan annexed Nabataea (see chap. 1), and he later annexed Armenia (114), Agrippa's kingdom of Judaea, the kingdoms of the Caucasus, and the Bosporan kingdom. Palmyra's position was no doubt secured at this time, though it had been formally annexed much earlier. Trajan's attention to the Far East of Rome exceeded that of any of his predecessors and seems to have had both military and economic motives. His reorganization of the customs and frontier dues on the Tigris and the Euphrates[16] followed his father's construction of a road across the desert. Palmyra's prosperity in the second century, and the lack of reference to trouble from nomads in the dedicatory inscriptions there, suggests that it benefited from the increased military presence in Syria.

A garrison was present, then, in Palmyra and the other kingdoms. The legions were XVI Flavia Firma at Samosata, III Gallica at Raphaneae near Apamea (replacing the X Fretensis, which had been Syria's third legion under Vespasian and was now in Jerusalem), and IV Scythica twenty miles north of Zeugma.[17] With this base, Trajan marched on Ctesiphon.

Trajan's short-lived conquest of Parthia secured the frontier behind him—a frontier that was, to be sure, more rational than the last. The line Euphrates-Araxes does not effectually enclose anything, for Rome could only control a strip one hundred miles or so inland from the coast, and the land within, with its tumbled rocks and bands of brigands, was not worth having. E. Luttwak writes:

> Trajan's Parthian war (A.D. 114–17) has been explained as an attempt to establish a 'scientific' frontier beyond the river. The only possible line that would satisfy the requirements of strategic depth, rear-area security, and economy of deployment was a perimeter that would follow the course of the river Khabur to the western edge of the Jebel Sinjar, then continue east along the high ground toward the Tigris and north again into Armenia. Though by no means straight, this frontier would have had advantages far greater than mere geographic simplicity.

This frontier would, Luttwak explains, provide a base for in-depth defense and a salient to "interdict" the advance of armies moving westward; it was also an area of adequate rainfall. This policy could have been successful if Armenia had been left as a client, "buffer" kingdom. Luttwak concedes, however, that Trajan's war was probably not a purely "rational" enterprise.[18]

The area was too great to be successfully consolidated with existing manpower, and Rome did not hold it long. Even with Roman garrisons present, Parthian troops could move to the Euphrates much more easily than Rome could march to it eastward across hostile desert.[19] Two hundred years later Julian experienced the danger of crossing the Euphrates and being cut off in hostile territoy with the enemy river behind him. He died there. Trajan was luckier; but one victory does not secure a desert. What was needed was a system of roads and castella, not a Maginot Line. Rome eventually established such a system of in-depth defense to the west of the Euphrates, but they did not have the forces to do it to the east. Nakedly exposed to the rage of Ctesiphon, Trajan's conquest did not last.

Gibbon's Golden Age of the Antonines may be regarded as due essentially to the quiescence of Parthia, but Rome did not learn its lesson. Septimius Severus tried again to extend the frontiers into Parthian territory. In fact his conquests created a border very close to Luttwak's ideal, though his achievement was not admired by Dio.

> Severus . . . was in the habit of saying that he had gained a large additional territory and made it a bulwark for Syria. But the facts themselves show that it is a source of continual wars for us, and of great expenses. For it provides very little revenue and involves very great expenditure; and having extended our frontiers to the neighbours of the Medes and Parthians, we are constantly so to speak at war in their defence.[20]

There lay the rub: Rome maintained two legiones Parthicae beyond the Euphrates in Mesopotamia and remained continually on the alert for the invasion that the Parthians show little sign of having desired. Put another way, it remained ready to launch a war whenever the mood took it. Rome wanted conquest more than defense.

The next occasion for conquest came in the reign of Caracalla. The emperor, arriving in Antioch after a short detour to Alexandria to massacre half the population,[21] decided to sue for the hand of the daughter of the new king of Parthia, Artabanus V.

> In his letters he alleged that he was anxious to marry the king's daughter because it was proper that he who was an emperor should not become the son-in-law of some private person of low birth, but should marry a princess, the daughter of the great king. The

two most powerful empires were those of the Romans and Parthians. If they were united by marriage, he would create one invincible power no longer separated by a river. . . . They would surely have no difficulty in ruling the whole world under a single crown. Furthermore, the locally grown spices of the Parthians and their wonderful clothes, and on the other side, the metals produced by the Romans and their admirable manufactured goods would no longer be difficult to get and in short supply, smuggled in by merchants. Instead both sides would have commerce and unimpeded advantage from the unification of their countries under a single rule.[22]

This passage is a beautiful argument for the view that Roman interests in the East combined military and economic motives in equal measure. The idea of a union of empires is raised again by the *Historia Augusta* in its account of Zenobia's motives; with what authenticity we may however be doubtful.

Unfortunately Caracalla's dream cut little ice with the Parthian king, and the emperor embarked on a "phoney war" against Parthia. In the summer of 216 he marched as far as Adiabene, but he "never saw an enemy"[23] and retired to Edessa. The following spring he was murdered at Carrhae, and his successor Macrinus, after being defeated at Nisibis, bought the Parthians off.

So a modus vivendi was established until 224, when the Parthian Empire was overthrown by one of its vassal kings, the Sassanid Persian Ardashir (whom the Romans called Artaxerxes, the Greek form of his name).[24] The murder of the last of the Arsacid kings threw the east into turmoil. Their supporters fled to all quarters—to Azerbaijan and Armenia. Two of the Arab tribes, the Tanukh and the Kuda'a, fled to Syria, and the former became an important player in the struggle of Rome against Palmyra. It is highly likely that the family of Odenathus of Palmyra also came west at this time, establishing itself in its new home and rapidly acquiring a dominant position. Who were these people who had destroyed the status quo at such an inconvenient time?

The Sassanian Empire

The name Sassanian or Sassanid[25] derives from that of Ardashir's father, who according to Tabari was called Sasan. Sasan married the daughter of Papak (who elsewhere appears as Ardashir's father). Establishing a new capital at Firuzabad in southwestern Iran—which he called

Ardashir-Khwarreh ("Ardashir is the Greatest")—he embarked on a rapid campaign of conquest. The Romans were quickly driven out of Mesopotamia. In 231 or 232 young Emperor Severus Alexander led an army against Persia, but the climate and disease created at least as much havoc as the enemy and he retired. Neither side had decisively gained the upper hand. In 237 Ardashir extended his conquests across the Tigris, taking Nisibis and Carrhae, and three years later he also took the Parthian capital of Hatra. He extended his conquests to Merv and the kingdom of the Kushans, and southeast to Kerman and Seistan. But he failed to hold Hatra and the Roman border cities of Palmyra and Dura-Europos. The Palmyrenes rapidly recognized their real enemy and prepared to resist.

The Persian army was a formidable new opponent for the Romans. "It should be explained," writes Herodian, "that the barbarians do not have a paid army like the Romans, nor do they have permanent, standing garrisons, trained in military techniques. Instead there is a general muster of all males, and sometimes women too, when the king gives the order." In fact the Persian army, like its society, was feudal: peasant soldiers provided infantry for their lord, and aristocrats provided the cavalry. "At the end of the war," according to Herodian, "everyone returns to his own home enriched by his share of the plunder."[26]

Their armor was as medieval as the structure of their army. Besides the light-armed bowmen already familiar to the Romans, they had heavily armored, mounted warriors dressed in helmets that covered the entire head and in chain mail constructed of scales of overlapping metal plates sewn onto a leather surcoat. Their legs were clad in boots that were attached to the upper garment to leave no chink free. The horses also wore armor—a solid metal plate in front, and a leather coat covered with metal rings over the rest of the body so as not to impede movement. In time these armored warriors, or cataphracts, became even more heavily armored, until the fourth century when the Romans dubbed them clibanarii, "oven-men"—a graphic description of what it must have been like to fight in such a metal casing under the broiling desert sun.

A Persian army on the march at this period is vividly described by Heliodorus in his novel *Aethiopica:*

> The sun just rising shone upon the Persians and gave such a wonderful brightness to their panoplies that it rebounded on those who were a great way off. . . . (The commander) took the centre, sitting in a brave scythed chariot and for safety surrounded by troops of

spearmen on either hand, while in front of him were posted the mailed horsemen, upon trust of whom he ventured to join issue with his enemies. For these men are the most valiant of all the Persian fighters and are set before the others as it were an invincible wall. . . . He leapeth not up himself, but others help him, so encumbered is he with the weight of his arms. When the time of battle comes, he gives his horse the reins and spurs him with his heels and rides upon his enemies at full speed like a man made of iron or a statue fashioned with hammers. His great staff is tied at its pointed end with a cord to the horse's neck and the hinder end is made fast to its buttocks, so that in the conflict it does not yield but helps the horseman's hand, who does but guide the same aright. Thus it gives the greater blow and runs through every man it hits, and often carries away two men together pierced by one stroke.[27]

A century later Ammianus adds that

all parts of their bodies were covered with thick plates, so fitted that the stiff joints conformed with those of their limbs; and the forms of human faces were so skillfully fitted to their heads that, since their entire bodies were covered in metal, arrows that fell upon them could lodge only where they could see a little through tiny openings opposite the pupil of the eye, or where through the tips of their noses they were able to get a little breath.

In the midst of this formidable but uncomfortable army, the king marched to war seated

alone on a golden car in the resplendent blaze of shimmering precious stones, whose mingled glitter seemed to form a sort of shifting light. . . . He was surrounded by dragons, woven out of purple thread and bound to the golden and jeweled tops of spears, with wide mouths open to the breeze and hence hissing as if roused by anger, and leaving their tails winding in the wind.[28]

Though the tanklike figures of the cataphracts were almost invulnerable to weapons, they were severely susceptible to heat stroke—a fact Aurelian used to his advantage in his campaigns against the similarly armored Palmyrenes. In addition, the Persians were far more skilled than the Parthians had ever been in siege warfare.

In 241 Ardashir abdicated in favor of an even greater warrior, Shapur I. Shapur extended his conquests as far to the west as Konya (ancient Iconium) in central Turkey, to the north to Gilan and Khwarazm (Matthew Arnold's hushed Chorasmian waste now resounding to the clash of war), and to the east to Kandahar, Kashgar, Sogdiana, and Tashkent. He conquered Peshawar and perhaps reached even to Quetta. From the Caucasus to Oman, the peoples bowed down to the Sassanid king. Why should not Rome itself yield to his sway and let his empire stretch also to the Mediterranean?

Shapur's own account of his achievements is inscribed on a rock at Naqsh-e-Rustam near Persepolis, in Parthian, Middle Persian, and Greek. Its central section reads:

When at first we had become established in the Empire, Gordian Caesar raised in all of the Roman Empire a force from the Goth and German realms and marched on Babylonia against the Empire of Iran and against us. On the border of Babylonia at Misikhe, a great "frontal" battle occurred. Gordian Caesar was killed and the Roman force was destroyed. And the Romans made Philip Caesar. Then Philip Caesar came to us for terms, and to ransom their lives gave us 500,000 denars, and became tributary to us. And for this reason we have renamed Misikhe Peroz-Shapur.

And Caesar lied again and did wrong to Armenia. Then we attacked the Roman Empire and annihilated at Barbalissos a Roman force of 60,000 and Syria and the environs of Syria we burned, ruined and pillaged all. In this one campaign we conquered of the Roman Empire fortresses and towns: the town of Anatha with surroundings . . . Birtha of Asporakan, the town of Sura, Barbalissos, Manbuk (Hierapolis), Aleppo, Qennisrin, Apamea, Rhephania, Zeugma, Urima, Gindaros, Armenaza, Seleucia, Antioch, Cyrrhe, another town of Seleucia, Alexandretta, Nicopolis, Sinzara, Hama, Rastan, Dikhor, Dolikhe, Dura, Circusium, Germanicia, Batna, Khanar, and in Cappodocia the towns of Satala, Domana, Artangil, Suisa, Sinda, Phreata, a total of 37 towns with surroundings.

In the third campaign when we attacked Carrhae and Urhai [Edessa] and were beseiging Carrhae and Edessa Valerian Caesar marched against us. He had with him a force of 70,000 from Germany, Raetia, Noricum, Dacia, Pannonia, Moesia, Istria, Spain, Africa (?), Thrace, Bithynia, Asia, Pamphylia, Isauria, Lycaonia, Galatia, Lycia, Cilicia, Cappodocia, Phrygia, Syria, Phoenicia,

Judea, Arabia, Mauritania, Germania, Rhodes [Lydia], Osrhoene,
Mesopotamia.

And beyond Carrhae and Edessa we had a great battle with
Valerian Caesar. We made prisoner ourselves with our own hands
Valerian Caesar and the others, chiefs of that army, the praetorian
prefect, senators; we made all prisoners and deported them to Persis.

And Syria, Cilicia and Cappodocia we burned, ruined and
pillaged.[29]

The capture of Valerian so near to Carrhae (ill-omened name for
Rome) was a triumph for Persian self-esteem. The battle makes an
episode in the *Shahnameh* of Firdausi[30] which claims 10,000 slain and
1,600 taken prisoner. The victory was proudly recorded for all time on
reliefs at Bishapur and at Naqsh-e-Rustam. But for Roman pride it was
a cataclysm even greater than the death of Crassus three hundred years
before. A great and much admired emperor had been made to kneel
before a barbarian and according to some accounts had been taken into
permanent captivity. Other, uglier rumors had it that he "lived long
enough for the Roman name to become the mock and game of the
barbarians," then was flayed alive and his skin stained red and exhibited
in the temple of the gods to the merriment of the peoples of Persia.[31]

Sapor is accused of treating his prisoners with wanton and unre-
lenting cruelty. Deep valleys were filled up with the slain. Crowds
of prisoners were driven to water like beasts, and many perished
for want of food. . . . He despaired of making any permanent establishment in the Empire, and sought only to leave behind him a
wasted desert, whilst he transported into Persia the people and the
treasures of the provinces.[32]

At Shushtar, on the western edge of the Zagros, one may still see
the bridge (now known as Band-e-Kaisar) that the Roman troops constructed (according to Firdausi it took them three years) at the other
end of the world from their fertile Mediterranean, close to the sweltering
marshland of southeast Iran. Here the temperature rises to 107 degrees
as early as April. The Romans in their specially built four-square city
went native and suffered in the heat and dust. They married Arab wives
and tended their dusty fields in the Karun valley, as it slides down to
shimmering Abadan. Among the captives were a number of Christian
priests from Antioch, and their growing flock erected churches and

monasteries under the very eye of the blazing divinity of Persia.[33] There are still Roman mosaics at Bishapur and at Gundeshapur, which at that time was called Weh-Antiok-Shapur ("Greater-than-Antioch-of-Shapur"). So much did the betrayal and conquest of Rome's eastern capital mean to the barbarian king.

Yet Shapur's Persia did not exist solely for conquest and slaughter. Internal politics preoccupied him, and he took an interest in religious matters—interest in which we may discern as much policy as devotion. The inscription at Naqsh-e Rustam insists on the aid of the gods, with which "we have searched out and taken so many lands, so that in every land we have founded many Bahram fires and have conferred benefits on many magi-men, and we have magnified the cult of the gods."[34] Shapur knew that a universal religion was one of the soundest means by which to unite a vast empire. Though dutiful to the ancient Mazdaean religion, he was impressed by a new prophet, who might have changed the face of Iranian spirituality.

Mani

Out of the marshes of the Tigris delta came Mani.[35] In his priestly uniform of yellow-and-green striped trousers, a sky blue cloak, and a long ebony cane, he preached the strife of God and Matter and the redemption of Man through Revelation (Gnosis). His system contained all the complex detail that obsession can create or credulity perpetuate. He presented himself as a prophet of Christ yet a greater than Christ, "the envoy of the true God in the land of Babylon," one who would be for the Eastern world what his admired model Paul had been for the Western.

Mani was born in 216, the son of a Parthian prince Patik (or Futtuq), in the marshlands of the lower Tigris, probably into one of the baptist sects whose secret traditions still survive (apparently with recognizably Manichaean elements) among the Mandaeans of modern Iraq.[36] He received his first revelation at the age of twelve, when an angel brought him a message from "the King of the Paradise of Light" and dubbed him the twin of the Holy Ghost. The twin or guardian angel is an important concept in early Judaeo-Christian thought; Mani was especially favored to have such a high figure in the spiritual hierarchy as his patron.

Light was to be the central emblem in Mani's cosmology: all human striving should aim at the cultivation and increase of the particles of

Light embedded in the darkness of Matter and the impurity of the body. He takes from Mazdaeism the opposition of Good and Matter, but he makes the Good superior in power and certain of ultimate triumph. Redemption—the conquest by Light—is through the power of Jesus but can be assisted by such practices as the avoidance of sexual intercourse (which disperses the particles of Light in the outflow of semen) and adherence to a correct diet, including in the main such receptacles of Light as bright melons. Altars of the Manichaean religion were commonly heaped high with these holy and delectable fruits. Redemption would be rewarded by the reception of the soul in Paradise, where eighty angel-houris awaited its pleasure—a striking anticipation of Mohammed's Heaven.

Because of this intense awareness of light, we should not perhaps be surprised that Mani was famed as a painter (some said that he had spent a year in Heaven to learn the art). His skill is reflected in the calligraphy and ornamentation of the surviving Manichaean gospels, where delicate flowers serve as punctuation marks. And it is possible to trace a direct line to the exquisite miniatures of later Persian art, with their striking refusal of the Muslim taboo on figural representation.

Mani's books were many, including seven in Aramaic—the *Shabuhragan*—which were summarized in Middle Persian for the benefit of Shapur I. Fragments of these were discovered in this century in Sinkiang, as well as later versions in Chinese, Latin, Coptic, Sogdian, and Uighur. They embody a fully worked-out (if entirely personal) cosmology, which, as a systematic and rational doctrine, for many years captivated the mind of young Augustine. So we should not be surprised at its attraction for Shapur, to whom many of its motifs were already familiar from Mazdaeism.

Mani's missionary work began in 240/1 with a visit to India. The shah of Turan, when he met him, mistook him for the Buddha. His encounter with Shapur took place at Ctesiphon: the king perceived the Light that sat on Mani's shoulders and gave him freedom to travel throughout his empire. The prophet went with him in his campaigns—as did the mobedh (Magian priest) Karter, later his enemy.

Shapur was succeeded briefly in 273 by his son Ohrmizd, but a year later Vahram I became king. Vahram evidently saw no future in Manichaeism. He appointed Karter his chief mobedh, and the latter developed the full-fledged form of Zoroastrianism that remained the religion of the Persian Empire until the Arab Conquest, and which still survives in isolated parts of Iran, notably Yazd, and among the Parsees.

Mani was imprisoned in 276 by Vahram. He died—or was tortured to death—within the year. His body was chopped in pieces and the fragments impaled above the gates of Bet-Lapat. Manichaeism survived in central Asia and China into the present century, but in Persia it was no more. A religion that might have displaced that of Christ awaited its successor, and it awaited one in vain. Rome and Persia were not to be united in faith.

The Crisis of the Third Century

The rise of Persia coincided with the nadir of the fortunes of the Roman Empire. Not only modern historians use these terms to speak of the confused and destructive third century. An anonymous rhetor whose work has been attributed to the middle of the century said the empire was "like an ill and rotting body, or like a bolting horse . . . in total confusion."[37] The rot was felt to have set in with the reign of Valerian's son Gallienus. This emperor was unpopular with the senatorial class, who provided the historians whose writings we read, such as the author of the *Historia Augusta*. The poet Commodian expected the annihilation of the empire in the seventh year of the joint reign of Valerian and Gallienus (the year of the capture of Valerian), and only the benefit of hindsight enabled the author of *Sibylline Oracle* 13 to take a longer and more optimistic view. The historian Orosius neatly sums up the accelerating disasters of the century.

> Suddenly, with the permission of God, the peoples surrounding the empire, feeling the loosening of the reins, invaded all the frontiers of the Romans. The Germans crossed the Alps and penetrated Raetia and the whole of Italy as far as Ravenna; the Alamanni crossed Gaul and also entered Italy; Greece, Macedonia, and parts of Africa were ravaged by the inundation of the Goths; Dacia across the Danube was permanently removed from the empire; the Quadi and the Sarmatians depopulated Pannonia; the further Germans ravaged and overpowered Spain; the Parthians removed Mesopotamia and began a war of attrition on Syria. Even now [Orosius is writing at the beginning of the fifth century], there are in several of the provinces poverty-stricken settlements amid the ruins of great cities, which function as indications of those miseries, from among which we can now display, in Spain, our own Tarraco, as consolation for more recent miseries.[38]

The ever-expanding balloon of Rome's power was assailed by constant pinpricks on all sides, and its tension and confidence lapsed with every assault. Fundamental to the whole process was the necessity that an emperor conduct foreign wars himself. This had been a satisfactory situation when the barbarians were quiescent. Trajan and even Septimius Severus were untroubled in the north and could concentrate on the glory of eastern conquest. Even Hadrian, with his assiduous program of visits to all the borders of the empire, was faced with no more serious threats than the local unrest of Northumbrian or Numidian tribesmen. The strain began to show with Severus Alexander, who yielded to the growing might of Persia and the turbulence on the Rhine, and who added to the expense of war the loss of manpower and the ignominy of retreat.

In succeeding generations the Persians were not alone in posing a threat to the frontiers, though Severus Alexander, the Gordians (from 242), and Valerian (255–59) were successively embroiled in wars on this front. In Pannonia, in Moesia, and in Gaul, the European barbarians were continuing their inexorable pressure westward and southward, from the plains of Prussia and Hungary to the pastures and sunny fruitfulness of the lands south of the Rhine and Danube. The emperors were constantly engaged far from Rome, in wars on one border after another. Since Galba, it had been a public secret that an emperor might be made elsewhere than at Rome. The corollary now naturally followed that wherever there was a successful army its general might be proclaimed emperor, and the exhaustion of foreign campaigns compounded the agonies of civil war between the pretenders.

After the assassination of Caracalla in 218, Emperors Macrinus, Elagabalus, Severus Alexander, and the three Gordians ruled and were murdered within the space of twenty-six years. The situation became more unstable in the following twenty years, as claimants to the throne rose and were eliminated before they could properly earn the title of emperor; their power bases remained local. The *Historia Augusta* contrived to identify as many as thirty such pretenders, or "tyrants" (admittedly by the expedient of inventing one or two).

The military and political crisis was perceptible to the ancient writers, but an equally fundamental crisis —the financial crisis of runaway inflation[39]—receives no discursive treatment from them but must be pieced together from scattered evidence. In the third century the Roman Empire was running alarmingly short of money. Its economy was monetized perhaps only to about 40 percent. Its level of tax collection, like that of many premodern economies, was at the inefficient level of 5 percent of the gross national product; yet its expenditure was constantly increasing due to the demands of war on the frontiers and, not least, due to the need for huge donations to the army at the accession of every new emperor. Transport, road building, commissariat, supplies, and storage ate up cash. "Crisis had become a ruthless creditor,"[40] and the state's monetary obligations may well have doubled by the mid-third century. The frontier troubles further impeded tax collection.

One of the main purposes of coinage was to pay the soldiers of the Roman army. In an age when many lived largely by subsistence farming or barter at various levels of sophistication, and when many taxes were paid in kind, the legionaries and auxiliaries were among the most numerous regular recipients of cash. They received a daily wage, an allowance for supplies, and donatives on the accession of every new emperor and on retirement. Peasants and smallholders, shopkeepers, and suppliers of services were always willing to make exchange for the good bronze, silver, and gold of the legionaries. The bronze and gold could be computed accurately by their weight as bullion, but the silver had a fiduciary element. Imperial coinage could always be changed at the tables of the money changers who sat at the entrance to the markets of provincial cities.

The eastern mints increased their output as the wars demanded coin. Yet, inexplicably, as the aurei and denarii increased in number, so prices rose too—not just due to periodic shortages of grain, but in a natural economic response to an increase in the money supply. At the same time the value of the coins declined. The turbulence of the century must have made commercial contacts more difficult (as Caracalla had observed), and that too would tend to drive up prices. What was the emperor to do? His solution compounded the problem.

Caracalla's first response was to reduce the silver content of the coins in response to the shortage of silver. Silver was alloyed with bronze, and the size of coins was reduced to that of the antoninianus (which itself shrank by the decade as the empire reeled). Of course this only accentuated the slide of the currency. A glance at a series of the coinage of the Roman emperors is enough to illustrate the rapid decline of value—of purity of metal, of size, and of artistic skill—that follows the last fine portraits of Severus. With no understanding of the behavior of money, and with an economy that was still not fully monetarized, here was a recipe for crisis.

By the time of Aurelian a further expedient was tried, the stamping of coins with a fixed value. This was the first groping attempt at a fiduciary currency like the modern banknote, worthless in itself but a pledge of exchange value ("I promise to pay the bearer on demand . . ."). The invention of the aurelianianus, stamped "five denarii' but less than twice the weight of the one and a half or two denarius antoninianus, concealed a further inflation of 150 percent or more. It has been calculated that by the end of the third century it would have cost sixteen tons of bronze to buy fifty pounds of wheat.[41]

Not all suffered equally from the inflation. The poor could still rely on the produce of their fields or on barter. But the middle classes, who handled more coin, were hard hit; and the government was in a vice. More and more of the soldiers' pay was offered in kind, and yet to remain secure at home the emperor had to buy the support of the plebs. To the long-standing bread dole, lately increased with allowances of oil and wine, Aurelian added regular handouts of pork, which he could ill afford. In the circumstances, Aurelian's achievement in arresting decline and securing Rome's frontiers is all the more remarkable.

These paragraphs have taken us beyond the end of our story. Already in the 250s the military and economic crisis was well under way. To the demoralization of constant invasion, army billeting and requisitioning, and inflation and food shortages was added the horror of the plague that swept through most of the southern parts of the empire in the years 252–54. In north Africa desperation was such that, it is alleged, people resorted to human sacrifice in an attempt to allay the anger of the gods.[42]

A Leader Sent from the Sun?

In the decades following 240 it began to seem that Syria might have a major role to play in the destiny of the empire. The shift of focus began with the accession to the throne (244) of Emperor Philip the Arab, a native of Shahba near Bostra in southern Syria. Though his father is described in an anonymous fourth-century source as "a leader of brigands,"[43] he was also a distinguished Roman general, and his opportunity came when Emperor Gordian III died on campaign against Persia and Philip took his place. In the five years of his reign he turned his native village into a magnificent Roman city, with temples, a theater, and prosperous villas. At Rome he celebrated the Secular Games for the thousandth anniversary of the city's foundation.

The mystic sacrifices were performed, during three nights, on the banks of the Tiber; and the Campus Martius resounded with music and dances, and was illuminated with innumerable lamps and torches. Slaves and strangers were excluded from any participation in these national ceremonies. A chorus of twenty-seven youths, and as many virgins, of noble families, and whose parents were both alive, implored the propitious gods in favour of the present, and for the hope of the rising generation; requesting, in religious hymns, that, according to the faith of their ancient oracles, they would still maintain 'the virtue, the felicity, and the empire of the Roman people.[44]

A curious feature of our testimonies about Philip is the persistent suggestion that he was in fact a Christian. This would not in itself be disproved by his participation in pagan ceremonies (even Theodosius did that), but the evidence is shaky. It indicates, however, the feeling among the senatorial class of Rome that almost anything could be expected of Syrians and Arabs.[45]

The murder of Emperor Philip opened what Gibbon called "twenty years of shame and misfortune." The reigns of Decius, Valerian, and Gallienus saw the rise of pretenders and invasions of the empire from east and north—"the blind fury of foreign invaders, and the wild ambition of domestic usurpers."[46] Shapur profited from the domestic confusions and prosecuted the war to the very coastline of the Mediterranean. His two major campaigns fell in the years 252 and 256, and the Syrian attempts on the imperial power are entwined with Syria's role in the resistance to Shapur.

Syria profited from the uncertainty of the times and was encouraged by the success of Philip to raise more than one pretender to the imperial power. The first was Jotapian (248–50?), who seems to have been related to the Sampsigeramid house of Emesa, the priest-kings of the sun.[47] His pretext was the high taxation and extraordinary levies of Philip's brother Priscus in the province.[48] His fall was swift, and he was beheaded during the reign of Decius.

More significant, but more enigmatic, was the career of another Emesene pretender. Uranius Antoninus,[49] a Roman citizen, claimed descent from the priest-king family of the Sampsigerami of Emesa, and in 253 he rallied what forces he could and repulsed the Persians from Emesa. Malalas describes the rout as the result of a lucky shot by a stone-slinger on the person of the Persian king. In 253/4 Uranius minted a series of gold coins proclaiming himself emperor. His career is allusively described in *Sibylline Oracle* 13.150–154:

> Then there will be a flight of Romans, but afterward
> the last priest of all will come, sent from the sun,
> appearing from Syria, and he will accomplish everything with
>   deceit.
> Then there will be a city of the sun.

A maximal interpretaton of Uranius' activity sees him as an eminent Arab effectively opposing Persia and taking it as "a suitable occasion for proclaiming himself Emperor and . . . restoring the Arab domination of the central government."[50] A minimal interpretation is that Uranius was adopting the symbols of Roman power to convey a purely local importance—not a medieval baron calling himself a king but a Middle Eastern dictator calling himself ruler of the world.[51] By the same token, Odenathus' assumption of the title King of Kings, or even Zenobia's of Augusta, would be of purely local significance. The bearer lays claim to an effective power at least equivalent to that of the distant emperor. We do not know what became of Uranius.

A more severe threat to Roman authority was posed by the traitor Mareades,[52] a senator of Antioch. He is referred to by the *Historia Augusta* as Cyriades, which seems to be a Grecization of his Syrian name. He was banished by the citizens for embezzlement of public funds and troubled the tragic reign of Valerian by betraying Antioch to the Persians. Shapur had advanced as far as Nisibis, when Mareades deserted to his cause and (probably in 256)[53] conducted the Persian army as far as Antioch.

> Then when a deceitful man comes, a foreign ally,
> Appearing as a bandit from Syria, an inconspicuous Roman,
> he will also deceitfully approach the race of Cappadocians
> and will besiege them and press them hard, insatiable for war.
> Then you, Tyana and Mazaka, will experience captivity.
> You will be in servitude, and will place your neck under the
>   yoke for this man.
> Syria also will weep when men perish,
> nor will Selenaea then save its sacred town.
> But when a wanton man flees from Syria in anticipation before

the Romans, fleeing through the streams of the Euphrates,
no longer like the Romans but like the proud arrow-shooting
Persians, then a lord of Italians
will fall in the rank, smitten by glittering iron,
letting go his decorum. His sons will perish in addition to him.[54]

The studied obscurity of these lines—written after the event but cast in the form of the Biblical prophecies of old, and combining a knowing precision of detail with a deliberate indeterminacy of allusion—have generally been taken to refer to Mareades. The scene at Antioch is vividly described by Ammianus.

One day at Antioch, while a comedian and his wife were on the stage performing some scenes from common life before a hushed and admiring audience, the woman said, "Unless I am dreaming, the Persians are here." The spectators all turned their heads and then fled in confusion to escape the missiles raining down upon them. The city was set on fire, and many people who were strolling at large, as one does in time of peace, were cut down. The neighborhood was burned and ravaged, and the enemy returned home without loss and laden with spoil. Mareades, who had rashly guided them to destroy his fellow citizens, was burned alive.[55]

As the *Sibylline Oracles* express it:

Wretched Antioch, they will no longer call you a city
when you fall under spears by your own folly. . . .
And you, Hierapolis, will be a triumph-spectacle, and you,
   Beroea,
you will weep with Chalcis for her newly slain children.[56]

These three pretenders, if such they should be called, had made no headway as rulers of Rome, whatever they might have done for their reputation at home. Persian power only grew more insistently menacing. The author of *Sibylline Oracle* 13 was right to perceive the atmosphere as laden with doom for Syria, and he concluded that Odenathus would be its savior.

The year 256 was an *annus mirabilis* for Shapur. It looked as if the lands of Syria might be permanently lost to Rome. Reaching the Mediterranean coast for the first time, the Persian king captured several major towns along the way, including the border towns on the Euphrates, Barbalissus and Dura-Europos.[57]

The excavation of Dura-Europos has taught us a great deal that was unavailable to earlier historians.[58] Dura was the southernmost fortress on the Euphrates, garrisoned by the twelfth cohort of Palmyrenes but a sizable town in its own right. Its population was unusually cosmopolitan, and every religion of the Roman world is represented in its temples, which range from those of Artemis-Azzanathkona, Jupiter Dolichenus, and the Palmyrene gods, through temples of Zeus, Mithras, and the Gadde, to a Christian baptistery and a synagogue whose frescoes of Old Testament scenes are among the finest and most spectacular examples of ancient painting found anywhere.[59] Here is the vision of Ezekiel in the valley of bones; the building of Solomon's temple at Jerusalem, represented in the exact form of a classical peristyle temple, complete with acroteria; the crossing of the Red Sea; Moses striking the rock; Jacob wrestling with the angel; the anointing of David by Samuel; and many others. These paintings testify to the strange forms religious observance might assume in the distant deserts of empire; for such figural representations are unique in Jewish art.

The city was a Macedonian foundation (under the name Europos) that, like Palmyra, had profited by the caravan trade and had become a sizable and prosperous city by the first century A.D. The Parthians had captured it from Seleucid rule in 113 B.C. but had continued to administer it on the accustomed lines; documents of this period continue to be in Greek. Dura's prosperity must have deterred the Parthians from making any great alterations, which in any case would have run counter to the tranquil Parthian manner of dealing with their conquests. Lucius Verus captured the city from the Parthians in A.D. 165 and made it into a garrison post. By the 250s it had been Roman for ninety years.

Dura was passed by, though somewhat damaged, by Shapur's first invasion of 253. Its garrison, the excavators sardonically observed, hastened rather to keep the baths in good repair than to rebuild the tumbled walls. The end came in 256, when Shapur put into action his siege techniques, battering and starving out the inhabitants. It cannot have taken long. At the southwest corner of the city a tunnel was discovered under the walls. In it lay half a dozen skeletons, one of them with a handful of Roman coins that had fallen from his now disintegrated tunic. Were these a group of Romans making a night sortie, crushed by the collapse of their hasty tunnel through the dusty soil? Or were they Persians tunneling into the city to surprise its garrison from within, as the alignment of the skeletons might suggest? Why then the Roman coins? The questions are unanswerable. Persian bones or Roman bones, they are not to be distinguished in death, and their mute message from the desert dust is the facile but incontrovertible, unavoidably moving reminder that war is no fun for those who die.

In the year 256, then, Dura fell, never to be rebuilt. Its handsome gateway leads from desert to desert, and the sheep pasture indifferently on either side of the walls. The monuments of ancient piety grace the museums of Damascus and New Haven. The walls crumble slowly into the wadi. And the single gaunt wall of the Palace of the Dux stares sightlessly across the Euphrates.

Between Dura and Palmyra there is only desert. If Dura lay ruined, could Palmyra be far behind? Many in the cities of Syria must have debated hard whether to maintain their loyalty to the disintegrating Roman Empire or to throw in their lot with the Persians, who looked set to gain the upper hand in any case. If the Romans could offer no protection, perhaps it would be better to trust the mercy of an acknowledged master than the brutality of a conqueror. Racial affinities in the Iranian stocks of these Eastern regions may also have played a part: Vorodes, the second-in-command of Palmyra, may have been influential in pursuing a pro-Persian policy in Palmyra.[60]

More certain are the actions of Odenathus, the undisputed leader of Palmyra. His fealty to Rome had been emphasized by the grant of the title vir consularis in (or before) 258; and in 261 he was responsible for putting down a rebellion of no less than three usurpers who rose up after the capture of Valerian at Carrhae in 259. Valerian's prefect Ballista (or Callistus) acted as kingmaker and elevated Macrianus—who was putting the shattered Roman forces together again—and his son Quietus to the role of emperor. These pretenders, more Roman than the Emesenes or Mareades, commanded more support, and their proclamation was well received in the East. Macrianus, however, immediately set out toward the Danube, where he was defeated by Gallienus' general Aureolus. Quietus and Ballista fled to Emesa, presumably relying on the same support that city had offered to earlier pretenders. At this point Odenathus moved in and overthrew the two in the name of the emperor of Rome (261). Ballista was killed in battle, Quietus by the Emesenes. This action shows that Odenathus understood where his interest lay, and on Rome's behalf he took the desert law into his own hands. According to the *Historia Augusta* he was thus made "emperor over almost the whole East."[61] At this point Syria truly became the determinant of whether the Roman Empire survived or was rent asunder.

Peace with Persia or her containment by warfare were Odenathus' only options. His first instinct was for friendship, a policy less costly than war and more fitting to his dignity as a king who held the balance of the East in his hand. He sent to Shapur

> a long train of camels laden with the most rare and valuable merchandises. . . . "Who is this Odenathus" (said the haughty victor, and commanded that the presents should be cast into the Euphrates) "that he thus insolently presumes to write to his lord? If he entertains a hope of mitigating his punishment, let him fall prostrate before the foot of our throne, with his hands bound behind his back. Should he hesitate, swift destruction shall be poured on his head, on his whole race, and on his country."[62]

So Odenathus' option was removed. Gathering an impromptu force "from the villages of Syria, and the tents of the desert," he pursued the mailed might of Shapur back across the Euphrates, recapturing Carrhae and Nisibis (262). If Roman arms had found warfare difficult against the armored horses and archers of the Persians, the slow and heavy Persians had equal difficulty in standing to battle with the lightly clad and armed skirmishers of the Bedouin tribes. Urgency lent enthusiasm to their onslaught, and the weary Persians retired to their capital. Odenathus was widely hailed as the savior of the empire. From the new emperor of Rome, Gallienus, he received the titles dux Romanorum and restitutor totius Orientis.[63] His power was now both established and recognized. He used the title king or lord.[64] Gallienus needed his support in the East while he struggled with invaders in the West. It would not have been surprising if he had followed the example of earlier compatriots and had himself proclaimed emperor. But he was more cautious than that, despite the accolades that greeted his action.

The conclusion of *Sibylline Oracle* 13 celebrates Odenathus' defeat of Macrianus and Ballista, and it looks forward to his supremacy among the Romans and to peace on the battlefield of Syria.

> Then will come, sent from the sun,
> A lion, terrible and frightful, breathing a great flame.
> Then indeed he will destroy with much shameless daring

the stag, well-horned and swift, and the greatest beast,
the frightful venomous one that issues many hissing noises,
and the goat that goes sideways. Him will glory attend.
He himself, unblemished and great,
will rule over the Romans, and the Persians will be powerless.[65]

Such success was not to be; but a century later Odenathus' memory
was still alive in Antioch, and the orator Libanius referred to him in
a letter as "Odenathus, who made the Persians' hearts tremble. Conquering his enemies everywhere, he overthrew cities and snatched from
the hands of his opponents their land and their safety, returning them
to them only in their hopes."[66]

In these crisis-ridden decades, this was not the only occasion on
which Rome had benefited from the private armies raised by local chief-
tains and landed proprietors. Many of the latter had had to take the
law into their own hands in resisting the barbarians, and the actions
of Postumus in Gaul and Odenathus in Syria are simply an enlarged
version of the same response, dictated by a sense that Rome had abandoned them.[67]

There is, however, little reason to take at face value Gibbon's presentation of Odenathus' army as a scratch army of peasants. This picture
first occurs in Festus, a century later, and thence in Orosius, who calls
it a *manus agrestis*.[68] It is surely exaggerated considering the success of
this army in driving Shapur's forces back; and the resources with which
Zenobia conquered southern Syria, Egypt, and Asia Minor cannot have
been essentially different. Since he was dynast of Palmyra, Odenathus'
own troops cannot have been few, and there is no reason to suppose
them ill-trained or ill-equipped.

As dux Romanorum, Odenathus had Roman troops formally under
his command, perhaps a remnant of Valerian's army. With these he
conducted a second campaign against Persia in 267, this time driving
the Persian army back as far as the gates of Ctesiphon itself. Still he
was far from wishing to set himself up in opposition to Rome. In this
he differed from Postumus in Gaul, who rewarded himself for suppressing a German uprising in 260 by claiming the title of emperor for
himself. Separatist movements were common in the empire at this time
(Spain and Britain also made short-lived breakaways), and Odenathus'
restraint is remarkable. An interesting inscription attests to his support
in distant Tyre.[69] It must nevertheless have seemed to some that the
moment for such a move would not be long in coming.

In the first part of 267, Odenathus was returning from his victory at Ctesiphon, in which Herodes, his son by his first wife, had fought at his right hand. He stopped at Emesa for a birthday party and was murdered, along with Herodes, by his cousin Maeonius.[70] Of ancient writers only the twelfth-century Byzantine chronicler Zonaras gives an explicit motive,[71] making Maeonius the bearer of a long-standing grudge against Odenathus, resulting from a quarrel on the hunting field, in which Maeonius had breached etiquette by throwing his spear first and had been unhorsed by the king. The tale is borrowed, whether in ineptitude or guile, from the historical tale of the conspiracy of the pages against Alexander—a neat example of how history is written through topoi. The shadowy Maeonius must conceal the instigators of a conspiracy, either of a rival for the throne or perhaps of a group who disapproved of Odenathus' accommodation with Rome. Inevitably there were those at Rome and elsewhere who implicated Zenobia,[72] an ambitious mother best placed to profit from the deaths of her cautious husband and her stepson. But she lost no time in bringing Maeonius and his associates to trial and execution.

One of the anonymous continuators of Dio's *Roman History* states that the death of Odenathus was encompassed by the Roman governor of Arabia, Rufinus.[73] This could be either Q. Aradius Rufinus, governor of Syria Phoenice and then Coele-Syria in about 230, or more likely Cocceius Rufinus, governor of Arabia 261/2. Most authorities have neglected this because the historian actually says that Rufinus obtained the murder of "the elder Odenathus" who was plotting rebellion; the "younger Odenathus" then complained to Emperor Gallienus and sought justice. The "elder Odenathus" has been shown to be a figment,[74] and even if he existed he could scarcely have been alive in the reign of Gallienus. The "younger Odenathus" would be an oblique reference to Odenathus' son Wahballath. Since the latter is only mentioned once in the other literary sources, it would not be surprising if this one got his name wrong. Alexander Baron, to his credit, picks up this tale and enlivens it with a deathbed confession by Rufinus to Aurelian that he arranged the murder of Odenathus and allowed all Rome to think that Zenobia was the perpetrator.

Gallienus may have been behind the murder.[75] But Odenathus' son presumably did not believe in the complicity of Gallienus, since he took his complaint about the governor to that very emperor. The case for Roman involvement remains very shaky, and there is little reason to believe that Odenathus was plotting rebellion. That, of course, would not necessarily deter the Roman government from obtaining the death of one who was innocent of the crime of which even their suspicion was a secret.

If Zenobia was not privy, at least she was politic enough to draw the full benefit of the circumstances and to act in a way that, perhaps, Rome had not considered a possibility—her ambition proved far greater than her husband's. Perhaps, too, if Rome had contrived to implicate her in a murder they had canvassed, her bitterness toward Rome would have encouraged secessionist tendencies. The reign of the most glamorous ruler of Syria for many centuries thus opens amid blood, suspicion, and mistrust. Four centuries later the Islamic poet El-Acha could still lament the extinguishing of Odenathus' throne and the "exile" of his son.[76] But whatever posterity might say, the future now lay with Zenobia.

5

Zenobia: The Warrior Queen

The fame of Odenathus' wife far exceeds his own. Zenobia has gone down in history as one of the great queens of the Orient, renowned alike for her beauty and her bravery, her virtue and her tragedy. Gibbon's paean, which closely follows the detail of the *Historia Augusta*, has already been quoted in the introduction. No less enthusiastic is the assessment of Geoffrey Chaucer in his *Monk's Tale:*

> Of Kynges blood of Perce is she descended.
> I seye nat that she hadde moost fairnesse,
> But of hir shap she myghte nat been amended . . .
>
> Hir riche array ne myghte nat be told,
> As wel in vessel as in hire clothyng.
> She was al clad in perree and in gold,
> And eek she lafte noght, for none huntyng,
> To have of sondry tonges ful knowyng,
> Whan that she leyser hadde; and for to entende
> To lerne bookes was al hire likyng,
> How she in vertu myghte hir lyf dispende.[1]

Chaucer's passage sums up three of Zenobia's most lauded traits: her beauty, her enthusiasm, and her love of learning. Her very name is said to mean in the Arabic form Al-Zabba, "one with beautiful long hair."[2] Her name appears in Palmyrene inscriptions as Bat-Zabbai, daughter of Al-Zabba; must we suppose her mother was even more beautiful than she? At any rate her own beauty is well attested—the lustrous black eyes and pearly teeth that shone out of a dark olive complexion may still often be met among the girls of eastern Syria. We will see more of her learning and intellect in chapter 6.

Perhaps Zenobia's beauty alone attracted the widowed and already middle-aged Odenathus to her. Odenathus is presumed to have been born about 220, and the first dedication to his elder son Hairan, who has as yet no formal titles, dates from 251: he was perhaps eleven or so. Six years later Hairanes is honored as patron of the tanners and makers of inflatable hide rafts (by modern Euphrates dwellers they are called *keleks*), still without formal titles.[3] We do not know the date of Zenobia's birth or of her marriage. If her son Wahballath was still a child when Odenathus was murdered at the age of forty-six in 266, he may have been born about 256. Assuming he was born soon after his mother's marriage, and that she married at about the age of fourteen, as was normal in the classical world, we may place her birth around 241 and her marriage around 255. At the time of his marriage to Zenobia, Odenathus was at the peak of his reputation as chief among the sheikhs of Palmyra: she could expect a share in absolute power and the best possible future for their sons—a prospect dimmed only by the existence of Odenathus' son by his first marriage.

Perhaps Zenobia's youthful beauty would have caught Odenathus' eye even if she had been a commoner, but in fact she claimed descent from the family of the Ptolemies and Cleopatras, the Macedonian rulers of Egypt. The important honorific inscription mentioned earlier calls her not only Septimia Bat-Zabbai but "daughter of Antiochus IV Epiphanes."[4] The latter had been king of Syria from 175–64 B.C.; his wife, Cleopatra Thea, was the daughter of Ptolemy VI of Egypt. There is no reason why Zenobia would have invented such an obscure connection: if one is going to invent an ancestry it will be more direct than this. We may assume at least that Zenobia had reason to believe it to be true. When she became sole ruler of Palmyra she made much of this lineage. It casts a piquant light on cosmopolitan Palmyrene society to envisage the hardy race of the mountain dwellers of Macedon turning through soft Egyptian luxury to an eventual alliance with a Bedouin chieftain.

On several aspects of her interests and character we are given plentiful information by the *Historia Augusta*—though it must be remembered that little of the colorful detail that work offers us should be believed, since the author, like many ancient historians, wrote what he felt ought to have been true. We are told that, like Odenathus, Zenobia was passionately addicted to hunting, which she pursued from childhood on, achieving feats only equaled by the heroines of Greek mythology:

She dorste wilde beestes dennes seke,
And rennen in the montaignes al the nyght,

And slepen under a bussh, and she koude eke
Wrastlen, by verray force and verray myght,
With any yong man, were he never so wight.
Ther myght no thyng in hir armes stonde.[5]

Hunting has always been the sport of kings, but this passion of
Odenathus and Zenobia allies them more with Persian mores than with
Roman: one thinks of the unforgettable relief of Taq-e-Bostan portraying
the Persian king Shapur II in pursuit of the wild boar, accompanied by
his bowmen and lancers, his dogs and beaters. This is indeed marvelous
riding country, provided water is assured.

Zenobia had surely received the education appropriate to a Palmyrene girl of noble family. Unfortunately, we know next to nothing
of what that was. Besides fluency in her own Palmyrene language, a
variant of the Aramaic and Syriac of Roman Syria, she had a good
knowledge of Greek, which she improved in later life when she invited
to her court the rhetor Longinus, with whom she "familiarly compared
the beauties of Homer and Plato."[6] She also is said to have known
Egyptian, a circumstance that could strengthen the probability of her
connection with the Ptolemies and that could have facilitated her intel-
ligence arrangements and negotiations with Firmus when she made herself ruler of Egypt. She did not know Latin, though her younger son
Timolaus (if he really existed) is said to have been good at it.

One of the more curious features of the portrait in the *Historia
Augusta* is Zenobia's extreme chastity[7]—a feature mentioned by
Chaucer:

They lyved in joye and in felicitee;
For ech of hem hadde oother lief and deere,
Save o thyng, that she wolde never assente,
By no wey, that he sholde by hire lye
But ones, for it was hir pleyne entente
To have a child, the world to multiplye;
And also soone as that she myghte espye
That she was nat with childe with that dede,
Thanne wolde she suffre hym doon his fantasye
Eft-soone, and nat but oones, out of drede.[8]

In other words, Zenobia submitted to sexual intercourse only for the
purposes of conception. As soon as she was sure that she was not

pregnant, she would allow her husband to come to her again, but if she became pregnant he might not touch her until after the child was born.

This severe attitude to the duty of procreation is one of the virtues in Judaeo-Christian thought. Such behavior is praised by the Alexandrian Jewish writer Philo and is developed as a general object of striving by Augustine,[9] though it is not to be assumed from Augustine's discussion that many put the theory into practice.[10] Perhaps more pertinent here is the belief of the Sabians, the planet-worshipers of nearby Harran, that procreation is the sole purpose of marriage.[11] The Sabians were regarded by Muslims as the only true pre-Judaic monotheists: it is not irrelevant that Abraham, the ancestor of the Jews, dwelt at Harran. Perhaps this is another fragment of evidence for Zenobia's attachment to monotheism.

A similar chastity is attributed to the Arab queen Zebba (who has acquired most of the features of Zenobia) by the Arab writer Ibn-Nobata,[12] though he states that she preserved her virginity completely after marriage—as some extreme Christian couples are known to have done. He does not explain how she came by her sons. Ibn-Nobata's excesses apart, it is clear that Zenobia has been credited with characteristics appropriate to a Christian heroine. Even the *Historia Augusta,* which begins its account of Zenobia with a rhetorical flourish ("Now all shame is exhausted . . . for a foreigner, Zenobia by name, cast about her shoulders the imperial mantle"),[13] goes on to paint what can only be regarded as a flattering portrait of her beauty, bravery, chastity, and wisdom. One sees the pagan senatorial historian fighting with the philosopher in the composition of this curious passage.

Not long after her marriage Zenobia gave birth to a son who was named Wahballath, Gift of Allat, or in Greek, Athenodorus. The existence of this son, attested from the coins minted in his name after the death of Odenathus and from a number of milestone inscriptions in Palestine and Arabia, is one of the strongest indictments of the credibility of the *Historia Augusta.* In the *Life of Gallienus*[14] the latter makes no mention of Wahballath, and states that Zenobia ruled in the name of her two very young sons, Herennianus and Timolaus. Herennianus might be intended as a Latin version of the name of Odenathus' own son Hairan, except that the Latinized name of that son in the *Historia Augusta* is Herodes.[15] A complicating factor is the record of another son, Herodianus "King of Kings," who is not the same as Herodes, since the reference is later than the latter's death.[16] He is associated with

Zenobia on a lead seal, but he must have died soon after Odenathus. Alföldi suggests that Herodianus may be the same man as the *Historia Augusta*'s Herennianus. Timolaus might then be a Greek form of the Semitic name Thaimilu,[17] but more probably of Taimallath, in which case it could be a doublet of Wahballath, Gift of Allat. However, in the *Life of Aurelian*[18] the *Historia Augusta* distinguishes Wahballath (the Latin form is Vaballathus) from Timolaus and Herennianus, perhaps in a deliberate "correction" of this passage. The simplest course may be to reject the testimony of the *Historia Augusta* altogether. The author may have known that there were two sons of Zenobia but may have made up their names.[19] We would then have to assume that the lead token and the dedication by the tanners were posthumous honors to Hairan. This is hardly a satisfactory solution. See the genealogical table for a schematic presentation of the ancestry and progeny of Odenathus.

It appears that Zenobia may have been made party to Odenathus' rule even in his lifetime, though the pair of statues of them in the colonnade was erected only in 271, five years after Odenathus' death, suggesting that their association in this context is intended at least partly to legitimize Zenobia's own position. There are a few hints that Zenobia may have had influence on Odenathus even while he was sole ruler. In general Odenathus remained within the bounds of his obligations to Rome, but two pieces of evidence indicate expansion in his reign: between 259 and 263 Odenathus sacked the city of Nehardea, outside the territory of Palmyra;[20] and at an unknown date the city of Tyre erected an inscription in honor of Odenathus.[21] Professor A. C. Vaughan envisages Odenathus systematically consolidating the chora of Palmyra, encouraging irrigation and bringing one village after another under his sway. Villas and villages accommodated the growing population; public buildings arose at his command. The evidence is insufficient to support this picture, and most of Palmyra's building is of a date earlier than 250. Odenathus' power was supreme because of his military might. He had little time to become a second Augustus, who had found Rome a city of brick and left it one of marble. Much of Palmyra was marble already. Odenathus was a cautious man.

His wife was not cautious. It is tempting to see in her a Lady Macbeth, urging her husband to more ambitious deeds and the canvassing of empire. Like Lady Macbeth, perhaps she did not stick at murder, though in this case it would have been the murder of her own husband that she plotted or connived at. There were those who were ready to accuse her of this, though more pointed the finger at Rome.

Genealogy of Odenathus

The following seems the most economical way of reconciling the conflicting evidence on the ancestry and the progeny of Odenathus.

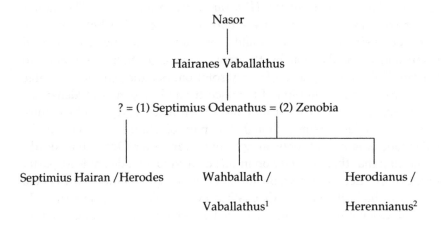

Nasor

Hairanes Vaballathus

? = (1) Septimius Odenathus = (2) Zenobia

Septimius Hairan / Herodes   Wahballath /   Herodianus /

Vaballathus[1]   Herennianus[2]

1. Timolaus, named in the *Historia Augusta*, might be a Latin version of Thaimallat, a doublet of Wahballath.
2. Herennianus may be the *Historia Augusta's* incorrect stab at the name of Herodianus, who is epigraphically attested.

The straightforward explanation, rivalry by another Palmyrene noble, is a perfectly reasonable assumption. Besides impatience at her husband's caution, a stronger motive might be found in her ambitions for her own son Wahballath, now approaching puberty. Herodes, the carefully groomed heir to Odenathus, was an obstacle to Wahballath's elevation, and the mother might well be tempted to risk everything to secure Wahballath's succession. The motive for the crime is there; but the shaky evidence (see chapter 4) points the other way. In this crucial item, our judgment of Zenobia's character can only be ill-informed.

The result of the assassination of Odenathus and Herodes was, as expected, the elevation of Wahballath to the position of *ras tadmor*, with his mother Zenobia as regent ("glorious queen," as two inscriptions of 271 call her)[22] in his minority. It is intriguing that from this moment on Worod is completely eclipsed. After the inscription of 266 detailing his *cursus honorum*, the record is silent. Clearly there was no place for him under the new absolutism of the queen.

The complicated development of the constitutional position can be traced through the coins issued under Palmyrene auspices and in the dating formulae of other documents of Roman rule. The coinage is the most significant.[23] At this time there were about twenty-two mints operating though the Roman Empire—mostly in the East, some with as many as fifteen separate workshops (the case of Antioch)—with the authority to issue coins in the name of the reigning emperor with reverses sometimes according to local taste. The first evidence of Zenobia's revolt, which began with her invasion of Egypt in late 269 or early 270 (see chapter 7), is her suspension of the mint of Antioch on the death of Claudius in 270. It reopened under Palmyrene control on the accession of Aurelian, when it began to issue coins in the joint names of Aurelian and Wahballath. They celebrate the year 4 of Wahballath and the year 1 of Aurelian, thus dating Wahballath's accession to 266/7, the year of Odenathus' death.

The coins of Antioch of this period exhibit Wahballath alone, backing the head of Aurelian on coins with a double obverse. Wahballath wears the laurel wreath of a Roman general, not the Persian tiara. His head is encircled by the enigmatic series of letters VCRIMDR, probably to be interpreted as Vir Clarissimus, Rex, Imperator, Dux Romanorum. The title Augustus is reserved for Aurelian on the reverse. It is not until five years later in 271/2, after Zenobia's revolt was well under way, that coins added the title Augustus to her son's portrait. Some Egyptian papyri date events by the regnal years of Aurelian and Wahballath jointly.[24] Though the coins show Aurelian as well, the titles assumed by Wahballath seem to defy directly the authority of Aurelian in the East.

Wahballath was not granted by Aurelian the additional title that had been his father's, Corrector totius Orientis. The latter title does however appear on the earliest inscription of Wahballath's reign. It is in Greek and Palmyrene and reads:

> [Greek] . . . for the safety of Septimia Zenobia, the most illustrious queen, the mother of the Emperor Septimius Athenodorus . . . [Palmyrene] for the life and victory of Septimius Vaballathus Athenodorus, the most illustrious King of Kings and Restitutor (Epanorthotes) of the entire Orient, son of Septimius Odenathus, King of Kings; and for the life of Septimia Bathzabbai, the most illustrious queen, mother of the King of Kings, daughter of Antiochus.[25]

This is also the first statement of an official position for Zenobia, though she is clearly treated as secondary to her son. An inscription erected by her generals Zabda and Zabbai in August 271 is the first to name Zenobia herself as queen in Palmyra. From this date on we can assume that Wahballath was merely a front for her own power. The coins too only show Zenobia as fellow-Augusta with Wahballath in the fifth year of the revolt, 271/2.

It has sometimes been supposed (not least by Alexander Baron) that Zenobia dreamed of a marriage between herself and Aurelian, which would give them jointly the unchallenged sway of the whole empire. If so, this was a remarkable anticipation of the division of the empire under the tetrarchy by Diocletian, who seemed to develop so many of Aurelian's initiatives in imperial organization and propaganda. Baron's conference on a ship moored in the Hellespont is pure fantasy and derives from Antony's meeting with Cleopatra on a ship in the river Cydnus. But it is not impossible that such a division of power was canvassed by the queen. Clearly it was not going to go very far, since a unilateral declaration of independence was Palmyra's only course to an increase of power.

Queens among the Arabs

The most interesting aspect of these events is the way in which a female ruler could rise to power in the male-dominated ancient world.[26] Zenobia never received sole honor as ruler within Palmyra. Even the statues erected in 271, four years after Odenathus' death, associated the two firmly as joint equals in the memory of Palmyra. Zenobia coined in her own name only in Egypt, from whose rulers she claimed descent, and where queens were a regular feature. Yet she was undoubtedly the real ruler of Palmyra in all but name.

To us this appears particularly remarkable among an Arab people, whose women have no chance of political or social prominence today. Yet history and legend can produce many examples of Arab queens and of queens in other Semitic nations. Most famous of all is one of Zenobia's own models, the Assyrian queen Semiramis. Semiramis' original name seems to have been Sammuramat, a Semitic name meaning "Sammu is exalted"; this name is recorded in inscriptions. She lived from about 850–790 B.C. and became the wife of King Ninus. Though she was probably a captive from Babylon, she was said to be the daughter of Derceto, the fish goddess of Askelon, and to have founded the temple at Hierapolis.

When Ninus died, closely followed by his first son in 812 B.C., Semiramis became regent for her minor son Adad-Nirari III. She led expeditions against Media, Guzara, and the Manaei. She introduced religious reforms—for example, by building the temple of Nebo, son of Marduk, at Nineveh. She built a road from Ecbatana to the Zagros, perhaps as a preliminary to the intended conquests of Persia, Ethiopia, Egypt, and even India. According to Ctesias—regardless of chronology—she built the Hanging Gardens of Babylon. And according to Moses of Chorene she built the Armenian city of Van and died after being defeated in battle by Zoroaster, turning into a rock and weeping like Niobe for eternity. Her virtue is measured, for Boccaccio, by the fact that she even regarded the defense of her kingdom as more important than the perfection of her coiffure: when Babylon rebelled while she was with her hairdresser, she marched forth instantly with her hair braided on one side and loose on the other.[27]

This Semitic trait of queenship can be traced to the civilization of Ugarit and is also found at Ebla. Notable among Assyrian queens were Naqia, the wife of Sennacherib, who secured the succession of his son Esarhaddon, and the charmingly named mother of Nabonidus, Adda-Guppi. In all these cases the position of the queen as regent prepared the way for her own political power.

Among the queens of legend, we may mention Nitocris, who built a bridge over the Euphrates.[28] Herodotus mentions a queen Nitocris of

Egypt who ensured her power by drowning the entire opposition in an underground chamber.[29] Another case is Dido of Carthage (an example Zenobia herself liked to recall). And there is the queen of Sheba, famous in both Jewish and Islamic legend;[30] though Saba (Sheba) is in South Arabia, Josephus made her queen of Egypt and Ethiopia. In general no Arab queens are attested from the southern regions of Arabia, but in the north they seem to be relatively common.[31]

Moving from legend to history, we find a significant number of ruling queens among the ancient Arabs, though regrettably little is known about any of them.[32] A thousand years before Zenobia there were queens in Arabia: Zabibi the queen of Aribi, and Queen Samsi, who paid tribute to Tiglath-Pileser III in 742 and 736 B.C. and was still paying it to Sargon II in 715. Queen Telkhunu ruled the Arab fortress of 'Adurna, conquered by Sennacherib in 688 B.C. One might also mention the Israelite prophetess Deborah and such other important Jewish queens as Bathsheba, Maacha, and Jezebel. Nearer to Zenobia's time, the Nabataean queen mother of Rabbel II seems to have ruled from A.D. 70–75, when Rabbel was in his minority.[33]

Zenobia liked to trace her ancestry to Cleopatra the Great, for the first Cleopatra (the wife of Ptolemy V) had indeed been a Syrian princess, though of course of Greek descent. There had been Greek queens too in Asia Minor: Artemisia of Salamis; Artemisia the mother of Maussollus, who became queen of Caria; and after her, Queen Ada, who adopted Alexander the Great as her son. Zenobia was not the last such Eastern queen, for a century later in the reign of Valens, the Christian Arab queen Mavia helped to protect Constantinople from the Goths.[34]

The Arabs seem to have been remarkably susceptible to the charm of a female leader. In the 1840s Lady Hester Stanhope modeled herself consciously on the queen of Palmyra and achieved an unrivaled influence over the sheikhs who dwelt around her mountain fastness in Lebanon. As an outsider, an exceptional creature, she was able to make herself a dominant political force, in a way not unlike that of those other freakish leaders, the stylite saints of sixth-century Syria. As Simeon the Stylite was in touch with the divine, so Zenobia in her austere sexuality represented the Other. Her authority has a charismatic element. It is worth pondering, too, the way in which warrior queens may be romanticized by contemporary and succeeding generations, so that their political power, great as it is, is further enhanced by the unusual nature of their position.

Zenobia could equally have looked westward to the valiant resistance of Boadicea to Roman arms, or to the role of Victoria, the mother of the Gallic emperor Tetricus. The author of the *Historia Augusta* thought the connection worth making; he has Zenobia quote the Gallic queen in her letter to Aurelian. The letter is of course fiction, on the Thucydidean principle of "what ought to have been said in the circumstances." It is notable that the Roman writers make the conflict more glamorous by making it one between Aurelian and Zenobia, ignoring the titular ruler of Palmyra, Wahballath.

In fact Zenobia, like Semiramis, owed her position entirely to the minority of her son, the legitimate successor of the previous king. Though the earliest coins show Wahballath alone as ruler, Zenobia would hardly have been without influence over him. Only Zosimus makes the point that Zenobia ruled, in the first instance, through the support of her husband's friends, and that in a truly "womanly" way she used them as scapegoats after her defeat, sacrificing Longinus and the others to save her own skin. In his view she was only a weak woman, led astray by her advisers.[35]

Besides these ancient queens and warriors, Zenobia probably remembered the example of Julia Domna, the Syrian wife of Emperor Septimius Severus, who had achieved an unrivaled political authority and influence without ever formally holding power. Whether Julia Domna also created a literary salon is disputed, and undoubtedly the extent of her literary and intellectual circle has been greatly exaggerated.[36] Zenobia certainly tried to draw intellectuals to her court. Rostovtzeff recalls that Catherine the Great, who likewise created a military and intellectual court, liked to compare herself to Zenobia (though she was certainly no match for Zenobia's fabled chastity).[37]

Zenobia's Court

Who then were Zenobia's court? First of all her son, or sons, were. If Timolaus is in fact to be distinguished from Wahballath, he was the clever one, excelling his mother in knowledge of Latin and equaling her in Greek (according to the *Historia Augusta*). This very fact might suggest a superior education: a woman whose claims included Greek-Egyptian descent might naturally know Greek, and even Egyptian, in addition to her native dialect; a man, who had a recognized position in Roman politics, could acquire a formal education that included Latin.

The sources, scanty as they are, make no mention of senate or magistrates under her rule. The loyal Tlass assumes that she governed constitutionally, but there is no evidence. That Odenathus had already assumed the title king suggests that the Roman pattern of government had already been superseded in Palmyra. The eclipse of Vorodes after the death of Odenathus is particularly interesting. It has been assumed that he, with his very considerable standing, had stood to gain from the death of Odenathus,[38] in which case he would doubtless have suffered in Zenobia's purge. However he may have represented a pro-Persian strand in Palmyrene policy,[39] in which case, if he survived, Zenobia's foreign war would have served as a distraction from domestic differences over policy toward Persia. Though she won both Armenia and Arabia (for a time) as her allies, the friendship of Persia was a last resort.

She seems to have had support from a considerable number of the neighboring Arab tribes, a feature of her revolt that has not been given the attention it deserves.[40] The *Historia Augusta* lists among her barbarian supporters the Blemmyes, Axumites, Arabs from Arabia Felix, Indians, Bactrians, Iberians, Saracens, and Persians.[41] There may be exaggeration here. Nevertheless, some problematic inscriptions suggest diplomatic ties between Palmyra and the tribes of the Hadramaut in the 270s,[42] and there are also suggestive connections with Judaea, where numerous Palmyrene names occur in the inscriptions from the cemetery of Beth She'arim, and perhaps with the Judaizing Himyarite kings of South Arabia.

The only notable figure we meet in this period is Septimius Apsaeus, who received a dedication from the city probably in 272.[43]

Besides the intellectuals, discussed in the next chapter, Zenobia's most important courtiers were her generals: Zabdas, the general-in-chief; and Zabbai, the commander of Asia. Not surprisingly, these two are confused and conflated in the Latin and Greek accounts. We really know nothing about Timagenes, who was the leader of her cause in Egypt, though both he and Zabdas figure prominently in the political play of the Abbé Hédélin. Zenobia could drink with the best of them, the *Historia Augusta* avers, and regularly attended the parties of the military and rode out with them to exercise and war.

One must envisage the queen surrounded by "the stately pomp of the courts of Asia" that Gibbon so vividly enumerated,[44] but with this she must surely have mixed the more popular manners of the Roman princes. Her court, no doubt, was staffed by eunuchs[45] (a few grave portraits seem to represent beardless, long-haired, effeminate men) and young girls, some of whom may even have had the role of foot-masseuse envisaged by William Ware, as well as officiating at the hot perfumed baths in the wet-lipped account of Alexander Baron. There certainly were silks, perfumes, and soft carpets, and gold plate and exquisite Syrian or Egyptian glassware. Her dinner service included the gold vases of her ancestor Cleopatra. Her economy and her luxury would alike be interpreted as avarice by her enemies.

The Image of a Queen

Besides her court Zenobia had an eye to the wider public, her Arab neighbors and the people of her realm. The image she presented to them can be discerned through public sculpture and architecture and through coinage. There seems to be no trace of ruler cult, no more than of the Roman imperial cult, in these easternmost lands of the Roman Empire. Possibly Zenobia's striking of a coin with a reverse portraying Selene might suggest an association with the moon-goddess or recall her admiration for her heroine Cleopatra (Selene), but on the whole the public image of the queen was expressed in secular terms. Her statue stood alongside that of Odenathus in a prominent position in the main street of Palmyra.

The *Historia Augusta* contains a few suggestive scraps, such as her fondness for hunting, essentially a king's pastime and one much practiced by the Sassanids. The *Historia Augusta* tells us that she had herself worshiped like a Persian king though wearing Persian garb. This might mean no more than an acceptance of proskynesis—prostration or the ritual blowing of a kiss, which horrified the Macedonians when Alexander the Great adopted it with the role of king of Persia. It might also be merely a recollection of the statues of the Palmyrene gods in Roman military garb. She dressed, we are told by the same source, in the robes of Dido[46] (though we are not told where she obtained these unlikely relics), a practice that would certainly proclaim her alliance to Dido's attitude toward Rome:

> Perpetual hate and mortal wars proclaim
> Against the prince, the people, and the name . . .
> Now, and from hence in every future age,
> When rage excites your arms, and strength supplies the rage,
> Rise some avenger of our Libyan blood;
> With fire and sword pursue the perjured brood.[47]

Unfortunately this anecdote tells us more about what a Roman, senatorial historian thought she ought to have felt and done than about her actual behavior. (Had she read the Aeneid?!) More tangible are her titles, "most glorious queen" and Augusta. She left it to Wahballath to advertise Victory on his coins and to include Aurelian on the reverse. She herself was linked only with the goddess Selene.

The use of buildings as public display must have been as important as anything else. Many travelers have eagerly sought to identify a "Palace of Zenobia" at Palmyra, and this title was often attached to the striking and elevated remains of the Camp of Diocletian at the northwestern end of the city, below the mountain. A forceful argument by Schlumberger identifies the shrine of the standards in the camp as the site of the Palace of Zenobia, comparing the architectural motifs, such as the tree of life, with those of other Middle Eastern palace buildings, especially with Imru 'l- Qais' palace at Mshatta.[48] More recent excavations suggest that the palace should be identified with another imposing group of columns just to the north of the colonnaded street and east of the tetrapylon, which has generally been known as the Baths of Diocletian.[49] If so, it is here we may join the imagination of William Ware in the scene where his hero is first presented to the queen.

> I was ushered into an apartment, not large, but of exquisite architecture, finished and furnished in the Persian taste, where sat Zenobia and Julia. At the feet of the queen, and supporting them upon an embroidered cushion of silk, crouched a beautiful Indian slave. It was her office to bear that light and pretty burden; it seems to be her pleasure too; for she was ever waving round it in playful manner her jewelled fingers, casting upward to her mistress frequent glances of most affectionate regard.

Equally wonderful is Ware's picture of Zenobia's dining hall, which again reflects the author's appreciation of the Victorian painters of imperial Roman scenes rather than direct acquaintance with the originals:

> The walls and ceiling of the room, and the carpets, represented, in the colours of the most eminent Greek and Persian artists, scenes of the life and reign of the great queen of Egypt, of whom Zenobia reckons herself a descendant. Cleopatra was all around, above and beneath. Music at intervals, as the repast drew towards a close, streamed in from invisible performers.[50]

Besides the city palace Zenobia seems to have boasted a spring palace at Batn-el-Medjiz in Osrhoene.[51]

Her building operations became the stuff of legend. Integral to her aim of securing an independent realm between Rome and Parthia was the consolidation of border defenses. It was with this aim that she founded the border fortress of Zenobia (modern Halabiye) on the west bank of the Euphrates. It lay some miles to the north of Dura-Europos, the main frontier station of the Romans, which had finally been destroyed by Persian troops in 256. The modern crossing of the Euphrates in this stretch is at Deir-ez-Zor, where French labor under the mandate built a fine suspension bridge in the 1930s. The banks here are level on either side and ideally suited to the construction of a bridge. But ancient considerations were different.

Zenobia, like Dura-Europos, takes advantage of the cliffs that line the Euphrates for much of its course and make crossing relatively difficult. But where Dura-Europos perches on a beetling precipice more than 100 feet above the river, making it unassailable except by an enemy that has already croseed the river and established itself on the west bank, Zenobia uses the cliffs on the eastern side to discourage a river-borne attack. Its own situation is nonetheless remarkable. Procopius, whose book *On the Buildings of Justinian* describes the restoration of the fortress by that emperor, writes:

> Zenobia stands beside the River Euphrates, which flows close to its walls on the eastern side. This river, surrounded by high mountains, has no space in which to extend itself, but its stream is confined among the neighbouring mountains and between its rugged banks. Whenever it is swollen by rain into a flood, it pours against the city wall and washes not merely against the foundations but as high as its very battlements.[52]

It seems from what Procopius says that the original city did not take advantage of the spectacular tactical advantage of the site, which encloses a pinnacle of mountain so steep it is unscalable except on hand and knees (*experto crede*), and which is topped by a walled garrison emplacement that could control the country for miles around. But this post on the west bank of the river was supplemented by a smaller fortress (now called Zalabiye) about a quarter of a mile downstream on the cliffs of the east bank, which could, though vulnerable itself, give advance warning of movements in the hills and wadis on the Persian side. So intimate was the strategic connection between the two that a legend arose in the Middle Ages that Zenobia had actually constructed a tunnel beneath the Euphrates to link the two castles.

Nothing remains of the buildings of Zenobia's period. Justinian razed the northern wall, which had become ruinous, and constructed a mole to protect the dilapidated walls on the eastern (riverine) side.

> He proceeded beyond the foundations of the (north) wall, beyond the outwork and the ditch itself, and there built an admirable and singularly beautiful wall, thus greatly enlarging Zenobia in this quarter. There was, moreover, a certain hill which stood near the city towards the west, from which the barbarians, when they made their attacks, were able to shoot with impunity down upon the heads of the defenders, and even of those who were standing in the midst of the city; this hill the Emperor Justinian surrounded with a wall on both sides, and thus included it in the city of Zenobia, afterwards escarping its sides throughout, so that no enemy could ascend it. He also built another fort upon the top of the hill, and thus rendered it altogether inaccessible to those who wished to assault the city, for beyond the hill the ground sinks into a hollow valley, and therefore it cannot be closely approached by the enemy.[53]

It is difficult to take this report at face value. One can scarcely believe that Zenobia would have founded a city between the river and the strongest tactical position in the vicinity without including that spectacular hill in the defenses. She may scarcely have had the resources to build a curtain wall—though there was clearly a wall on the lower ground—but the peak must have been held by a fort, however small. This would have been necessary, if for nothing else, to receive the signals from Zalabiye. I suspect that Procopius, anxious to glorify his hero, minimized the extent of the defenses already in existence—though, to be sure, they had been falling into ruin for three hundred years by the time of Justinian.

It is surprising that we do not know of any building by Zenobia in other parts of her empire, at Zeugma or Callinicum on the Euphrates, or at Hierapolis-Membij, which according to Procopius was quite undefended until Justinian's works there. She must have calculated that the Persians were on the defensive and that the mobile Palmyrene troops would have the advantage and little need of walls. The city of Zenobia, besides its role as a signaling base, was designed, like that other tactically puzzling monument, Hadrian's Wall, in large part to impress—to show both Persia and her own people the claims of Palmyra.

We know little of Zenobia's army. In Arab tradition it was composed of Jews, Arabs, and Amalika.[54] William Wright reports the local traditions on three encampments of Zenobia's Bedouin allies, the first due south of the fountain, the second on the plain opposite the Abu el-Fawaris springs, and the third on the road to Emesa at a place called Marbat 'Antar, where, in a cleft in the mountain, there is a fine spring of water.[55] The association of these vague indications with Zenobia must unfortunately remain doubtful. But wherever Zenobia's troops actually lay, the Roman legions at Antioch and Samosata must have gazed with anxiety on the increasing militarization of their doubtful ally.

On her side, then, were the soldiers, a part of the desert Arabs, and certainly some of the senators. But the easy succession after her capture suggests there were protagonists waiting in the wings. A scant few months after Aurelian had sacked Palmyra and taken Zenobia captive, a second revolution installed her kinsman Antiochus as figurehead. This does not necessarily suggest a continuation of her policy. Some, we know, had other views. One of those who warmed little to the imperial regime was Septimius Haddudan, chief symposiarch of the priests of Bel.[56] Like the princes of Palmyra, Haddudan was a senator. His father 'Ogeilu, son of Maqqai Haddudan, had been a loyal supporter of Odenathus. But Haddudan watched the growing hubris, the literary and philosophical discussions, the ambition, and the luxury of the Sun Queen with a jaundiced eye—biding his time in silence.

6

Of Philosophers, Oracles, and Bishops

A Cabinet of Intellectuals

Sir Ronald Syme entitled one of the chapters of his *Roman Revolution* "The Organisation of Opinion." Syme assumed that the onrush of Augustus to dictatorial power required the marshaling of poets and artists, priests and soothsayers, moralists, historians, and antiquaries to bolster his labile power. The chapter has met much criticism. Poets at least are not so easily led; and even religious leaders often have other springs of action besides their need to remain in the favor of the wordly great. Critics seem to suggest that Augustus organized no opinion and that no intellectual supported him.

We are in no danger of supposing Zenobia's power so divorced from the intellectual concerns of her contemporaries. For one thing we lack the evidence. Only a rash man would argue that she consolidated her leadership in the teeth of all the intellectuals. *Trahison des clercs* is too familiar a phrase for that. The stray fragments of evidence we have suggest a considerable loyalty of philosophers, orators, religious leaders, and historians. The inferiority of their productions to those of the age of Augustus has deprived us of the opportunity to judge them. We may consider both the loyalty of a rhetor and the opportunism of a bishop. Oracles will not be tardy in support. And after all, what had they to hold against a mighty and charismatic queen, when Rome was far away and at once beholden (to Palmyra) and beleaguered (by the northern tribes)?

Best known and best attested among the courtiers of Zenobia is the philosopher and rhetorician Cassius Longinus, whose most famous work is not by his hand. The treatise that excited the eighteenth century, *On the Sublime*, which contains the earliest literary appreciation of a passage of the Bible, and which has puzzled scholars with the hardness of its Greek, is falsely attributed to this critic, whose memory thereby becomes the duller. He must nonetheless have been a worthy scholar, with three lost books about Homer, commentaries on Plato's *Timaeus*, and an *Art of Rhetoric* to his credit. He often solemnly celebrated Plato's birthday with an intellectual dinner party.

Longinus came as a student to Athens when the Syrian Epiphanius headed Plato's Academy. Since he was likewise a Syrian (his mother was from Emesa), perhaps he received special attention from Epiphanius. By the time he reached maturity he had himself become head of the Academy and the tutor of another Syrian, Porphyry (born 234 with the Semitic name of Malik), who later abandoned him for the greater eminence of Plotinus. Eunapius, in his *Lives of the Sophists*, describes Longinus unforgettably as "a living library and a walking museum," an accolade that might seem only equal to the renown of Dominie Sampson as a "literary dumb-waiter."[1]

At the age of nearly sixty he received a call to Zenobia's court at Palmyra, which he accepted more readily since the Goths' invasion of Greece had made Athenian circumstances uncertain. His role, it appears, was primarily to instruct the queen in Greek, and, if the *Historia Augusta* is to be believed, to conduct her diplomacy with Rome in that language,[2] in which, to be sure, she was considerably more proficient than in Latin. He enthused about the climate of Palmyra, though it can hardly have been more pleasant than that of Athens before the nephos of the twentieth century—except in winter—and invited his pupil Porphyry to join him there out of consideration for his health. The letter, also requesting copies of the works of Plotinus, casts a vivid light on the difficulties of a scholar far from home and libraries.

> Send them (Plotinus' works) when you like, or, better, bring them: for I shall never stop asking you to give the journey to us the preference over any other, if for no other reason—for surely there is no wisdom that you could expect to learn from us as a result of your visit—for the sake of our old friendship and of the climate, which is particularly good for the ill-health of which you speak.... There is such a shortage of copyists here that really all the time I have been trying to complete my set of Plotinus and have only just managed it by taking my manuscript-writer away from his usual tasks and setting him to this one only.[3]

Longinus' discourses included lectures on the interpretation of Plato: Gibbon imagined how Zenobia "familiarly compared the beauties of Homer and Plato under the tuition of the sublime Longinus."[4] Another favorite theme was the Demiurge or Creator as the emanation of the Universal Mind (a doctrine that developed into Porphyry's Neoplatonism and influenced both Emperor Julian's religion of the sun as chief of the gods and the Christian theology of the Word that proceedeth from the Father). The excellent, if pious, William Ware, in his novel on Zenobia, imagines Longinus dilating to his Roman visitors at Palmyra on the certainty of a future life, and he consecrates to him in the dungeon of his last hours before execution a nobility of discourse worthy of the dying Socrates.[5] At least as welcome to Zenobia would have been Longinus' lengthy oration on the virtues of Odenathus.[6]

Longinus was vilified as the architect of the queen's ambition—even by the queen herself, who saved her skin after the fall of Palmyra by blaming her advisers—scorned for his bombastic style, and condemned to neglect as a thoroughly second-rate thinker. His position was the living embodiment of the hired intellectual, "the great man's licensed friend" mocked by the satirist Lucian: from snobbery, or desire of luxury, the scholar would impart to his philistine patron an "air of Grecian culture," only to be outfaced by a singer and rejected when the patron tired of him.[7] One hopes Longinus had never read this acid little tract.

Among Zenobia's motives we must surely consider a desire to emulate that earlier empress from Syria, Julia Domna, who gathered around her a glittering firmament of Greek men of letters, chief among them Philostratus, author of *Lives* of his contemporary philosophers and of the wonder worker of Apollonius of Tyana. It was not Zenobia's fault if the pool of talent available to her was less than that of her countrywoman a century before. The size and importance of Julia's coterie should not be overrated: "Great and ambitious men of the age did not settle down to diverting an Empress."[8] But it was the best model Zenobia had.

Who now knows of Callinicus of Petra, another sophist who practiced at Athens, wrote an account of Roman antiquities, and seems to have dedicated his Greek *History of Alexandria* to Zenobia. The dedication is in fact "to Cleopatra"; the work written at the time when Zenobia extended her rule to Egypt. That is of peculiar significance, since we know that Zenobia saw herself as an heir of Cleopatra.[9] Callinicus found at Palmyra a rival in another citizen of Petra, the sophist Genethlius, who may be the author of the treatise on speech making that survives under the name of Menander Rhetor.[10]

What should we make of the historian Nicomachus, known to have written a biography of Apollonius of Tyana, and also credited by the *Historia Augusta* with having translated into Greek from "Syrian" one of Zenobia's letters to Aurelian.[11] If not an invention of the *Historia Augusta*—if the man himself existed—perhaps he was another pale sophist at her court.

At about this time Nicomachus of Trebizond wrote a history of the period from Philip to Odenathus, concluding with the resounding victories of the latter. He too may not have been unwelcome at the court of Zenobia.[12] It would be going too far to suggest that the author of *Sibylline Oracle 13*, who concludes in a similar vein, also moved in these circles. Though he was certainly a Syrian, he says nothing of Zenobia herself.

Less evanescent than these men's labors was the Neoplatonic school of Apamea, founded by Plotinus' pupil Amelius, with Zenobia's support and Longinus' blessing. The city already had an intellectual tradition, represented in the second century A.D. by Numenius of Apamea, the Platonist philosopher and critic of Homer.[13] Here the long-robed philosophers paced beneath the colonnades that still extend for more than a mile through fields of asphodel and anemone, the barley sugar twisting of the columns reflecting the intricacies of their thought. It was a wealthy city. Five hundred years before, it had housed the stables for the six hundred elephants of the Seleucid king. Now Roman villas, baths, and temples of the Roman gods sprang up to cosset the traders and administrators of this fertile plain, while the hot sun beat down from a brazen sky, paring thought down to an awareness of simplicity and unity. At Apamea was a famous hydromantic oracle in the temple of the sun and moon, where bronze tablets had foretold the elevation of Julia Domna to empress. Apamea was a good city for an ambitious queen to cultivate.

Literature in Third-century Syria

The number of these Greek intellectuals deserves comment. The Greek tradition in the literature of Syria was not a negligible one. It went back to the Epicurean Philodemus of Gadara, a profound influence on Latin poetry of the age of Cicero and Augustus, and to the delicate Antipater of Sidon (also first century B.C.) In the first century A.D., another poet, Meleager of Gadara, was proud to proclaim that he was an heir of both Greek and Syrian culture and that he came from what then might well be called the Athens of Syria:

A foster child of Tyre's fair isle;
    The land that gave me birth

> Was where the suns of Syria smile
> On Gadara's Attic earth . . .[14]

In the second century most literary pretensions were punctured by the humorous Lucian of Samosata, who spoke only Syriac until he was fifteen years old, when he left Samosata to make his fortune. Also, though his date is disputed, the novelist Heliodorus had probably flourished in his home town of Emesa, where he celebrated his descent from the sun himself, not long before Zenobia's rule in Palmyra. Heliodorus exhibits a knowledge of both Egypt and Athens; perhaps he studied in the latter city when Longinus headed the Academy? Another Syrian writer, author of a novel entitled *Babyloniaca*, was Iamblichus (the name is known at Palmyra, though the origin of this Iamblichus is undiscovered). He wrote about A.D. 160-80. The *Phoenician History* of the contemporary Philo of Byblos is lost to us.

The Syrian connection in Western letters extended to the next generation also, when Iamblichus (another one) of Chalcis in Coele-Syria (ca. 250-325) studied under Longinus' pupil Porphyry. He founded a school, perhaps at Apamea, and wrote voluminously on philosophy: books are known on the life of Pythagoras and on mathematics. The intellectuals of Zenobia's court were heirs to a long and distinctive tradition.

While West looks to East for inspiration, East looks to West for respectability. Palmyra was unusual in bringing eastward the Greek-trained intellectuals of western Syria, whose natural home was the Hellenic West. The fact that they came at all must indicate something about the power and prestige of the city, as well as about the difficulties of living in the Roman Empire at this period. There are a number of pieces of evidence suggesting a traffic in the other direction, of intellectuals of Palmyrene or at least Syrian origin who made it in the West. We do not know the native town of Odenathus the philosopher, mentioned by Damascius in his *Life of Isidore*,[15] but is is not improbable that he was a Palmyrene. There are also two candidates for possible Palmyrene origin among the bishops of Jerusalem in the third century, Mazabanes (253-64) and Zabdas (297-301).[16] The name Zenobius is found more than once in the years after the fall of Palmyra: Libanius' teacher bore this name, as did the architect of the Church of the Holy Sepulchre under Constantine. A century later, Libanius refers to a rhetor Odenathus who was a descendant of the great Odenathus.[17] These scattered facts may suggest that a considerable degree of literary culture and education in Palmyra found employment in other parts of the Roman Empire after the destruction of the city.

Such Greek writings and traditions were unusual in third-century Syria. By this time the native tradition had established itself, and there was an extensive literature in Syriac. Though the authors of these works had no connection with Zenobia, the character of Syriac literature provides a context for the cultural amalgam in which the queen was operating and in which her ideas were formed.

Syriac literature, though often translated into Greek, had almost nothing in common with Greek literature as far as its themes were concerned. An exception was the *Epistle* of Mara bar Serapion, a collection of maxims from the early Stoa. By and large Syriac literature inherited the Judaic tradition (the Book of Enoch is one of the earliest Syriac writings), and its essence was the burgeoning Christian philosophy of those eastern churchmen whose grasp on orthodoxy was often tenuous and whose ascetic habits earned the scorn of Gibbon.[18]

The Syrian region can boast the first Christian monarch in the person of King Abgar of Edessa (now Urfa in Turkey). According to legend, a correspondence was preserved between Abgar and Jesus, and the apostle Addai converted Abgar to Christianity; Abgar thereupon banned the wilder excesses of the Syriac religions, such as self-mutilation, decreeing that anyone who castrated himself (or circumcised himself?) should lose also his right hand. It seems more likely that Christianity took root among the Jews of Edessa around the middle of the second century—perhaps the silk merchants were the first to receive it.[19]

Other rulers are said to have toyed with Christianity. Julia Mamaea invited Origen to Antioch to discuss theology.[20] Several reports (but only in Christian writers) state—without much plausibility—that Emperor Philip the Arab was a Christian and likewise had corresponded with Origen.[21] Origen had other connections with Syria too: he converted Gregory, later to be named wonder-worker, whose alma mater was the law school of Berytus.[22]

Edessa was the home of the highly influential Bardaisan (Grecized as Bardesanes) (154–222).[23] Bardaisan was an exact contemporary of the eunuch bishop Melito of Sardis, who addressed a defense of the Christian religion to Emperor Marcus Aurelius. Bardaisan's own position with regard to Christianity was more complex. Regarded by Eusebius as an able defender of the faith, notably against the hyper-Paulinism of the heretical Marcion and his followers, his thought nonetheless contained a strong mixture of Stoic physics and Semitic astrology. His cosmology of five elements was fundamental, as was his belief, resembling that of Mani, in a good and an evil God. He also denied the resurrection of the body. Attractive features of his doctrine include free will, the naturalness of Good to man, and his insistence on an active striving to do Good (in contradistinction to the Manichaean and monachic insistence on ascetic practice). He regarded sexual intercourse as a valuable means of spiritual purification, and knowledge as the route to salvation.

Hints that he was not as orthodox as Eusebius makes out appear in his connections with Valentinianism (in which the soul is good and the body evil), which he later repudiated, and in his curious account of the Incarnation, in which God made the Mother pregnant in the form of a fish and she bore the "Son of Life." This Father and Mother are identified with the sun and moon, and therefore with the Syrian Gods Hadad and Atargatis (to whom the fish was sacred). Bardaisan seems to represent one of the attempts, very common in the early centuries of Christianity, to weld inconsistent and disparate religious traditions into a unity.

Bardaisan interests us here for his literary achievement. His most famous work is the *Book of the Laws of Countries*, which may have covered some of the same ground as his dialogue *On Fate*. In these he attacked astrology, in particular geographical determinism, the idea that the climate or Zodiac sign in which one is born determines one's nature.

> In all places, every day and at all hours, men are born in nativities which are distinct from one another, and the laws of men overcome the Decree, and they govern themselves according to their customs; and Fortune does not compel the Seres to kill at all when they do not wish; nor the Brahmins to eat flesh; nor restrain the Persians from marrying their daughters and their sisters; nor the Hindus from being burnt; nor the Medians from being devoured by dogs; nor the Parthians from taking many wives; nor the Britons from many men taking one wife; nor the Edesseans from being chaste; nor the Greeks from practising gymnastics; nor the Romans from always seizing upon countries; nor the Gauls from marrying one for another; nor constrain the Amazons to bring up the males; neither does the Nativity compel any at the circumference of the world to use the art of the Muses; but as I have said, in every country, and in every nation, all men use the Free-will of their

Nature as they wish, and do services to Fortune and to Nature, on account of the body with which they are clad, at one time as they wish, at another as they do not wish; for in every country and in every nation there are rich and poor, and rulers and subjects, and healthy and sick, each of them, according as Fortune and Nativity has reached him.[24]

Bardaisan also wrote a book on Indian customs and one hundred and fifty hymns, the number being clearly an imitation of David of Judah. His position at the court of King Abgar gave him the leisure to write, and we know from the account of a Roman envoy to Abgar that Bardaisan also endeared himself to the king by his skill in circus archery: he could outline a man's portrait in arrows on a shield. How many other theologians could claim skill in any sport more dangerous than croquet?

Bardaisan's son was the appropriately named Harmonius, a composer of hymns who was the first to introduce Greek musical forms and melodies into Syrian song. The followers of Bardaisan met regularly in caves to sing these hymns and the psalms of Bardaisan and to read from his writings. This continued for two centuries, until the meeting places were destroyed by Bishop Rabbula of Edessa in the fifth century. The harmonies of Harmonius were adopted by the orthodox St. Ephraim to sweeten his own fine Christian poetry,[25] though the tunes of the son were attached to fierce metrical denunciations of the father. A typical passage is "Let us pray for Bardaisan, who departed this life in heathenism—a legion of demons in his heart, and our Lord on his lips."

Other writings that have been, surely wrongly, attributed to Bardaisan, include two very famous works, the *Hymn of the Soul* and the *Odes of Solomon*. By its references to Parthia, the *Hymn of the Soul* can be dated to the period preceding the end of the Parthian kingdom in A.D. 224. It represents Gnosticism at its peak and is an allegorical account of the self-transfiguration of the Soul by the search for the Pearl of Knowledge, Understanding ("Gnosis").

1. While I was yet but a little child in the House of my Father,
Brought up in luxury, well content with the life of the Palace,
Far from the East, our home, my parents sent me to travel,
And from the royal Hoard they prepared me a load for the
    journey,

Precious it was yet light, that alone I carried the burden.

2. Median gold it contained and silver from Atropatene,
Garnet and ruby from Hindostan and Bactrian agate,
Adamant harness was girded upon me stronger than iron;
But my Robe they took off wherewith their love had adorned
 me,
And the bright Tunic woven of scarlet and wrought to my
 stature.

3. For they decreed, and wrote on my heart that I should not
 forget it:
  "If thou go down and bring from Egypt the Pearl, the
   unique one,
  Guarded there in the sea that envelopes the loud-hissing
   Serpent,
  Thou shalt be clothed again with thy Robe and the Tunic of
   scarlet,
  And with thy Brother, the Prince, thou shalt inherit the
   Kingdom."

After being led astray by temptation, forgetting his quest, a letter comes
from the King to arouse him again.

11. High it flew as the Eagle, King of the birds of the heaven,
Flew and alighted beside me, and spoke in the speech of my
 country,
Then at the sound of its tones I started and rose from my
 slumber;
Taking it up I kissed and broke the Seal that was on it,
And like the words engraved on my heart were the words of the
 Letter.

The eagle is the holy bird of the sun-god in Semitic religion, and in
this stanza we clearly see the adaptation of a Syrian motif to a Christian
purpose.

13. Then I seized the Pearl and homewards started to journey,
Leaving the unclean garb I had worn in Egypt behind me;

> Straight for the East I set my course, to the light of the
>   homeland,
> And on the way in front I found the Letter that roused me—
> Once it awakened me, now it became a Light to my pathway.[26]

The singer's robe is restored, glorious as ever, and he enters the gate of
the Kingdom to dwell with his Father.

The *Odes of Solomon* were probably composed in the second century by a Syrian Jew, but by the mid–third century had been translated
into Greek, suggesting the spreading tentacles of the Syriac tradition
into the dominant Greek culture. Number 15 is significant in its invo-
cation of God as Sun, a Syrian idea stemming from Arab sun-worship:

> As the Sun is a joy to those who seek its day,
> So my joy is the Lord;
> Because he is my sun, and his rays roused me,
> And his light dispelled all the darkness from my face.
> I obtained eyes by him, and I saw his holy day.

Even St. Ephraim is not above invoking Christ as Sun:

> For the Sun—that sun of Yours—
> announces Your mystery as if by mouth.
> In the winter, as Your type, it descends to a low level;
> In summer, like You, it ascends to the height and rules over
>   all. . . .
> In January the Pair of Lights emerged:
> You from the womb and the Sun with You from within the
>   dark.[27]

From the next generation comes Tatian's *Diatessaron* or *Harmony of the
Four Gospels*, as Syrian Christianity becomes steadily more orthodox.
Acts of Judas Thomas (the Apostle of India) seems also to have been
written during the third century, probably in Syriac to begin with, then
later translated into Greek like the *Odes of Solomon.*

Religion in Third-century Syria

The strongly religious content of such literature prompts a consideration
of the complex religious scene of third-century Syria. The old Arab

worship of the heavenly bodies and the sun mingled with the distinctively Syrian ecstatic cults and the dominant cults of the Greek gods. The Christian doctrine opposed both but at the same time exploded into fission in innumerable heresies. The new religion of Mani encountered all these head-on as well as the extensive Jewish population of the major cities. And even the Persian worship of Mithras and the Zoroastrian religion made its inroads. It would be no easy task for a ruler to create a united people. There was no tradition, as in the Roman cult of the emperor, by which religious observance could be given a political content. As throughout the pagan world, neighbor gods coexisted peacefully. A good example is the city of Dura-Europos, where in the narrow confines of its walls one could find, within a stone's throw of each other, a synagogue, a Christian baptistery, and temples of Artemis Azzanathkona, of the Palmyrene Gods, of Mithras and Zeus-Baalshamin, of Bel, and of the Gadde (Fortunes) of the city. We are hampered in our interpretation by the lack of literary evidence for most of these cults, but we gain the impression that religion was a matter of personal choice, an affair between man and his god, or of small groups and their gods, not of public social practice. As Posidonius said, "The purpose of man is to study the heavens." This gnostic tendency was inimical to the political organization of cult.

It is instructive to consider the diversity of these cults. The best known of the old pagan cults of Syria is that of the Syrian goddess at Hierapolis-Membij.[28] Usually she was identified with Atargatis (in Greek Derceto), a goddess to whom fish were sacred, and who might even take on the form of a mermaid. The cult of the Nabataeans focuses on such a fish-goddess. The legendary Semiramis, according to one story, traced her descent to the fish-goddess herself and was the founder of the temple at Hierapolis. The Greeks characteristically regarded Derceto as a nymph, or the goddess Aphrodite, transformed into a fish to escape the pursuit of Typhon. In another version a fish saved the goddess Dione while crossing the Euphrates.[29]

Fish therefore were taboo and were not eaten by Syrians. Plutarch tells us that 'if anyone eats herrings or sardines the Syrian goddess devours his shins, inflames his body with ulcers, and consumes his liver."[30] Musaeus called Atargatis a "cruel queen" because of this ban on the eating of fish, normally an important source of protein for the Greeks.

Astarte also received worship through fish, with dedications of golden or silver fish or with carefully cooked real fish, and as far west as Labranda in Caria there was a pool sacred to Zeus where the fish were adorned with golden necklaces and golden earrings. (How do you fix an earring onto a fish?) In Astarte's case a fish meal seems to have been part of the worship, just as in many Syrian cities the main religious function was a communal meal. At Dura-Europos and Palmyra there were dining rooms with couches for as many as forty-five persons, and special kitchens were attached to the temples.[31]

Another important god was Jupiter Dolichenus, whose worship was carried abroad by Syrians wherever they went, as far as Spain and even Caerleon in Wales. Like the Persian Mithras, he became generally popular among the Roman army.[32]

More visible to outsiders than the dinners were the ecstatic rites of the Syrian goddess, vividly described by Lucian. Before her temple stood pillars on which crouched ascetic stylites, just as Christian saints would do a century later. Votaries danced to the sound of timbrel and pipe and in the ecstasy of devotion severed their genitals (the purpose being not, as Christian doctrine might lead us to suppose, to enforce chastity on themselves but in Greek theory to preserve the body's quota of *pneuma*, spirit, which would otherwise flow out in seminal emissions). St. Augustine admits to having been rapt more than once by the frenzy of these rites, despite their obscenity.[33]

When I was a young man I used to go to sacrilegious shows and entertainments. I watched the antics of madmen; I listened to singing boys; I thoroughly enjoyed the most degrading spectacles put on in honor of gods and goddesses. . . . Certainly these mountebanks would be ashamed to give a rehearsal performance in their homes, before their mothers, of these disgusting verbal and acted obscenities. Yet they performed them in the presence of the Mother of the Gods before an immense audience of spectators of both sexes.

Our reaction to the accounts of such pagan rites is so conditioned by the Christian revulsion that began with Augustine that it is hard for us to enter sympathetically into the minds of the participants in such rites. Easier for us to grasp, perhaps, is the typically Arabian worship of the heavenly bodies—planets, moon, and above all the sun. The goddess Astarte at Aphaca was identified with the moon.[34] There was a more famous Temple of Sin (the Moon) at Harran (Carrae), where Abraham lived with Sarai, and where Jacob married the daughters of Laban the Syrian; where Crassus was slain by the Parthians and Valerian taken captive by the Persians. This Temple of Sin was one of the holiest and best-known shrines of pagan Syria. The worshiper must approach the god in a mood of humble sorrow, clad entirely in black, and drenched in a perfume made of incense, opium, and the grease and urine of a goat.[35] It attracted even emperors to its cult, and Caracalla was murdered on his way to pay homage to the god.

The worship of the heavenly bodies was closely linked with the practice of astrology, a specialty of Semitic peoples, among whom the Babylonians were renowned for their expertise. The Sabaeans and Mandaeans were planet-worshipers, and we know from St. Paul that planet-cult was prevalent as far west at Colossae.[36] Its importance at Palmyra is reflected in the zodiac reliefs adorning the roof of the Temple of Bel, and a mosaic at Philippopolis/Shahba is also full of astral imagery recalling Philip's association with the god Aion.[37]

Not immediately identifiable with the heavenly bodies were goddesses like Manah, Allat (often = Athena), and al-'Uzza, the strong one (often = Venus). Both the latter appear in dedications all across the Hauran and in Palmyra. The Islamic writer Ibn al-Kalbi (d. A.D. 821/ 2) refers to them as daughters of Allah, as does the Qur'an.[38] This illustrates the difficulty Islam had in extirpating the pagan gods, for it merely relegated them to a subordinate position. Allat, Ibn al-Kalbi tells us, "was a cubic rock beside which a certain Jew used to prepare his barley porridge."[39] Both Allat and al-'Uzza were local in origin, and as their cult spread they were represented by idols as well as the original baetyls or stones.

The Black Stone of Elagabal

The black stone, like that in the Ka'aba at Mecca, is the fundamental object of cult to the Arab peoples. The volcanic region of the Hauran consists almost entirely of a litter of black stones; consequently there were gods aplenty in Roman Syria. St. Ephraim once compares Christ to a stone—"the Perfect Stone that went up and stood upon the stone that fools rejected."[40] Antonin Artaud devotes a remarkable passage of his odd book on Emperor Heliogabalus to these black stones.

> There are black stones in the form of a male phallus, with a female sex chiseled below. These stones are vertebrae from the precious corners of the earth. The black stone of Emesa is the largest of these vertebrae, the most pure, the most perfect.

But there are stones that are alive, like animals or plants, and like, one may say, the sun, with its spots that move about, inflate and deflate, and dribble into one another.... The spots are born in it like a cancer, like the effervescent buboes of the plague.... All this is alive; and one may say that some stones are alive; and the stones of Syria are alive, like the miracles of nature; for they are stones hurled from heaven.

There are many miracles and marvels of nature on the volcanic soil of Syria—this soil, which seems carpeted and moulded entirely of pumice stone, but where the stones fallen from the sky live their own life, without being confused with the pumice. There are marvelous legends about the stones of Syria. Witness this text of Photius, a Byzantine historian of the epoch of Septimius Severus [sic]:

"Severus was a Roman.... It was he himself who related that he had seen a stone on which could be observed the varied figures of the moon, taking on every kind of appearance, growing and diminishing according to the course of the sun, and containing also the imprint of the sun itself."[41]

Another such tale is that of one Severus in Damascius' Life of Isidore.

I saw [says Severus] a baetyl moved by the air, partly hidden in its coverings but also partly carried in the hands of a servant; the name of this servant who looked after the baetyl was Eusebius, and he told me that there had suddenly and unexpectedly come upon him the violent desire to leave the city of Emesa, almost at midnight, and to go far away towards that mountain where the ancient and magnificent temple of Athena was situated. He arrived very quickly at the foot of the mountain and sat down to rest, when at that very spot he saw a ball of fire fall from the sky with great speed, and an enormous lion holding close to the ball of fire. The lion disappeared almost at once, but Eusebius ran up to the fireball which was now almost extinguished, took it and inquired to what god it belonged. It replied that it belonged to Gennaios (this Gennaios is adored by the people of Hierapolis who have erected to him in the temple of Zeus a statue in the form of a lion). He carried it home that same night, a distance of not less than 210 stades. Eusebius was not master of the baetyl, but he was obliged to pray and implore it; and the other heard his prayers.

It was a perfectly spherical ball of a whitish color; and its diameter was that of a palm's width. But at certain times it became larger or smaller; at other times it took on a purplish hue. And he showed us the letters traced on the stone, which had the colour of minium (or cinnabar). Then he fixed the baetyl in the wall. It is by these letters that the baetyl gave him the answers he sought. It emitted voices like a light whistling, which Eusebius interpreted to us.[42]

The most famous of these baetyls was indeed the black stone of Elagabal the sun-god of Emesa. His name means God of the Mountain, and it has been convincingly argued that the cult was only transformed into a solar one with the arrival of the nomad Arabs in Syria.[43] The mountain-god is a god of sedentary people, the sun quintessentially that of nomads. The same effect may be seen at other sites in Syria, and the overlay of solar imagery on many cults accounts for the difficulty we have in distinguishing one god from another at Palmyra and elsewhere. What was originally solar about the Jupiter of Heliopolis-Baalbek? The Palmyrene Yarhibol is "master of the months" and a god of the waters, yet depicted as radiate like the sun.

The attempt of the boy emperor Elagabalus to import the cult of his own native god, the sun, to Rome is a strange one,[44] and it anticipates the more successful attempt of Aurelian to turn his empire to sun-worship. Emperor Elagabalus (204–22) or as the *Historia Augusta* calls him, Heliogabalus, was born into the family of the sun-priests of Emesa. He was given the name Marcus Aurelius Antoninus. His mother was one of the quartet of imperial Juliae of the Severan dynasty, Julia Sohaemias, granddaughter of the high priest of Elagabal Julius Bassianus. Emesa had become part of the Roman Empire in the Flavian period and reached the supreme honor two generations before Elagabalus, when his great aunt Julia Domna became the wife of Septimius Severus. After the death of Emperor Caracalla, Macrinus succeeded to the throne and made his young son Diadumenian Caesar. Macrinus was then defeated by the army of Elagabalus, and the allegiance of the legions to the young man was won by his grandmother Julia Maesa, by a pretense that he was the illegitimate son of Caracalla. Military involvements in the East prevented him from reaching Rome for some months. His eventual arrival in July 219 was an extraordinary affair.

Invested with all the panoply of the priest of the sun—a long-sleeved, gold-embroidered tunic of purple silk reaching to his feet, gold and purple trousers, necklaces and bangles and a jeweled diadem on his head (no breastplate or toga)—the fourteen-year-old emperor pranced into Rome at the head of a procession whose centerpiece was the black stone itself, mounted in a chariot in which no human ever set foot. It was drawn by six white horses, and the emperor ran backward before them holding their bridles. The god was installed in a specially built temple on the Palatine. Having moved the statue of Pallas Athena to the god's quarters and then rejected her as "too warlike" to be the god's bride, the emperor had the goddess Astarte brought from Carthage to bear the god company. This he presented as "a marriage of the sun and moon."[45]

Godfrey Turton describes this as "a make-believe wedding of dolls and a hilarious romp, pelting the crowd with livestock and tableware."[46] But this trivializes what for Elagabalus was a deeply serious affair. Many of his practices were commonplace in Syria—the ritual dancing before the Lord and the wearing of "effeminate" clothes, even the ostrich dinners. Too young for power and drunk with pietistic enthusiasm, he set out to turn the Roman religion upside down, to infuse with religious fervor what seemed to him ossified, absurd, yet stately, rites.

For Antonin Artaud, this deliberate perversion of the social order made Elagabalus a hero of the absurd. Gibbon chided him for being not "a rational voluptuary," a connoisseur of women and sauces, but one who deliberately subverted all the laws of nature. Indeed it might seem that Elagabalus aimed to pollute and insult every convention of Roman life and to show up its hollowness, replacing it with a religion of more intense fervor and devotion. The view of Roman religion as a hollow sham is, rightly, no longer accepted by scholars, but its roots lie in the same Near Eastern view of religion that produced both Elagabalus' enthusiasms and the Christian biases of even quite recent historians.

Elagabalus' anarchism was also sexual. He practiced ritual indiscriminate copulation with both sexes, in which he forced senators and their wives to take part. He took as his wife a vestal virgin, one of the nunlike priestesses of the sacred fire. From his point of view it was natural thus to unite the religion of Rome with that of Emesa and to tilt the city at a different angle to the universe, to the universal sun.

The sun or his eagle avatar appeared on the coins Elagabalus minted at Antioch. The sun was the focus of his every act. But Rome was not ready to be converted forcibly, and was as shocked as Juvenal had been by the wilder excesses of west Syrian religion—not to mention the sexual employment of a vestal. It remained for the calmer devotions of the Palmyrene sun to win the allegiance of the people and senate of Rome. After four brief years of ecstasy and—in truth—pure debauchery, Elagabalus and his mother were murdered and their bodies hurled into a sewer. The black stone was bundled back to Emesa. Elagabalus was succeeded by a younger cousin, Severus Alexander, a much more responsible and cautious ruler. The *Historia Augusta* tells us that even he had a private chapel with images of Orpheus, Abraham, Apollonius of Tyana, and Alexander the Great; but the allegation is too bizarre to be other than fiction.[47]

Solar Religion

Elagabalus' devotion to the sun was not as outlandish as it is often made to seem. By this period the sun had become the increasingly dominant symbol of divinity, portrayed on temple fronts from Emesa to Bostra. This coincided with the increasing interest of philosophers in the heavenly bodies and especially the sun. Many philosophers and theologians were developing a religious position that accorded the sun supremacy over all the gods and men.

The early Stoic poet Cleanthes regarded the sun as "leader of the cosmos,"[48] while an anonymous inscription to Apollo from the first century B.C. or earlier already expresses the belief, to be developed later by Macrobius, that all deities merge in the sun.[49] Posidonius of Apamea (first century B.C.) was one of the most influential Stoic thinkers, and he must have found that the dominant cult of his native Syria dovetailed nicely with his monotheism. For him Man was quintessentially "the beholder and expounder of the heavens." This idea was adopted even by that conventional Roman Cicero, for whom the sun is "leader, ruler, and controller of the other luminaries, the mind and conscience of the universe."[50]

Other theological traditions developed a similar idea, such as is found in the Jewish author Philo,[51] that God is the Sun of the sun. Neoplatonists came to see the sun either as God or as an emanation of the Godhead, like the Word of God in the Jewish-Christian thought of Philo or St. John. This idea is fundamental to Emperor Julian's elaborate oration in praise of the sun, in which Helios is situated midway between the visible gods surrounding the universe and the intelligible gods surrounding the Good.[52] Not only is he for Julian begetter of the Greek savior god Asclepius, but his association with the desert gods Monimos and Azizos (identified with Ares) at Emesa is equally important. Much of Julian's theology is explicitly derived from another Syrian philosopher, the Neo-Platonist Iamblichus.

The use of the solar calendar was an important support to the dominance of solar religion, and it profited from the prevalence of astrology in Syria.[53] We have already touched on the importance of astrology in the theology of Bardaisan. It is inescapable in Syria. The ceilings of the Temple of Bel at Palmyra, for example, exhibit the signs of the zodiac. From its origins in Babylon, astrology penetrated Persian and Semitic religion as well as acquiring considerable sway at the popular levels of Greco-Roman paganism. Septimius Severus was an adept. The dominance of the sun could be seen in scientific as well as religious terms.

According to Josephus,[54] the Essenes of Qumran addressed prayers to the sun. So did the wonder-worker and sage, Apollonius of Tyana. Emperor Vespasian greeted the sun solemnly every morning. Even the queen of Sheba is claimed by the Qur'an as a sun-worshiper.[55] As the development of both Neo-Platonism and Stoicism led thinkers to a monotheistic position, the sun seemed the most natural candidate for that role.

Firmicus Maternus, the author of an astrological handbook who was later converted to Christianity, suggested in his earlier phase that the worship of the sun was the most satisfactory religion yet developed— only its rites were degrading. The sun should be regarded as a way to approach the nature of a higher God still. "Before religion reached the point where it proclaimed that God should be sought in the Absolute and the Ideal, one cult only was reasonable and scientific and that was the cult of the Sun," wrote Ernest Renan.[56] The cult of the sun was therefore nothing new in Rome and was well established in Syria. The worship of the sun at Palmyra occupied one of its finest temples and did much to set the tone of religious life in the city.

A Christian Supporter of Zenobia?

Not less important in Syria was the growing force of Christianity,[57] itself subject to fission as it struggled to emancipate itself from its Judaic roots and spawned one heresy after another or branded as evil those pagan practices that too closely resembled Christian ones. One thinks of the Maiuma, the total immersion rituals at Gerasa (modern Jerash) resembling Christian baptism, which "degenerated" into mere nautical spectacles and mixed, nude bathing. Christian disapproval banned them until 396, and they were banned again in 399, finally resurfacing only in 535 in the new and innocuous form of a harvest festival.[58]

Few now would have the patience to distinguish in detail the heresies that plagued Antioch alone in the third century.[59] Besides the major deviations of Christianity—Gnosticism with its view of the world as evil and of personal revelation as the only route to salvation, and the Marcionites who saw Yahweh as evil and Christ as the son of a different, good God—most of the arguments focus on the nature of Christ. They include the Monarchian or "patripassian" view that the Son is wholly divine, hence it was the Father who (in him) suffered on the cross; the related Docetist views of Marcianus of Rhossos that Christ's humanity was an appearance only; the view of Satrumil that Christ as man truly suffered; and the view of Beryllus of Bostra that God the Son had no preexistence as did God the Father. One may see a Semitic opposition to Greek ideas of preexistence, which becomes more prominent after about 240 and reaches its climax in the doctrine of Paul of Samosata.

Further arguments raged around the question of baptism. There were numerous baptist sects, and in 217–22 one Alcibiades of Apamea brought to Rome a collection of baptismal formulae whose efficacy was multifarious and extended even to the curing of the bites of mad dogs.[60] Still more colorful opinions characterized the Sethians—with their blend of Orphic, Neo-Pythagorean and Semitic myth—and the Novatians and the Donatists—who "dream of clouds of angels and aeons."[61] Furthest of all from the Gospel stood the snake-handling sect of the Ophites of Asia Minor, and the Montanists, who continued the tradition of Phrygian ecstatic cults. The forms that Christianity might assume were so diverse that one can sympathize with people like Celsus,[62] who saw in Christian practice an almost infinite number of orgiastic practices, from the ritual slaughter of babies (swathed in pastry to disguise the crime) to promiscuous and incestuous coupling in a darkened room.

A vivid snapshot of the Christianization of Syria at this period can be gained from the life of the indomitable St. Abercius,[63] bishop of Hierapolis in Phrygia during the reign of Marcus Aurelius, who traveled through Syria and Mesopotamia from one church to another to encourage and correct their doctrine. He began his career with a dream vision, after which he smashed all the statues in the Temple of Apollo in Hierapolis with a big stick, thus becoming the first of many Christian destroyers of pagan sculpture. He became famous for his miracles of healing, eventually being summoned to Rome to cure the emperor's daughter Lucilla, and when already an old man, he was sent by the

Lord to Syria. He visited the young churches of Antioch, Daphne, Apamea, and Seleuceia—like Odysseus, he "visited all the cities of men" in Syria—and he even came as far as Nisibis on the Euphrates to dispute with Marcion. He met a delegation of Christians headed by Bardaisan, who dubbed him *isapostolos*, the "equal of the Apostles." His influence may have been as great as that of his predecessor Addai.

Not until sixty years after Zenobia's reign could the Syriac-speaking territory of Antioch be regarded as broadly Christian. This is the period of the first Christian inscriptions. The first cenobitic foundations also date from the 330s, but it is certain that some had already retired to the anchorite life as early as the 270s (when Antony, the father of all hermits, fled to the desert in Egypt). Until doctrine was certain, it was hard for a person to make that absolute commitment. In the mid and late third century, Christian teaching was still struggling to establish itself within the cities and the world of humankind. Even in the sixth century there was a governor of Edessa who hedged his bets by venerating an icon that portrayed Christ on one side and the sun-god Apollo on the other.[64]

One thing that united all these thinkers was a hatred of the "idolatry" of the Greeks. This hatred was as typical of Tatian, whom Renan characterized as "sombre, heavy, violent, full of wrath," as of Theophilus of Antioch, who disdained all Greek philosophy. For Bardaisan the main enemy was from the East: astrology—and perhaps Buddhism.[65]

In the Christian church of Antioch we seem to see the paths of religion and politics cross, prompting the question among scholars whether here at last we can see the patronage of Zenobia at work. This occurs in the story of Paul of Samosata, bishop of Antioch.[66] Samosata was the capital of Commagene, situated at the entrance of the gorge on the Euphrates some fifty kilometers north of Edessa. It was the headquarters of one of the three Syrian legions, XVI Flavia Firma. Although it produced one of the leading Greek authors of the second century, Lucian, it was not Hellenic in culture. Lucian tells us that he wore oriental clothes and spoke only Syriac until he left the city at the age of fifteen. We know that the worship of Jupiter Dolichenus was important at Samosata, and we may presume that other oriental cults were also practiced. Whether there was a large Jewish population, as there was at Palmyra and Edessa, we do not know, though it is likely.

Like Lucian a century before him, Paul went west to the Hellenic world to make his name. We first hear of him when he succeeded Demetrian as Bishop of Antioch (probably 260 A.D.). According to

Eusebius, "he held low, degraded opinions about Christ . . . regarding him as in his nature just an ordinary man." It has been argued that he also obtained secular office as procurator ducenarius of Antioch (i.e., as an imperial financial officer, on the exceptionally high salary of 200,000 sesterces) and became one of the most influential men in Antioch. All that the deposition of the bishops in Eusebius actually says is that

> he deck(ed) himself out with worldly honors and [was] anxious to be called ducenarius rather than bishop. . . . [He] swaggers in city squares, reading letters aloud or dictating them as he walks in public surrounded by numerous bodyguards, some in front and some behind. The result is that the faith is regarded with distaste and hatred because of his self-importance and inflated pride.

We may accept Paul's status as a notable public figure, even if the claim of important political office is dismissed, as it is by Millar, as a "fantasy."[67]

His comportment was not indeed such as befitted a humble servant of God.

> Nor need we judge the way this charlatan juggles with church assemblies, courting popularity and putting on a show to win the admiration of simple souls, as he sits on the dais and lofty throne he has had constructed for him [How unlike a disciple of Christ!] or in the *secretum*, as he calls it, which he occupies in imitation of the rulers of the world. He slaps his thigh and stamps on the dais. Some do not applaud and wave their handkerchiefs as in a theater, or shout and spring to their feet like his circle of partisans, male and female, who form such a badly behaved audience: they listen, as in God's house, in a reverent and orderly manner. These he scolds and insults. Those who have departed this life, but once preached the word, he assails in a drunken, vulgar fashion in public, while he boasts about himself as if he were not a bishop but a trickster and mountebank.

"All hymns to our Lord Jesus Christ," this letter in Eusebius goes on, "he has banned as modern, compositions of modern writers, but he arranges for women to sing hymns to himself in the middle of the church on the great day of the Easter festival." (Alexander Baron, in his lurid novel of Zenobia, *Queen of the East*, goes one better, and has the white-robed choir of virgins rise to welcome Paul as he enters the theater of Palmyra itself—an improbable location for a Christian sermon if ever there was one!) Not content with this bevy of adoring choristers, "who say that their blasphemous teacher is an angel come down from heaven," he took two of them as "spiritual brides" to live with him at home.[68]

What has all this to do with Zenobia? Three passages in fourth-century writers identify Zenobia as a Jewess or proselyte and give this as a reason for her political support of Paul. Athanasius writes, "Zenobia was a Jew and patron of Paul of Samosata." Filastrius mentions "a certain Zenobia, Queen in the East, [who] at that time seemed to Judaize"—an idea echoed in the fifth-century Theodoret. John Chrysostom speaks of Paul flattering a "certain woman" by his doctrines; and the apparent unitarianism of the bishop, influenced by the Jewish thought of many of his compatriots, has seemed to chime with the suspected Jewish sympathies of the queen.[69] The link of Paul and Zenobia has received considerable support from the recent identification of two passages from Paul's "Writings to Zenobia" preserved in the *Questions* of Pamphilus.[70] These concern the fundamental issue of the nature of Christ, and we find Paul arguing for a single nature against the bishops who claim for Christ the two natures of "god before all ages" and "man born of the virgin."

His unpopularity split the church in Antioch into two parties, the opposition to Paul being headed by Domnus and Malchion, who are supposed to have had Hellenizing tendencies. Eventually the whole Origenist school denounced Paul at two Councils at Antioch in 264 and 268/9. He was deposed, and Domnus took over the ministry of the Antioch church.

> But Paul absolutely refused to hand over the church building, so Emperor Aurelian was applied to and gave a perfectly just decision on the course to be followed: he ordered the building to be assigned to those to whom the bishops of the religion in Italy and Rome addressed a letter. In this way the man in question was thrown out of the church in the most ignominious manner by the secular authority.[71]

According to the *Ecclesiastical Chronicle* of Gregory Bar-Hebraeus, he fled to "a certain Jewish woman by the name of Zenobia, who had set out from the Persian regions of Syria against Rome, and to whom the opinions of Paul were most sympathetic."[72]

The traditional interpretation of the ancient sources is that Paul's assumption of the dignities of a procurator ducenarius indicates a formal political role in Antioch under the sponsorship of Zenobia. This interpretation is rightly discounted in recent writing: Paul's assumption of honors was a way of impressing his own townsmen, not a political statement in imperial terms.[73] The traditional view further requires that Paul continued to act as viceroy of Zenobia in Antioch until Aurelian made his judgment when he was in the region in 272. The judgment against Paul would be part of the elimination of Zenobia's support in 272. More recently Fergus Millar has proposed a minimalist interpretation that Aurelian's role here has no power-political implications but simply shows the emperor acting as ultimate authority in yet another little local dispute. Its chief significance then becomes the fact that this is the first acknowledgement by an emperor of the Christian church as a legal body.

It is difficult to imagine how the synod could have appealed to Aurelian in 272, when Antioch was firmly under the control of Palmyra. One must suspect that the appeal to the emperor was made when he was still far away, at the beginning of his reign. Paul would then have fled to Palmyra at this time, say late in 270. He (with his choirgirls) would then be present in Palmyra in the crucial years of the revolt. Through his links with Antioch, he might perhaps have been able to consolidate Zenobia's position there. But since he seems to have been notably unpopular in Antioch, this is hardly a strong possibility. If Paul's political importance is slighter than has been supposed, he nonetheless adds one more to the tally of fugitive intellectuals at Zenobia's court.

Zenobia the Jew?

Let us return to Zenobia's interest in Judaism. There was certainly a large—if barely orthodox—Jewish colony at Palmyra, as well as colonies of most other religions (as also at Dura-Europos). At least one Jew named Zenobius is known from inscriptions at Palmyra. In addition, Zenobia is known to have paid for the restoration of a synagogue in Egypt,[74] and to have restored the privilege of asylum at another synagogue in the Delta.[75] She also—probably—restored the shattered colossus of Memnon—from which date it ceased to sing at dawn as it had done for millennia[76]—so this might represent rather a concern for old buildings than any doctrinal leanings. However, Photius says that Longinus converted her to Judaism from "the Hellenic superstition."[77]

Further hints of the importance that Jewish opinion held for Zenobia come from the Jewish necropolis at Beth She'arim in Galilee, from which a number of Palmyrene names are known, suggesting a significant Jewish component among Palmyrene families. Names include the banker Leontius of Palmyra, several women called Zenobia, and Isaac of Palmyra, on the walls of whose tomb his sons Samuel and Germanicus are depicted in, respectively, gladiatorial gear and Roman military uniform. These Jews probably fled to Galilee after the fall of their native city of Palmyra. It is possible that Zenobia also had links with the Judaizing Himyarite kings of Sabaea, since Himyarites are also buried at Beth She'arim.[78]

Judaism is not the only faith with which Zenobia has been associated. The Coptic papyri surveyed in the 1930s, and now lost, contained the story that she was a convert to Manichaeanism, the Mesopotamian rival to Christianity that nearly became the official religion of the Persian Empire.[79] Again, though this particular tale was unknown to Cumont, he stressed the importance of Babylonian astrology in Zenobia's rule.

> The power of Palmyra under Zenobia, who ruled from the Tigris to the Nile, must have had as a corollary the establishment of an official worship that was necessarily syncretic; hence its special importance for the history of paganism. Although the Babylonian astrology was a powerful factor in this worship, Judaism seems to have had just as great an influence in its formation. . . . This influence of Judaism seems to explain the development at Palmyra of the cult of Zeus *hypsistos kai epekoos* [the highest, the listener], "he whose name is blessed for eternity." The name of Hypsistos has been applied everywhere to Jehovah and to the pagan Zeus at the same time. The text of Zosimus (1.61) according to which Aurelian brought from Palmyra to Rome the statues of Helios and Bel proves that the astral religion of the great desert city recognised a supreme god residing in the highest heavens, and a solar god, his visible image and agent, according to the Semitic theology of the last period of paganism.[80]

This falls short of being a watertight argument, and historians now do not much care for phrases like "must have had," but there is a general plausibility in this picture of the tendency to monotheism here as elsewhere.

Astrology remains an important part of the religious outlook of the nomad. Lady Hester Stanhope's growing adherence to astrology had as its purpose, at least in part, to strengthen the bonds between her and the Syrians she "ruled."[81] Of Zenobia's own leanings we really can say little. Perhaps she was as eclectic as her predecessor Julia Mamaea, who came of the priestly family of the sun at Emesa but nonetheless summoned Origen to Caesarea to instruct her in Christian doctrine.[82]

It is difficult to picture a world in which so many religions of widely differing nature were practiced side by side (though perhaps modern Britain is as good a parallel as any; and one suspects that the contiguity and equal status of many devalues them all). If Zenobia looked eastward to Judaism, and Manichaeanism, and orientalizing forms of Christianity, she also looked westward to the more traditional polytheistic cults. It is not clear how much authority we should attach to the reports in Zosimus that she consulted the oracle of Apollo Sarpedon at Seleuceia (Silifke) before the onslaught of Aurelian (he might after all be taken for another sun-god),[83] or to the omen of the Palmyrene mission to the pool of Aphrodite/Astarte at Aphaca, where the offerings to the goddess, which normally sank as a sign that the goddess had accepted them, on this occasion all rose to the surface. But a general assent to such pagan practices, even by a monotheist, would be no stranger than the superstitious rites practiced in present-day Christian or Islamic lands, though a more credulous age might attach greater weight to them than the modern. A wise ruler will not neglect any customs that seem appropriate to her people. Surely the water-oracle of Yarhibol at the spring Efqa at Palmyra continued to be consulted. Christians, Jews, astrologers, and adherents of sun and moon and the Greek cults all made part of Zenobia's dominion. The gods, it was to hoped, had been marshaled on Palmyra's side.

7

Revolt in the Desert

During the five years after the death of Odenathus in 267, Zenobia had established herself in the minds of her people as mistress of the East. Housed in a palace that was just one of the many splendors of one of the most magnificent cities of the East, surrounded by a court of philosophers and writers, waited on by aged eunuchs, and clad in the finest silk brocades that Antioch or Damascus could supply, she inherited also both the reputation of Odenathus' military successes and the reality of the highly effective Bedouin soldiers. With both might and influence on her side, she embarked on one of the most remarkable challenges to the sovereignty of Rome that had been seen even in that turbulent century. Rome, afflicted now by invasions from the barbarian north, had no strong man in the East to protect it. The reign of Gallienus, troubled by so many pretenders, was followed by that of Claudius, whose short reign (268–70) was occupied with wars on the Danube against the Goths, during which he died of plague. Syria was temporarily out of mind.

It is just possible that Zenobia had been extending fingers of control into Palestine as early as 260.[1] Emesa was also under Palmyrene sway by the end of the 260s. But the first decisive step was taken when Zenobia sent her general Zabdas to invade Egypt. The date of this event is uncertain. It is possible that the uncertainty following the death of Claudius in early 270 gave Zenobia the opportunity to raise the standard of revolt. But the breach with Rome may have come before the death of Gallienus, in 267.[2] And the invasion of Egypt is likely to have taken place in late 269 rather than early 270.[3]

At the same time as Zenobia invaded Egypt, the young St. Antony sold his possessions and retreated to the desert to become a hermit and wrestle with his demons. This is an interesting conjunction of two radical and extreme expressions of dissatisfaction with the empire of Rome, one a rejection of Rome's values by retreat from the world and the contumacies of village society, the other an attack on Rome's military might from a power that claimed equality with it. Who is to say whether

Zenobia or St. Antony inflicted the deeper wound on the worldly dominion of Rome?

The Arabic traditions on Zenobia are relevant to the understanding
of her rise to power and the context of her revolt.[4] The earliest version
is by the sixth-century author 'Adi ibn Zayd, whose work was the
source both for Ibn Habib and for the well-known *Chronicle* of Tabari
(A.D. 839–923). The legend is further elaborated by several writers of
the Middle Ages. Al-Ya'qubi, a near-contemporary of Tabari (d. after
890) gives essentially the same story. The tale is also told in the history
of Ibn al-Athir (1160–1234) and the encyclopedia of al-Nuwairi (1279–
1332). In all these writers we find an interesting convergence of the
legend of the queen of Sheba, Bilqis, with that of Zenobia. The story
in Ibn al-Athir is constructed to make the events of the conflict between
Zebba (Zenobia) and Jadhima (also famous in Arab traditions as a poet)
the origin of an enormous number of Arabic proverbs. The link with
historical events is reduced to the names of the principals, and the
Romans play no part at all in Arabic tradition: this is an entirely inter-
Arab dispute.

Tabari's account of Zebba gives us an account of her military campaigns against her neighbors and introduces us to the local tensions
that complicated her position on the world stage. According to Tabari,
she was of the tribe of Amila-el-Amalik like Odenathus and was daughter of 'Amr, who had lost his life in battle with Jadhima for control of
the two banks of the Euphrates. Jadhima was a sheikh who controlled
part of central Arabia. His historical existence has lately been confirmed
by inscriptions found at Umm el-Jimal in his territory. He was king of
the Tanukh, an Arab people who had deserted Ardashir after his accession in 224[5] and had settled in the area of al-Qatif in the northeastern
part of the Arab peninsula, west of the Euphrates. Rome, then, was
not Zenobia's only problem; her drive for power encompassed also the
aim of conquering the Tanukh.[6]

Tabari's account is based on the sixth-century writer 'Adi ibn Zayd.
Zebba, according to the legend in Tabari, wanted to take vengeance on
Jadhima for the death of her father 'Amr. Her sister Zainab (for whom
she had built a castle beyond the Euphrates and a tunnel to link the
two banks) advised her against war and recommended the use of guile
instead. So Zebba sent a message to Jadhima to the effect that she would
be willing to unite their two realms by marriage. One of Jadhima's
generals argued that she should be called to a meeting at Baqqa, where
he was encamped. But a second general carried the day with the proposal

that Jadhima go to meet her. As they crossed the Euphrates, Jadhima asked his first general, Qasir, what prudence would advise him to do now. "Prudence!" replied Qasir, in a phrase that has become proverbial, "You left your prudence behind at Baqqa."[7]

The two parties met at a place called Rabbat-Malik-ibn-Tauk. The accounts of the meeting vary slightly, but the central feature is that Zebba responds to Jadhima's assent to the idea of a marriage by lifting her skirts to reveal her private parts. The length and quantity of her pubic hair (the name Zebba means "with beautiful long hair") astonishes Jadhima, and Zebba remarks that one with such an appearance is hardly a suitable bride for him. The point being made is not altogether clear, but the scene recalls interestingly the meeting of Solomon and the queen of Sheba, when the king induces the queen to walk across a mirror that he pretends is a stream. As she lifts her skirts to do so, Solomon catches sight of her hairy legs and ceases to find her attractive.

A squadron of Zebba's cavalry now surrounded Jadhima, unhorsed him, and brought him to the queen. "How do you wish to die?" she asked. And he replied, "Like a king."[8] He was served a meal, with plenty of wine. As he began to doze off with the effects of the alcohol, he was placed on a leather blanket and the veins of his wrists were opened. His blood was collected in vases, since it was believed that the blood of kings had special virtues against madness.

The historicity of this story may be judged by that of its sequel. Qasir took his vengeance on Zenobia by an interesting variant of the stratagem of the Wooden Horse of Troy. He mutilated himself[9] and went to the queen, presenting himself as a renegade from the ill usage of his compatriots. Having gained her confidence, he announced that a train of a thousand camels, heavily laden with treasure of all kinds, was on its way to her. Each camel carried two large sacks, and the greedy queen admitted the caravan in delicious anticipation. Each sack proved to conceal an armed warrior. Once within the city, they emerged and massacred the garrison.

Zenobia attempted to flee via her tunnel under the Euphrates. But halfway along, Qasir was waiting for her. Behind her the way was blocked by Jadhima's nephew 'Amr ibn 'Adi. She evaded capture and torture by swallowing poison, and her kingdom passed to 'Amr. An inscription of Namara names these kings and 'Amr's successor Imru'l-qais "the first," who benefited to the maximum from Zenobia's eventual defeat, though they certainly did not procure it.[10]

If the second part of this legend is almost entirely fabulous, the first seems to contain some nuggets of historical information and shows the importance of the local Arab context for Zenobia's rise and fall. Both tales, of course, testify to the extraordinary imaginative hold that the figure of Zenobia took over later writers in the Arab tradition, as much as in our own.

Malalas' very scrappy account of Zenobia's campaign describes her as making war on Arabia (with no mention of her other conquests).[11] Signs of destruction at Bostra (the Temple of Jupiter Ammon destroyed,[12] the military commander killed, the legion III Cyrenaica destroyed) and at Petra[13] suggest the obstacles that Rome placed in the way of her march. See seems also to have destroyed Umm el-Jimal (Thainatha), the home of Fihr, the tutor of Jadhima.[14] The Tanukh, it is clear, took the side of Rome (and remained friendly to it into the next centuries—their Christian queen Mavia fought for Byzantium against the Saracens in the fourth century). But the Safaitic tribes of Hauran and Transjordan, such as the 'Awidh, are shown by the inscriptions to have taken Zenobia's side.[15] Most suggestive is a graffito reading "May God remember [her] for good," written above a drawing of a woman on a camel. Could this woman represent Zenobia? The position recalls to a modern student the way in which Mecca later rose to power by organizing the local tribes so as not to damage its trade: perhaps there is a hint here of a commercial motive in Zenobia's policy.[16]

We are slightly better informed about the continuation of the campaign into Egypt, though almost all we know of that campaign is contained in one chapter of Zosimus (corroborated by a similar but more muddled account in the *Historia Augusta*).

> Zenobia now became ambitious, and sent Zabdas to Egypt because Timagenes, an Egyptian who was working to hand Egypt over to the Palmyrenes, had raised an army of seventy thousand Palmyrenes, Syrians and barbarians, against whom were ranged fifty thousand Egyptians. In a fierce battle the Palmyrenes won a decisive victory and, after setting up a garrison of five thousand men, marched away. When Probus, who had been commissioned by the emperor to clear the sea of pirates, learned that Egypt was held by the Palmyrenes, he attacked the garrison with his own troops and all the Egyptians who opposed the Palmyrenes, and expelled it. When the Palmyrenes mounted a fresh campaign, Probus assembled an army of Egyptians and Africans. These were not only victorious but drove the Palmyrenes right out of Egypt. Probus occupied a

mountain near Babylon to cut off the enemy's escape into Syria, but Timagenes, who was familiar with the area, gained the summit with two thousand Palmyrenes and surprised and killed the Egyptians. Probus was captured, but committed suicide.[17]

Nothing else is known of Timagenes. The Babylon mentioned is not the famous city but a homonym on the borders of Egypt. The invasion may be presumed to have entered Egypt via Pelusium, continuing to Memphis to take Middle Egypt, then advancing to Alexandria. Probus (this is Tenagino Probus, not to be confused with the future emperor) cut the army off in the delta, but the Palmyrenes destroyed his opposition, and Roman power was thus eliminated. It is possible to associate with this campaign a letter on papyrus addressed to the Alexandrians by a usurper cautiously identified by P. J. Parsons as Wahballath.[18]

Alexandrians . . . good feeling towards me . . . you continued bearing in your hearts your (friendly?) disposition (?). So then I shall visit you, if fortune is kind, having been elected Emperor by the most valiant solders, and about to enter auspiciously upon the supreme command among you; and starting from you in particular my power to confer benefits, I have bestowed on the ancestral [*or* my mother's] city all that is right to bestow. First year, Pharmouthi.[19]

Zosimus' rather over-abbreviated presentation ends with the Palmyrenes in firm control of Egypt.

At this time the emperor of Rome, Claudius, died of plague. His brother Quintillus, who had been joint Augustus, also died after a reign of perhaps two months. Aurelian became emperor shortly before the end of August 270.[20] He was acutely aware of what had to be done, but for the time being he was engaged in fighting the barbarian tribes on the Danube.

Little is known of Zenobia's rule in Egypt, and even less about the conquest of Asia Minor. All we learn from Zosimus is that she gained control of Asia Minor as far as Ancyra (Ankara).[21] An attempt to hold Chalcedon in Bithynia, opposite Constantinople, was short-lived.

The chronology of these years is dependent on the interpretation of the coinage.[22] In the course of 270 Zenobia gained control of Antioch. Coins of Antioch showing Wahballath (Vaballathus) and Aurelian on opposite faces refer to year 1 of Aurelian and year 4 of Wahballath.

The year began on August 22, so Aurelian must have acceded to the throne before that date in 270, and Antioch came under Zenobia's control during the same year. In the course of 271 coins begin to appear with Wahballath and Zenobia Augusta and without Aurelian; but from 271/2 there are no Alexandrian coins of Wahballath, indicating that the recapure of Alexandria was complete by August 271. In short, in the course of the years 270 to 271 Zenobia gained control of approximately the eastern third of the Roman Empire. This remarkable feat of arms in the face of the usually indomitable Roman power requires some explanation.

Zenobia's Aims

The author of the *Historia Augusta* has the queen say to her conqueror and captor Aurelian:

> You, I know, are an emperor indeed, for you win victories, but Gallienus and Aureolus and the others I have never regarded as emperors. Believing Victoria to be a woman like me, I desired to become a partner [with her] in the royal power, should the supply of lands permit [*si facultas locorum pateretur*].[23]

The rhetoric and parallelism are neat: Victoria, the mother of Victorinus, seized the Gallic Empire from Postumus by murder and put Tetricus thereafter at its head. But it is in the highest degree improbable that there would have been any communication between the two queens. Postumus and his successors had sought to benefit from Rome's disorders by turning Gaul into an independent realm. In this way they hoped to secure more real protection against invaders than Rome seemed able to offer. They thus deprived Rome of its easy access to one of the most productive, and most fully Romanized, parts of its empire, as well as of access to its distant problem province, Britannia. But Zenobia went further than this, embarking on a campaign of active conquest of substantial parts of the Roman Empire outside her own borders.

The attack on Egypt struck at not so much the heart but the stomach of Rome itself. Egypt was the source of perhaps one-third of Rome's annual supply of grain (the province of Africa providing the other two-thirds).[24] The precise proportion alleged by Josephus may be doubted, as may the figures given by other sources for absolute quantities: twenty million modii of wheat under Augustus, and twenty-eight million under

Septimius Severus.[25] But the general point may stand: as Tacitus had remarked,[26] in the corn supply the life of the Roman people was entrusted to ships and the sea. If the plebs go short of bread, Pliny assures Emperor Trajan, they will riot.[27] The author of *Sibylline Oracle* 13 was aware of the importance of this factor when he wrote,

> the Persians are far from victory
> on that day, insofar as the dear nurturer of Italians,
> which lies in the plain of the Nile by the wondrous water,
> dispatches a seasonal tribute to seven-hilled Rome.[28]

William Ware put into Zenobia's mouth the touching motive that Zenobia aimed to prevent Rome's universal dominion, a moral lesson that would surely have been lost on those emperors who struggled to preserve even their city in security.[29] It may be attractive to see Zenobia's campaigns as a kind of crusade in reverse. But there is not a scrap of evidence for such an interpretation, and to make war purely for the sake of a moral concept is an uncommon occurrence in history.

The view of J. Schwartz is that Zenobia's main purpose was to protect the commercial interests of Palmyra's merchants in the face of the increasingly unsettled conditions of the frontier zone.[30] There certainly were problems, as can be seen from the increasing number of references to the threat from the nomads of the Euphrates region; but it is not clear how the conquest of Asia Minor or of the southern areas would serve that particular aim. Though Roman weakness had allowed an increase in border violence, there is no indication that the caravans had ceased to ply their trade from the distant East or to pay their dues in Palmyra—though what even the privileged aristocracy of the empire laid their hands on to pay for their spices, scents, and silks is hard to imagine.

Zenobia was not unique in raising rebellion. The explanation must lie in the political conditions. The *Historia Augusta* blames Gallienus' alleged debaucheries for the rise of the Twenty Tyrants[31]—which may be an inept way of suggesting that these numerous revolts were a natural result of Rome's inability to guarantee security on its borders. Zenobia's problems with the Tanukh were a strong reason for her to take the law into her own hands.

The most likely interpretation of the events is that Zenobia was aiming at independence from Rome in the manner of the Gallic Empire or of the later Carausius in Britain.[32] It is with the Gallic Victoria that the *Historia Augusta* itself draws the parallel. Macmullen astutely observes that it is when the Eastern subjects become Romanized—when Palmyrene archers become important and Aziz appears on coins—that they become a danger to Rome. The outsider wishes to become an insider; "The foes of the monarch rise from the midst of his friends."[33]

Yet some writers have seen a still more ambitious plan in Zenobia's actions. Beginning from the *Historia Augusta*, they have surmised that Zenobia aimed at the rule of Rome itself, as sole empress or as consort of Aurelian. Alexander Baron has developed the supposed "romantic interest" between Aurelian and Zenobia, and it appears also in the Abbé Hédélin's prosy drama of 1647. W. Marsham Adams' play (1870) actually ends with Aurelian's coronation of Zenobia, queen no longer of

> this our island home
> Girt by the ocean of uncompass'd sand

(echoes of John of Gaunt!). But a revolt is raised at this very moment by the priest of the sun, and Aurelian stabs Zenobia instead of marrying her. Melodramatic fantasy apart, the idea that Zenobia should become empress of Rome was not absurd. Precedents could be cited. Her model Julia Domna had virtually ruled the empire from her position as imperial consort and mother, and other imperial Juliae had wielded equal power over their emperor's sons.

Emperors from Syria were, of course, commoner than empresses. Emperor Vespasian had been proclaimed as such by the legions of Syria, with whom he greeted the sun every morning with prayers and oblations. In the reign of Marcus Aurelius, the commander of the Syrian legions, Avidius Cassius, had himself proclaimed emperor, prompting the caustic comment Herodes Atticus enshrined in a letter to him on hearing the news: "You have gone mad."[34] Indeed he had not lasted long. But this did not stop other legionary commanders from following the same path. Syria was far from Rome. The troops concentrated there, if idle, were numerous, and a general could consolidate considerable strength before the news reached Rome. In Syria, near the temple of the moon at Carrhae, Caracalla had been murdered, to be succeeded by Macrinus. Pescennius Niger rose here when Pertinax was murdered, though he was quickly extinguished when Severus' power was consolidated. New heart could be given to Syrian hopes by the success of the Syrian dynasty that followed Severus, the success of Elagabalus and his brother Severus Alexander, and the success of Philip the Arab. In her own lifetime, or that of her husband, Zenobia had witnessed three unsuccessful but not contemptible attempts at the rule of this portion of Rome's Empire.

It must be remembered that revolt against the emperor and a claim to the throne was not a peculiarity of the Syrian East. The pattern of rebellion that was so damaging to Rome began on the Rhine with Maximin (235–38), and we have already met several equally powerful pretenders from Gaul and the Danube. The readiness of the provinces to raise pretenders should be seen in the light of Rome's inability to offer protection on all frontiers at once, and it is a fact about the third century as much as it is about the "volatile East."

Though these numerous attempts could hardly been seen as certain auguries of success, Zenobia's position was without doubt stronger than that of any of these legionary commanders. She could take on Rome, it seemed, as an equal, for she (or Odenathus) had protected Rome as an equal. Having brought down Persia, she could hold her own against Rome and bring Palmyra to a point of world dominance. Such must have been her plan. Controlling the balance of two empires, she could aspire to create a third that would dominate them both.

Aurelian

The interregnum following the death of Claudius saw the elevation of Aurelian to the throne of Rome.[35] His brief, four-year reign marks a turning point in the fortunes of the empire, and it assured Zenobia's nemesis in a way she could perhaps never have foreseen.

> The task awaiting him was one to tax even his powers. The restoration of the empire, begun by Claudius, was as yet far from complete. . . . Behind the problems of military recovery lay those of political and economic life. The government of the provinces, the relation of emperor and senate, the ruined coinage—all these demanded attention, as soon as a breathing space could be obtained from war. The empire was in a state of transition. The old empire of the princeps and senate, of Rome and Italy as queens of the provinces, was dead or dying; a new society, with new social and new religious ideals, was being born.[36]

According to the *Historia Augusta*, Aurelian was born in Sirmium in the Danubian province of Pannonia on September 9, A.D. 214. This may be incorrect; an alternative candidate for his birthplace is Moesia.[37]

Another unverifiable statement by the *Historia Augusta* is that his mother had been a priestess of the sun. A conventional military career brought him to the rank of dux in the reign of Gordian III. In the 240s he may have taken part in an embassy to Persia, which would have been his first sight of the difficult conditions under which the Eastern armies must fight, so different from the lush agricultural land, plentiful water, and plentiful cover of his native Danube lands. According to the *Historia Augusta*,[38] he acquired his first elephant in the course of this embassy. But the episode is probably fiction. Sir Ronald Syme draws attention to the parallel with Stilicho's visit to the East in 383, which resulted in the arrival of elephants at Rome in 384.[39] The latter event was fresh in the mind of an author writing in about 395.

Aurelian was still with the Danube army when Gaul revolted to form an independent "Gallic Empire" in 258, when the East was lost with Valerian in 260, and during the revolt of Macrianus in Egypt in the same year. The reigning emperor Gallienus could bless Odenathus of Palmyra for his repression of the latter, but the Gallic Empire was not to be recovered until Aurelian's reign. Postumus had, like Odenathus, assisted Rome by his repulsion of the invaders, but unlike Odenathus, he had gone on to proclaim an independent empire that lasted through the succeeding reigns of Victoria and Tetricus. When Claudius died of plague at Sirmium in 270, his commendation of Aurelian, already fifty-five years old, as his successor, united with the public perception of his abilities, ensured his accession to the imperial throne. A reign of less than five years was to see the most remarkable reconstruction of Roman power and authority that can be imagined.

Aurelian's success on the northern frontiers was followed by his successes in the East against Zenobia. The development of Roman domestic politics is much less clear. One of his main achievements, probably in 270, was the suppression of a revolt of the guild of moneyers at Rome (in which seven thousand are said to have been killed in a battle on the Caelian Hill). What lay behind it is quite unclear. All we are told is that the mint officials had "debased the coinage."[40] It seems likely that this revolt was caused by a first stage in the coinage reform that became far-reaching in 274 with the introduction of the new denomination, the aurelianianus. Now, in 270, a preliminary attempt was made to halt the continued decline in the precious metal content of the coins. The revolt was crushed, and the mint was closed until 274. Reform could not begin until Aurelian had control of the other major mints of the empire, notably Antioch and Alexandria.

At the same time, to prevent a recurrence of the crisis of barbarian invasion of Italy, Aurelian began the construction of the walls that still surround the old city of Rome. The senate's approval was obtained, and work began in 271. Twelve miles long, twenty feet high and twelve feet wide, with eighteen gates and numerous towers and sally ports,[41] they were built with civilian labor—a corvée of the guilds of the city— because the legions were needed elsewhere. They were not finished until the reign of Probus, but the name of Aurelian is still rightly attached to their magnificent and durable structure.

The Campaign against Palmyra

Zenobia's conquest of Egypt in 269/70, followed by Wahballath's assumption of the title of Augustus in 271, put a halt to the exercise of the arts of peace. The driving ambition of Zenobia created Aurelian's most formidable challenge yet. Aurelian despatched Probus (the future emperor) to Egypt to recapture it for Rome, while he himself advanced through Thrace and Illyricum to Byzantium, the first—and easiest— stage of the long march to Palmyra in the desert.

The chronology of the campaign is uncertain. The conventional view is that Aurelian left Rome late in 271 and reached Palmyra in time to besiege it in August of 272.[42] It has been calculated that the march from Rome to Antioch by this route, through the northern Balkans and across the forbidding plateau of central Turkey, would at this time have taken 124 days for an army with all its equipment and supplies.

Thus far the terrain was broadly familiar. We do not know what kind of maps and other information were available to Aurelian for the most difficult part of the march, that from Antioch to Palmyra. The most famous Roman "map," the Peutinger table, probably goes back to an original of the second century A.D., but its proportions are so dis- torted that its value is largely as an itinerary rather than as a means of strategic planning. The itinerary scratched on the reverse of a shield found at Dura-Europos—one soldier's memorandum of the route from the Black Sea to the Euphrates—suggests that such information was rarely systematic and usually in the form of an "AA Recommended Route" rather than a scale map. The strategic writer Vegetius "advises that all troop movements should be planned with the assistance of good *itineraria picta*,"[43] but it would have been impossible with such maps to conceive of a military situation in "global strategic terms." However, the region had been under Roman control for some time. It had been surveyed for the building of the Via Nova Traiana and the network of other routes observed by Père Poidebard in his aerial reconnaissances of the region in the 1920s and 1930s,[44] and we can be sure that Rome's military efficiency included proper strategic information.

Nonetheless, safe passage was by no means assured. The imperial posts must have crossed the desert from time to time, but for a single runner or horseman to find his way in time of peace was very different than for an army to march through hostile lands with expedition. Aurelian must have had to rely a good deal on local guides. Scouts (exploratores) do not receive much mention in our sources, though it was customary for an army on the march to send plentiful advance parties to spy out and secure their routes.

At Antioch Aurelian could expect to be joined by troops experienced in desert conditions, if not in desert warfare. But those with him were the Illyrian legions, who had fought only in the hills and forests of central Europe, where water never ran short (after the fall of Palmyra, Aurelian established some of these troops permanently in Arabia). Though he might look forward to the accession of the thirsty troops of Syria, he could not be sanguine about their fighting condition.

Since the time of Vespasian, Syria had been defended by three legions: the XVI Flavia Firma at Samosata or Sura, the III Gallica at Raphaneae near Apamea, and the IV Scythica, which was probably stationed about twenty miles north of Zeugma. To these had been added the III Cyrenaica at Bostra (from 106) and the VI Ferrata at Caparcotna (from Trajan's reign). Two Mesopotamian legions (I and III Parthica) had been stationed at Singara and Nisibis under the Severi, but they had probably been driven out by Shapur's campaigns of the 250s; II Parthica sometimes wintered at Apamea. XV Apollinaris seems to have been at Satala in Armenia in the third century, too far north to be of much use.[45] The troops in Antioch had been a byword for idle luxury since the days of Nero, when Corbulo had had to struggle harder against the slackness and cowardice of the soldiers than against the treachery of the Parthian enemy.[46] The long habit of peace had indisposed them for war; and a century later Fronto had advised his emperor Lucius Verus to attend to the demoralization of his Syrian legions.[47] At this time they may perhaps be pictured as more occupied with drink, baths, gambling, and women, the temptations of the fleshpots of luxurious Antioch, which were unavoidable for an army that was, unusually, stationed within the city rather than outside it.[48]

The legionaries were undoubtedly slowly going native in the settled conditions and comforts of Antioch and in the remote regions of the frontier. Soldiers had acquired native wives and had retired, after twenty years, to citizenship and a donative of land near their lifelong place of employment; they raised sons, half-Syrian and half-Roman, who in their turn joined the army; and through the generations since Trajan the process had continued. The auxiliary troops in Syria also contained a number of native soldiers, including the *cohors XX Palmyrenorum sagittariorum* formerly stationed at Dura-Europos. It is uncertain whether these legions remained loyal to Rome in the crisis. Having been under the command of Odenathus, it is quite possible that they did not.[49]

Aurelian's first setback in his march across Asia Minor—which did not prove difficult to detach from Zenobia—came at Tyana, the home of the legendary wise man and wonder-worker Apollonius, whose trial as a sorcerer under Domitian had culminated in his magical disappearance from the courtroom. When Aurelian came to the city, he found its gates closed against him. "In this town," he swore, angry at their defiance, "I will not leave even a dog alive."[50]

It was not long before the city was betrayed by one of its citizens, Heraclammon. The conquest was marked by a characteristic mixture of clemency and ferocity. Aurelian declined to slaughter a population of now loyal citizens and compromised by killing all the dogs as he had sworn. But Heraclammon was put to death—for a traitor once may be a traitor again and can never be trusted.

This action added to Aurelian's reputation for cruelty, which had served to terrorize his own troops into obedience. It is related that he punished a young legionary discovered in the act of adultery, by bending two saplings to the ground, tying a leg of the unfortunate victim to each, then releasing the trees so that the man was torn apart.[51] Other such tales were told and contributed to the variant versions of his treatment of Zenobia, as we shall see.

The army rested at Tyana. Here the *Historia Augusta* inserts one of its most egregious pieces of novelistic invention: the author has perhaps been reading the works of Nicomachus, to whom he attributes the translation into Greek of Zenobia's letter to Aurelian, and whom we know to have written a biography of the Tyanean sage Apollonius. As Aurelian was retiring to sleep, a vision of the long-dead sage Apollonius appeared to him and spoke (in Latin): "Aurelian, if you wish to conquer, there is no reason why you should plan the death of my fellow citizens. Aurelian, if you wish to rule, abstain from the blood of the innocent. Aurelian, act with mercy if you wish to live long."[52]

Aurelian promised the sage honorific statues and even a temple, and he took the wise man's words to heart.

The army marched on—in advance the scouts, followed by the pioneers who made the roads and passes negotiable for man, cavalry, wagons, and artillery. The pioneers were accompanied by those who would mark out and pitch the next night's camp. Behind them came the baggage of the chief officers, with its escort. Close by them was the commander in chief himself, with a bodyguard of cavalry and infantry armed with lances. The central place of the army was taken by the cumbrous weaponry of ballistas, catapults, onagers, and mantlets. Then, in columns of six, came the mass of the army, with officers alongside to maintain order and discipline. Then came grooms and beasts of burden—mules, horses, and perhaps even oxen. Though it is not recorded, it seems not improbable that once the army reached Antioch the beasts were supplemented by the indispensable camels of the desert. The merits of these animals, according to Vegetius,[53] included the ability to recognize roads even when they were covered in sand and obliterated. This group of grooms and beasts might include a walking larder, especially in view of the barren country ahead, and would be followed by the butchers, the provisioners, and the crowd of camp followers, ranging from merchants—grocers, ironmongers, and clothiers—to concubines and prostitutes. These too received an escort of cavalry, largely mercenaries.[54]

Much of the secret of Roman success in arms lay in the rigid discipline of their daily routines. Even on the march, time would generally be found for a daily routine of drill. As Josephus wrote, their battle drills differed scarcely at all from the real thing: "It would not be far from the truth to call their drills bloodless battles, their battles bloody drills."[55]

Aurelian knew that the difficult part of his march lay beyond Antioch. It was particularly important to secure that city and its resources, not only because it was needed as a supply base for the march across the desert, but because it was the capital of the Eastern Empire. The great generals are those who have understood logistics and commissariat. Alexander the Great never, but once, let his army run short of food. Aurelian would have had that model—as well as the disaster of the Gedrosian desert—in mind. Beyond Antioch lay Emesa (Homs), and that was the last possible source of provisions, and even of water, before Palmyra.

The army had to carry with it a large part of its supplies and equipment. Barley, wheat, lentils, meat, and chaff for the animals must be secured. Wine must also be carried. A mobile bakery was needed. Hides for clothing, tents, and defenses must be supplied. Metals must also be carried in sufficient quantity to replace broken weaponry. All this was likely to be obtained through forced requisitioning from the peoples through whose territories an army passed.[56] It was no light task to supply, move, and store such quantities of equipment. No wonder marching was generally slow. To ease the supply of weapons at least, Diocletian had several arms factories built at Antioch a few years later.[57]

After four months on the march, Aurelian's European legions turned the corner of the Mediterranean at Issus and crossed the last pass over the Nur Dağ to see Antioch shining in its rich valley below them. Its general appearance was probably not very different from when Gertrude Bell arrived there at the beginning of this century:

> . . . one of the loveliest of places, with its great ragged hill behind it, crowned with walls, and its clustered red roofs stretching down to the wide and fertile valley of the Orontes. Earthquakes and floods have overturned and covered with silt the palaces of the Greek and of the Roman city, yet as I stood at sunset on the sloping sward of the Nosariyyeh graveyard below Mount Silpius, where my camp was pitched, and saw the red roofs under a crescent moon, I recognized that beauty is the inalienable heritage of Antioch.[58]

When Aurelian mounted that same hill, the palaces were still standing. The colonnades and temples of the city stood out bright against the paradisaic suburb of Daphne with its green laurel groves, where Alexander the Great had drunk from a spring so sweet that he named it Olympias "because it reminded him of his mother's milk."[59] Here were the gambling dens and brothels that for centuries had been softening up Rome's soldiery. And here Zenobia awaited him with an army of seventy thousand men.

Our only detailed source for the Battle of Antioch is Zosimus, and I cannot do better than quote his summary account.

> Aurelian found Zenobia well prepared with a large army, and since he also was prepared for battle, he advanced to engage her as honour obliged him. Seeing, however, that the Palmyrene cavalry felt very confident of its heavy, strong armour and also greatly surpassed his own in horsemanship, he set his infantry apart somewhere over

the Orontes river, and ordered the Roman horse not to engage the fresh Palmyrene cavalry immediately, but to take their charge and pretend to flee until they saw that both their pursuers and their horses were abandoning the chase, exhausted by the heat, and the weight of their armour. This is exactly what happened. The emperor's cavalry obeyed his order, and when they saw the enemy giving up, with the horses wearied and the riders hardly able to move, they checked their horses, wheeled and charged, trampling them as they fell from their mounts. The slaughter was varied, some being killed by the sword, others by their own or the enemy's horses.

Thereupon, the survivors fled to Antioch. Zabdas, Zenobia's general, fearing that the inhabitants would turn on his forces if they heard of the defeat, found a middle-aged man who resembled the emperor, and dressing him as Aurelian was likely to look in battle, led him through the middle of the city as if he had captured the emperor alive. The Antiochians were taken in by this trick, and at night he slipped out of the city with the remnants of his army and Zenobia, and retired to Emesa. When day came, the emperor intended to call up the infantry and attack the routed enemy on both sides, but hearing of Zenobia's escape, he entered Antioch and was kindly received by the citizens.[60]

The Roman troops, the *Historia Augusta* assures us, were spurred on during the battle by the appearance of a "divine form" among their ranks, who spread encouragement throughout the foot soldiers and rallied even the horsemen.[61]

The chroniclers refer to a second battle at Immae ('Imm, Bab el-Hawa), forty-two kilometers from Antioch, which is not in Zosimus or the *Historia Augusta*. It has often been supposed that they have confused Immae with Emesa, the scene of his next major battle, though why an obscure village should replace the name of a famous city is not easy to understand. G. Downey has argued that Zosimus' reference to Aurelian sending his cavalry "across the Orontes" is crucially vague.[62] The Roman feinting retreat, according to him, continued for the forty-two kilometers southward to Immae before the cavalry turned and inflicted its defeat on Zenobia. If that is so, the Roman legions had to come all the way back again for the immediately subsequent battle outside Antioch, in the suburb of Daphne.

The return of the exiles to Antioch was not the end of the story.

A party of Palmyrenes had occupied a height overlooking the suburb of Daphne, thinking its steepness would enable them to block the enemy's way. He commanded his soldiers to make the steep ascent with their shields held close together and in tight formation to ward off weapons and stones that might be thrown down on them. The climb was managed accordingly, and when they stood against the enemy on equal terms, they immediately put them to flight. Some fell from the crags and were dashed to pieces and others were killed by their pursuers, both those at the top and those still making the ascent.[63]

The famous Roman military maneuver, the testudo, which had failed Crassus in these lands three centuries before, had shown its effectiveness on this occasion. Zenobia's forces retreated down the Orontes Valley to Emesa, a pleasantly situated town dominated by a small acropolis, on which stood the temple of the sun-god. The priest kings of the city had thrown in their lot with Zenobia, and their army was gathered in the plain before the city.

> When the armies engaged, the Roman cavalry decided to give way somewhere to prevent the Roman forces being encircled unawares by the Palmyrene horse, which was numerically superior. The Palmyrene cavalry, however, pursued them so strongly as they gave way that they even broke their own ranks and the Romans' plan turned out contrary to their own expectations; for they were much inferior in numbers to the enemy and most of them were killed. Then, indeed, the whole burden of the battle was borne by the Roman infantry, and seeing that the Palmyrene line was broken when the cavalry concentrated on pursuit, they wheeled about and fell upon the Palmyrenes scattered in disarray. There was enormous slaughter because the Palmyrenes fought with their usual weapons, while the Palestinians used clubs and maces against their iron and bronze breastplates. In a way, the chief cause of the Roman victory was the enemy's amazement at the strange attack with maces. The Palmyrenes fled headlong, trampling each other and being killed by the enemy as well, so that the plain was filled with the bodies of men and horses; those who could escape made for Emesa.[64]

Aurelian entered Emesa and took possession of Zenobia's treasure while the queen retreated to Palmyra. Entering the Temple of Elagabal to fulfil his vows, "he beheld the same divine form that he had seen supporting his cause in the battle."[65] Like Constantine a generation later with his vision of Apollo (only later was Constantine's adherence to Apollo shaken by a second vision, that of the cross), this emperor found Rome supported by the bright god of the East. Aurelian vowed thereupon to build a temple of the sun at Rome on his return.

The next stage occupies one sentence in Zosimus: "He then immediately set out for Palmyra, which on his arrival he encircled and besieged, securing an abundance of provisions from the nearby peoples."[66] This was the trickiest operation of all: an army of, it seems, six legions plus auxiliaries (forty thousand men at least) must cross 140 kilometers of waterless desert. At the normal marching speed of the Roman legions, this would take a minimum of three days. The season was now high summer. The day's march would be parching and dusty, the night's camp made trying by the prevalence of scorpions (in 1745 William Beawes claimed knowingly that squeezed garlic juice would cure their sting) and the howls of the jackals, though some alleviation might be had by the lucky chance of hunting down an oryx or an ostrich, the latter a popular local dish. When Emperor Julian crossed this same Syrian desert on his march against Persia, his army encountered a herd of "deer" (presumably gazelles), but most of them escaped capture by swimming across the Euphrates.

In summer the discomfort of the desert is made greater by the hot southerly wind, and still more by the northwest wind known as the semeil, whose blasts begin in July and last about forty days. They blow the dust about the traveler and into his nose and eyes. This is vividly described by a merchant traveler of the eighteenth century.

> The heat of the sun is not the most incommodious circumstance you will meet with on the road, but that of the north-west wind; for this blows directly in your face, and is as violent as if it came from a glass furnace, and penetrates into your very lungs. This may be probably owing to its passing over such a vast tract of barren land heated by the sunbeams. The Arabs turn a part of their turbant before their mouth and nostrils, by which they find a small alleviation. It likewise greatly affects the eyes; which perhaps might be remedied by green glass, worn like spectacles, and tied behind the head to keep them fast.[67]

The Romans had no sunglasses, not even turbans, and it says much for legionary discipline that they could still fight effectively at the end of the march.

The cavalry could not feed their horses on the camel-thorn, which would sustain a camel for four to ten days without water, and the men might grow faint on barley-cakes and dates, the staple of the desert. Survival, let alone success, could only be obtained by the attachment of the nomads to the Roman side. These were no doubt the Tanukh rather than the indigenous tribes, who supported Zenobia. By all accounts their provision was ample. (In the 1930s the Rualla Bedouin were able to pasture 350,000 camels in the Syrian desert.)[68] The variety of the assistance the Romans might receive is suggested by the help the nomads gave Emperor Julian a century later, teaching him the trick of making sheepskin rafts in order to cross the Euphrates. But the "brigands" (as the *Historia Augusta* calls them, following the usual classical designation for nonagricultural barbarians),[69] gave the army a hostile reception. Aurelian himself is said to have been once wounded by an arrow, though whether on the march or later in the siege is uncertain.

Meanwhile Zenobia was preparing Palmyra for a siege. A circuit wall was hastily constructed around the buildings that previously had looked onto the open desert, and soldiers were set to patrol it. When the Roman army arrived, one of these sentries

> even abused the Emperor himself. Then a Persian [archer] standing near the Emperor asked: "How would you like to see that insolent fellow dead?" When the Emperor bade him try, the Persian, setting several men in front of himself for concealment, shot the man as he was looking over parapet hurling insults, and he toppled down dead from the wall in front of the Emperor and the army.[70]

Oriental archery had proved itself a valuable addition to the massive might of Rome and an assistance in the matter of a siege where most of the legions must necessarily be idle. Also, Roman artillery and siege machinery were highly developed and effective, and they could do the work of many men. Ammianus' description of the instruments used at the siege of Circesium in 363 gives an indication of the resources Aurelian would have brought against Palmyra.[71]

A number of different machines were used to bombard the walls. First and most famous is the ballista, a gigantic crossbow in the groove of which a huge iron-tipped bolt was placed. The bolt was drawn back by ropes twisted onto rollers. When these were released, the arrow flew forth, "sometimes emitting sparks because of the excessive heat."[72] Next was the scorpion or onager (wild ass), a frame in which a beam was secured by twisted cords at one end; the other end held a sling into which rocks could be placed. This end was pulled back by ropes that were secured by a peg. When the moment came to fire, the peg was struck out with a hammer, the sling sprang forward, and the stone was catapulted out against the walls. A third instrument was the ram. A tall fir or ash trunk was tipped with a long, hard iron in the shape of a ram's head. This was suspended between two beams,

> so that it hangs from a third beam like the pan in a balance. Then a number of men, as great as the length of the pole permits, draw it back and then shove it forward again with powerful blows, just as a ram charges and retreats, to break everything in its way.[73]

More popular than the ram in Ammianus' day was the helepolis or "city-taker," which had been in use since Hellenistic times.

> A huge mantlet is constructed of strong planks of great length fastened together with iron nails, and covered with ox-hides and hurdles of green twigs; and over these is spread mud, in order to protect it from fire and falling missiles. On its front side are set very sharp, three-pronged spear-points, of the form which our painters and sculptors give to thunderbolts, made heavy with iron weights, so that whatever it attacks shatters with the projecting points. This powerful mass is guided by numerous soldiers within by means of wheels and ropes, and by their united efforts is brought up to the weaker part of the walls; and unless the strength of the defenders above is too great, it shatters the walls and opens great breaches.[74]

Finally the Romans used fire-darts made of reeds covered in an iron casing and containing inflammable material—an early form of the incendiary bomb.

All this Roman siege machinery was formidable to look on from the defenders' point of view. William Ware's Roman within Palmyra describes the "vast preparations" of the Romans:

> Every engine known to our modern methods of attacking walled cities was brought to bear. Towers constructed in the former manner were wheeled up to the walls. Battering-rams of enormous size,

those who worked them being protected by sheds of hide, thundered on all sides at the gates and walls. Language fails to convey an idea of the energy, the fury, the madness of the onset. The Roman army seemed as if but one being—with such equal courage and contempt of danger and of death was the dreadful work performed. But the queen's defences have again proved superior to all the power of Aurelian. Her engines have dealt death and ruin in awful measure among the assailants. The moat and the surrounding plain are filled and covered with the bodies of the slain. As night came on, after a long day of uninterrupted conflict, the troops of Aurelian, baffled and defeated at every point, withdrew to their tents, and left the city to repose.

The temples of the gods have resounded with songs of thanksgiving for the new deliverance, garlands have been hung around their images, and gifts laid upon their altars. Jews and Christians, Persians and Egyptians, after the manner of their worship, have added their voices to the general chorus.[75]

The exchange of letters between Aurelian and Zenobia in the *Historia Augusta* is an invention of the author and is full of rhetorical commonplaces, but it may still preserve some of the mood of the crisis.

From Aurelian, emperor of the Roman world and recoverer of the East, to Zenobia and all others who are bound to her by alliance in war. You should have done of your own free will what I now command in my letter. For I bid you surrender, promising that your lives shall be spared, and with the condition that you, Zenobia, together with your children shall dwell wherever I, acting in accordance with the wish of the most noble senate, shall appoint a place. Your jewels, your gold, your silver, your silks, your horses, your camels, you shall all hand over to the Roman treasury. As for the people of Palmyra, their rights shall be preserved.

From Zenobia, queen of the East, to Aurelian Augustus. None save yourself has ever demanded by letter what you now demand. Whatever must be accomplished in matters of war must be done by valor alone. You demand my surrender as though you were not aware that Cleopatra preferred to die a queen rather than remain alive, however high her rank. We shall not lack reinforcements from Persia, which we are even now expecting. On our side are the

Saracens, on our side, too, the Armenians. The brigands of Syria
have defeated your army, Aurelian. What more need be said? If
those forces, then, which we are expecting from every side, shall
arrive, you will, of a surety, lay aside that arrogance with which
you now command my surrender, as though victorious on every
side.[76]

The siege continued, unaffected by the diplomatic maneuvers of the
two principals, who had yet to set eyes on each other. Morale was
lowered by the omens that preceded the revolt and were now publicly
known. A consultation of the oracle of Apollo Sarpedon at Seleuceia
had elicited the response "One hawk commands the chill lament of
many doves; they shudder at their slayer."[77] Furthermore, the annual
procession with gifts to the shrine of Aphrodite Aphacitis near Heliopolis
had been rejected by the goddess: instead of allowing the gifts of gold,
silver, linen, and silk to sink in the waters of her sacred pool, she had
sent them floating back to the surface. For Zosimus, who tells these
stories, the gods were on the Romans' side as long as they maintained
the pagan cults.

The next blow to Palmyra was the desertion of its Armenian allies
to the Roman side. From the walls, the defenders watched as their
northern neighbors folded their tents and transferred their impediments
to the Roman lines, where they were welcomed by officers who outlined
their dispositions in their new role. William Ware's Piso wrote to his
friend at Rome:

> Cries of indignation, rage, grief, and despair then burst from the
> miserable crowds, as with slow and melancholy steps they turned
> from the walls to seek again their homes. Zenobia was seen once
> to clasp her hands, turning her face toward the heavens.... This
> last has proved a heavier blow to Palmyra than the former. It shows
> that their cause is regarded by the neighbouring powers as a losing
> one, or already lost, and that hope, so far as it rested upon their
> friendly interposition, must be abandoned.[78]

This calamity was shortly followed by desperate measures: the
queen herself fled toward Persia to summon further aid. She mounted
a dromedary under cover of darkness and, with a small escort, pounded
eastward to the Euphrates. At the river there was some delay in finding
a boatman to ferry her across to Persian territory. The Romans, who

had got wind of her flight, came up with her and took her small party prisoner. Perhaps the sophist Callinicus, who "died beside the Euphrates,"[79] was one of the party: his name was given to the place, thence known as Callinicum.

When this news became known, the city surrendered. Opening the gates, the people poured forth with gifts and sacrifices: "Aurelian respected the sacrifices and accepted the gifts, and sent the bearers away unharmed."[80] Among the first citizens to turn their allegiance to the conqueror were the priests of Bel, as an inscription found before the main entrance of the temple shows. It refers to the high priest "Septimius Haddudan, illustrious senator, son of Septimius Ogeilu Maqqai, who had aided the army of Aurelian Caesar."[81] It was erected in 274, two years after the destruction of Palmyra, and refers to officials of the years 273 and 274. Thus Aurelian came into possession of the jewel-encrusted garments, the Persian dragon-banners and headdresses, and the robes of purest purple that were later put on display in the temple of the sun in Rome.

Still mindful of the admonition of Apollonius in his vision, Aurelian took control of the city peaceably, installing as commander Marcellinus, the prefect of Mesopotamia and rector orientis, with a garrison of six hundred archers led by one Sandarion. Zenobia and the leading members of her court (including General Zabdas and the philosopher Longinus) were led in captivity to Emesa for trial.

The bloodthirsty soldiery demanded the blood of Zenobia but were appeased by that of Longinus and others, whom, perhaps, Zenobia implicated more deeply in order to save herself.[82] The rudimentary Roman chivalry balked at the execution of a woman, while the glory of the general required a conquered foe to exhibit at his triumph in Rome. For this reason one must be skeptical of the conclusion of the account of Malalas, who condenses the whole campaign into a single battle at Antioch. He avers that Zenobia was paraded through "all the districts of the East" mounted on a camel. He says Aurelian

> brought her to Antioch the Great. After he had watched the chariot-racing there, he brought her in on a dromedary. He built a structure in Antioch and placed her on top of it in chains for three days: he called the structure he built "Triumph." He took her down from there and led her off to Rome as empress of the barbarian Saracens. After parading her in his triumph in Rome in the old manner, he beheaded her.[83]

Though Aurelian was surely not averse to a spectacular display of his success, there is good evidence that Zenobia did not die at Aurelian's hands.

The Roman army started back to Rome with its precious booty and prisoners. While crossing the Propontis, many of the prisoners were drowned, but it seems that Zenobia and her sons survived to grace the triumph.

By autumn 272 Aurelian was on the Danube again to repulse an invasion of the Carpi. At this time the news reached him of a second revolt in Palmyra, under the leadership of Septimius Apsaeus.[84] The purple had been offered to Marcellinus, who prevaricated and used the delay to send a messenger to Aurelian informing him of events. Meanwhile the Palmyrenes clothed Antiochus, a relative of Zenobia, in the purple. Sandarion and his archers were massacred.

At the same time Egypt had again risen in revolt, under Firmus, whose purpose was to reunite the remains of the Zenobian "party." Firmus is the subject of one of the most colorful pieces of description in the *Historia Augusta:* it is a pity that there is no reason to suppose one word of it to be true. According to our friend, Firmus was a rich merchant of Alexandria, by birth a native of Seleuceia (which one is not stated). He traded in glass, paper, and other oriental products, and he may not have been without interest in the grain trade also. He was the living disproof of the Roman assumption that trade never brings real wealth—and certainly not status.[85] Firmus was a very rich man, and a colorful character as well.

He is memorably described in the three chapters of the *Historia Augusta* devoted to him.[86] A huge, swarthy, hairy—and curly-haired— pop-eyed giant of a man, he drank only water but was capable of eating a whole ostrich at a sitting. He was renowned for such strongman tricks as supporting an anvil on his chest, but he devoted most of his energy to the more rational pursuit of amassing wealth by trade. His vessels reached to the Blemmyae of Lower Nubia, the Saracens, and even India. His wealth was such that he was even able to adorn his house with glass windows (glass being one of the rarest of luxuries in antiquity, a particularly fine sort coming from Syria). He "owned so many books that he often used to say that he could support an army on the paper and glue."[87]

Most remarkable of his possessions were two, ten-foot long elephant tusks. These tusks have a history of their own. When Aurelian defeated Firmus they were one of the most prized items of his booty. With them, he planned to build a throne for a statue of Jupiter in the temple of the sun in Rome. But a later emperor, Carinus, gave them away to a "certain woman" who had them made into a couch instead: "So the gift of the Indians, consecrated to Jupiter best and greatest, became both the instrument and the reward of lust."[88]

Recently found papyri show a man named Firmus assuming the title of epanorthotes or corrector,[89] the same title Odenathus had been granted in Palmyra. This may be proof at least of the existence of our hairy hero. Alexandria was nonetheless divided. Not all the population supported Firmus. But for a while he succeeded in again severing Egypt from the empire.

Instant action was necessary. Aurelian turned his army about and marched back across more than one thousand kilometers of mountain, steppe, and desert, until he stood once more before the walls of Palmyra. The inhabitants were amazed at the speed of his return. The walls were battered down and dismantled, the city pillaged, and many of its inhabitants massacred or driven to flight. Antiochus was spared, presumably as an opponent worthy of a monarch, but the city was left to relapse into insignificance. It was stripped of all its wealth. The caravans plodded no more through its weed-covered colonnades, and the desert grouse nested among its stones. Shepherds and Bedouin camped among its palaces and temples.

Aurelian must have marched instantly from Palmyra to Alexandria—the chronology is unclear in our sources—and suppressed the Egyptian revolt. The district of the Bruchion was laid waste, and the palace therein, including the Museum of Alexandria, severely damaged.[90] Firmus committed suicide. Now Aurelian could make the proclamation that the *Historia Augusta* attributes to him:

> There is nothing now, fellow citizens, sons of Romulus, that you need fear. The grain supply from Egypt, which has been interrupted by that evil brigand, will now continue undiminished.[91]

In fact the corn dole was altered to a bread ration of two pounds, increased by one ounce by a special tax imposed on Egypt.

Meanwhile, Zenobia, dragging from camp to camp in her golden chains, waited for her first sight of Rome.

A Villa in Tivoli

Not until the following year (273) did Aurelian arrive in Rome with his prisoners. Besides Zenobia and a number of other leading citizens of Palmyra, there was the Gallic chieftain Tetricus, who had surrendered his own troops at the onslaught of Aurelian. According to the *Historia Augusta*, though he had assumed the imperial title on the urging of his mother Victoria, he was "unable to bear the impudence and shamelessness of his [own] soldiers".[1] This may be taken to mean that his own authority was shaken—one of his governors, Faustinus, was proving troublesome, and the barbarian invasions were falling directly on his own troops. His best chance of survival lay in once again throwing in his lot with the Roman Empire.

These two prisoners were the central spectacle of Aurelian's triumph. The *Historia Augusta* describes the procession in detail.

It is not without advantage to know what manner of triumph Aurelian had, for it was a most brilliant spectacle. There were three royal chariots, of which the first, carefully wrought and adorned with silver and gold and jewels, had belonged to Odaenathus, the second, also wrought with similar care, had been given to Aurelian by the king of the Persians, and the third Zenobia had made for herself, hoping in it to visit the city of Rome. And this hope was not unfulfilled; for she did, indeed, enter the city in it, but vanquished and led in triumph. There was also another chariot, drawn by four stags and said to have once belonged to the king of the Goths. In this—so many have handed down to memory—Aurelian rode up to the Capitol, purposing there to slay the stags, which he had captured along with this chariot and then vowed, it was said, to Jupiter Best and Greatest. There advanced, moreover, twenty elephants, and two hundred tamed beasts of divers kinds from Libya and Palestine, which Aurelian at once presented to private citizens, that the privy purse might not be burdened with the cost of their food; furthermore, there were led along in order four tigers and also giraffes and elks and other such animals, also eight hundred pairs of gladiators besides the captives from the barbarian tribes.

There were Blemmyes, Axomitae, Arabs from Arabia Felix, Indians, Bactrians, Hiberians, Saracens and Persians, all bearing their gifts; there were Goths, Alans, Roxolani, Sarmatians, Franks, Suebians, Vandals and Germans—all captive, with their hands bound fast. There also advanced among them certain men of Palmyra, who had survived its fall, the foremost of the State, and Egyptians, too, because of their rebellion. There were led along also ten women, who, fighting in male attire, had been captured among the Goths after many others had fallen; these a placard declared to be of the race of the Amazons—for placards were borne before all, displaying the names of their nations.

In the procession was Tetricus also, arrayed in scarlet cloak, a yellow tunic, and Gallic trousers, and with him his son, whom he had proclaimed in Gaul as Emperor.

And there came Zenobia, too, decked with jewels and in golden chains, the weight of which was borne by others. There were carried aloft golden crowns presented by all the cities, made known by placards carried aloft.

Then came the Roman people itself, the flags of the guilds and the camps, the mailed cuirassiers, the wealth of the kings, the entire army, and, lastly, the senate (albeit somewhat sadly, since they saw senators, too, being led in triumph)—all adding much to the splendour of the procession. Scarce did they reach the Capitol by the ninth hour of the day, and when they arrived at the Palace it was late indeed. On the following days amusements were given to the populace, plays in the theatres, races in the Circus, wild-beast hunts, gladiatorial fights and also a naval battle.[2]

Rome had equaled Syria in her ostentation. Surrounded by all this display, the emperor himself, in his stag-drawn chariot, was, we may presume, attired in the traditional garb of the Roman general in triumph—a purple tunic embroidered with palms, covered with a purple toga embroidered with stars. On his head was a laurel wreath. His face was painted red to resemble the face of Jupiter, whose clothes he wore. Traditionally, a slave stood behind the general, holding a golden crown over his head and constantly whispering in his ear the admonition that all human glory is fleeting.[3]

Huge tapestries and paintings were sometimes carried in triumphs—

notably in those of Julius Caesar and of Vespasian—portraying the battles in which the soldiers had won their victories. The carnival atmosphere was enhanced by cartoon representations of the leading figures of Rome and masquerades of the conquered peoples. We may doubt whether such lighthearted honors were considered appropriate for the glittering new dignity of Aurelian. Gallienus had had no time for foolery at his own triumph; and when some bystanders asked some Romans dressed as Persians where Valerian was, Gallienus had ordered them burned alive.

Aurelian assumed a string of titles—a record number—reflecting his remarkable achievements: restitutor orbis, pacator orbis, restitutor patriae, reparator et conservator patriae, conservator orbis, and restitutor Galliarum. Many of these legends appear on the coinage of this and the next year, along with that of oriens augusta. This latter encircles a type of the sun-god standing between two captives, and it clearly symbolizes the restoration of Roman sway to Zenobia's realm.

Sun-cult at Rome

The sun-god—Sol Invictus—was a major element in the propaganda surrounding Aurelian's return to the center of power in Rome. He had seen the sun-god Elagabal aiding his troops, like the Angel of Mons, at Antioch and Emesa. And when the city of Palmyra was sacked, he gave orders for the restoration of the temple of the sun there.

> Now as to the Temple of the Sun at Palmyra, which has been pillaged by the eagle-bearers of the Third Legion, along with the standard-bearers, the dragon-bearer and the buglers and trumpeters, I wish it restored to the condition in which it formerly was. You have 300 pounds of gold from Zenobia's coffers, you have 1800 pounds of silver from the property of the Palmyrenes, and you have the royal jewels. Use all these to embellish the temple; thus both to me and to the immortal gods you will do a most pleasing service.[4]

This letter is a fiction, but there is no need to doubt its substance.

What is this "temple of the sun"? At first it might seem to refer to the temple corresponding to the finds of the dedication to the sun-god Shams dating from the reign of Zenobia.[5] The brief sentence of Zosimus is, however, specific: "For Aurelian removed from this temple to new homes in Rome the statues of Helios and Bel."[6] It appears then that the Temple of Bel was to be restored, and this may partially account for its unusually fine state of preservation today (though it has since then been a Christian church and an Arab fortress). If Aurelian did restore the temple of the sun-god Shams, his restoration has left no traces. Is it possible that Aurelian thought that he was taking the effigy of Zenobia's patron god, when in fact he was taking that of Yarhibol from the Temple of Bel? Or did he take the image of Shams but decide that it would be enough simply to restore the finest and most conspicuous temple of Palmyra? It is unclear; but it is certain that Aurelian's capture of the sun-god of Palmyra was of special importance to him.

Even more significant than this honor to the sun at Palmyra was Aurelian's construction of a new and magnificent temple of the sun at Rome.[7] Though its site is the subject of some controversy, the most authoritative map places it on the east side of the Corso, at the corner of Piazza San Silvestro, roughly underneath the church of San Silvestro. Its size is conspicuous and striking. It followed the ground plan of the Temple of Bel at Palmyra, placed in a courtyard with a peristyle.[8] It housed the two cult statues of Bel and Helios, and Aurelian established a college of priests, the pontifices solis, equal in rank to the ancient pontiffs of Rome, to tend the two gods and organize their cult. We know no details of the cult, but it was surely a more restrained affair than the sun religion that the unfortunate Elagabalus had attempted to import to Rome, with its ecstatic dancing, orgies of bloodshed, and indiscriminate ritual copulations. Not the least of its purposes was to reflect and enhance the dignity and glory of the emperor.

The sun had for more than a century now been a dominant religious symbol in the empire. We considered some of the philosophical aspects of the worship of the sun in chapter 6. It was equally significant as a focus for power. As early as the first decades of the empire, the emperor had been associated with the supreme deity, the sun. Caligula demanded such acclamation, Dio Chrysostomus had encouraged Emperor Trajan to resemble the sun—all seeing and all beneficent[9]—and Trajan had consulted Jupiter of Heliopolis, the Syrian sun-god, before his Parthian war.[10] Commodus appears on coins of Smyrna wearing the radiate crown of the sun and riding in his two-horse chariot, and he shocked the people of Rome by dressing in purple and gold (and by dressing up as Hercules).[11] Caracalla used a real chariot adorned to look like the sun's own vehicle, and both he and his father were acclaimed in Egypt in the manner of Pharaohs, as "lords who have risen in their Egypt." In 155

Aelius Aristides could claim that the sun watched over the empire. Gordian and his wife are shown on coins of Arycanda as the sun and moon. Gallienus had virtually impersonated the sun-god—hero, redeemer, and Prince of Peace—scattering his hair with gold dust to resemble the bright deity.

> He went out in public processions with the radiate crown, and at Rome—where the emperors had always appeared in the toga—he appeared in purple cloak with jeweled and gold clasps.[12]

He had carried out alterations to the temple of the sun at Emesa.[13] The impressiveness of ceremony was slowly given a theological coloring. Around 260 Origen could see in the monarchy of Rome a psychological preparation of the world for monotheism.[14] If the worship of the sun was in the second century not altogether congenial to old-fashioned pagans,[15] and even smacked of Egyptian religion and the memory of the frightful Cleopatra, it was certainly in the emperor's interests to encourage monotheism.[16]

The cult of Sol took many forms. It is well known that one of the most widespread religions of the Roman army was that of Mithras, who was worshiped under the title Sol Invictus. This title was sufficiently all-inclusive to accommodate the Syrian sun as well as the Persian. And if Aurelian's sun-cult reflected primarily Syrian images, it would have been no disadvantage that the soldiers could see their favorite deity in Sol.[17]

The suggestion is not that Aurelian introduced the cult of the sun as worshiped at Palmyra into Rome[18] but that he borrowed the imagery of the Palmyrene sun to deepen and enhance his own solar religion. His High God borrowed attributes from a variety of existing gods.[19] His coins depicted Sol kicking a conquered enemy. The suggestion is perhaps that he had brought the god of Palmyra over to his own side. Did he carry out at Palmyra the archaic rite of Evocatio, calling the gods of his enemy to join the conqueror?[20]

A world state needed a world religion. Stoicism, the leading pagan philosophical system, believed in both and saw them as intertwined; and where philosophers led, emperors could follow. As Shapur had welded his diverse kingdom together with the Mazdaean religion, so Aurelian must now strive to center on a single god the patriotic devotion that the majority of his subjects could never feel toward the city of Rome.

There was a further consideration also. The preceding twenty years had shown that the making of an emperor on the strength of his military achievement was no longer reliable. Too many enemies meant too many armies. Not only could an emperor be made elsewhere than at Rome, but several emperors could be made at once. It was not enough to rest the authority of princeps on the achievements of imperator. The emperor must become a transcendent symbol.

People in the ancient world seem to have longed always for a present God, a visible helper in time of trouble. This was part of the explanation for the ready adoption in the Greek East of the cult of the Roman emperor. As the god of the philosophers retreated into the skies, far from human cry, the emperor became the controlling power of men's little destinies on earth. From the point of view of the common people of Rome, the city itself could no longer be a symbol of their might: that role now fell to the emperor in person.

> The venerable city, after humbling the proud necks of savage nations, and making laws, the everlasting foundations and moorings of liberty, like a thrifty parent, wise and wealthy, has entrusted the management of its inheritance to the caesars, as to its children.[21]

Aurelian made the god on earth a remote and dazzling being, which increased his authority in the non-Greek East, where emperor-cult had never caught on, but where regal pomp and splendor was assumed as a minimum requirement of royal rule. He took the first step toward that mysterious, elevated, and inaccessible glory that would characterize the emperors from Diocletian on, and which Gore Vidal so well evokes (in *Julian*) in his portrait of the remote Constantius. Elagabalus had been a priest, and Gallienus—had he lived—had planned the erection of a statue of himself as sun-god; but Aurelian surely perceived in his vision at Emesa a special relation, like that Constantine was to develop later, with his own god as patron of his power. Aurelian introduced a new costume for the Roman emperor, a diadem and cape studded with gold and gems, making of the tough Danubian soldier a glittering *Roi Soleil*. We have come a long way from the emperor as general, or even from that figure who emerges from the pages of Fergus Millar's epochal book—the emperor as managing director.

As part of his new religion, Aurelian established games—the Agon Solis, which was first celebrated in 274. It included among other entertainments no less than thirty chariot races. It was celebrated on the winter solstice, December 25, Natalis Invicti.[22] Between 354 and 360 the now Christian emperor Constantius II, anxious to extirpate a pagan remnant, transferred to this date the celebration of the birth of Christ, which had formerly been celebrated on January 6.[23] The turning of the world to new life was attributed to a second, longer-lasting Sun of Righteousness: "Light and Life to all he brings, Risen with healing in his wings . . ."[24]

The sun was not intended to displace the other cults of Rome. Polytheism was not exclusive, and Julian, who restored the pagan cults, was a devotee, above all, of the sun. The philosophic view was that the other gods were all emanations of the sun. Aurelian was no philosopher; but a golden diadem from Latakia portrayed the twelve gods ranged on either side of Sol Invictus—a royal diadem for an emperor or king.[25] More weight might be attached to the idea that the establishment of the sun was intended to stem the advance of Christianity. Aurelian had indeed, it is said, formed plans for a persecution of the Christians like that executed by Decius. But he was murdered before it could be carried out.

Zenobia in Retirement

What happened to Aurelian's prisoners? In the rough old days of the Republic, it had been the custom to butcher the prisoners on reaching the Temple of Jupiter Capitolinus, but there were a few precedents for clemency. Aemilius Paullus had spared King Perseus and his son: the latter went into business at Rome as a brass-smith. As far as Aurelian was concerned, Tetricus was no longer a danger. He was appointed corrector Lucaniae, a post of considerable distinction and some importance, which involved overseeing the affairs of one of the less populous regions of Italy.

Zenobia retired to an honorable and comfortable exile in a villa at Tibur (Tivoli), where the pleasant sound of streams and waterfalls makes music through the lush green chasms below the Temple of Vesta. Hadrian had made Tibur his favorite place of retirement, and Zenobia would not have been uncomfortable there. She may have married again. Eutropius tells us that her posterity were people of great reputation, and according the the *Historia Augusta*,[26] they were reckoned among the nobility of Rome in the reign of Valens. A dedication of the late third or early fourth century appears on a grave monument erected by a wet nurse to her "sweetest and most loving mistress,"[27] the resplendently named Lucia Septimia Patabiniana Balbilla Tyria Nepotilla Odaenathiana, who has been thought to be a descendant of the queen. However, the name may derive from, for example, a freed slave who started a family. A son by Zenobia by a new husband could not, in the normal way of things, inherit her first husband's name. But in this woman's name the memory of the prince of the East was not dead.

Not surprisingly, scholars have often puzzled themselves over the site of Zenobia's villa. Locating it became a parlor game for Renaissance erudition. Fulvio Cardoli placed it on Colle di Santo Stephano near the Villa of Hadrian. Andrea Bacci thought the queen made her home in the Baths at Conchae, where the bishop of Ferrara found "a jewel of gold, and an antique vessel, and other ornaments belonging to the ladies of those early times, with an inscription, that in that place one of the daughters of Zenobia was buried."[28]

Surely, as Zenobia sat at evening with her wine, overlooking the green glades where cicadas sang and swallows wheeled, the memory of her shattered city came constantly to her mind. I doubt if her Jewish learning extended to the study of the Book of Job, whose words seem to reflect so closely her own situation:

> Then the caravans, winding hither and thither, go up into the
>   wilderness and perish;
> The caravans of Tema look for their waters, traveling merchants
>   of Sheba hope for them;
> but they are disappointed, for all their confidence, they reach
>   them only to be balked.
> So treacherous have you now been to me.[29]

The caravans indeed no longer, or rarely, passed through Palmyra. The destruction of Dura and the reduction of Palmyra had reduced the artery of the desert to a shrunken trickle. The trade route probably reverted to Nabataea, and Aurelian may have transferred the legion X Fretensis to Aelana, perhaps to protect that trade.[30] But this was only a temporary measure. A series of military successes under Probus (276–82) and Galerius (298), strengthened the Romans' hand, and Diocletian was responsible for a massive military buildup in the region. In 297, the Roman government of Diocletian and the Persian king Narses established by international agreement a new silk mart at Nisibis.[31] The caravans now followed a line from Seleuceia-Ctesiphon, between the Tigris and the Wadi Tharthar, to the ruined city of Hatra, to Singara

(Sinjar), and thence to Nisibis (Nusaybin). It was a longer journey up the Tigris from the Persian Gulf, but it was effectually protected, not least by the chains of little brick forts erected on either side of the Tigris, on the right bank by the Romans, and on the left bank by the Persians. The Roman castella of Mesopotamia were still used to guard this road.[32] The two empires glared at each other across the blue waters but for many years made no move.

Then in 337 Nisibis was besieged by the Persians under Shapur II. With foot soldiers, horses, and a huge number of elephants, he "invested the city all the way round, set up engines, built batteries, and dug in palisades." Towers of earth were built for the archers. The river was diverted to batter against the city walls. However, we are told, the appearance on the walls of the holy man James of Nisibis brought all their plans to nothing. The walls were rebuilt overnight, plague assailed the besieging army, and Shapur returned home.[33]

A further expedition in 363 was more successful. Nisibis was shattered and evacuated.[34] The silk route moved north again to cross through Asia Minor to the new capital of Constantinople. Syria had become an irrelevant no-man's-land.

Palmyra was reduced to an unwalled, unprotected village, whose inhabitants squatted uneasily or uncomprehendingly among the monuments of its former greatness. A Roman garrison watched over the people as they returned to the life of eking a subsistence from the desert. The city ruled no territory, but it remained a market center for the villagers and nomads. Zenobia might think bitterly of the characterization of Roman military aims by the Gallic chieftain Calgacus, as recorded by Tacitus: *Ubi solitudinem faciunt, pacem appellant* ("They make a desert, and they call it peace").[35]

The Desert a City

It was not utter solitude in Palmyra. The nomad tribesmen, according to Arab tradition, found a new leader in 'Amr ibn Adi, a member of the family of Zenobia's former enemy Jadhima. Be that as it may, the kings of the Tanukh—perforce, if not willingly, allies of the Romans— no longer held the balance but were merely squeezed between the superpowers.[36]

Aurelian's repairs to the Temple of Bel were thorough but did not withstand the passage of the centuries. In addition, the city was rapidly becoming Christian. Tabari tells us that 'Amr ibn Adi's son and successor,

Imru'l-qais, "King of all the Arabs," was himself a Christian (but Tabari may have confused him with another ruler of the same name).[37] A bishop is referred to in the year 325. The temples of Bel and of Baalshamin were converted into churches, and other churches were built of the tumbled stone of the city. Zenobia's palace was converted into a bathhouse for the legionaries of Diocletian's army. The Temple of Allat stood until 385/6, when it was destroyed by Christians during the visit of Maternus Cynegius, the praetorian prefect of the East from 384–88.[38] The statue of the goddess was buried in the ruins and was discovered in the excavation season 1975–76.

"Black-robed tribes" of monks now rampaged through the Eastern Empire, attacking

> the temples with sticks and stones and bars of iron, and in some cases, disdaining these, with hands and feet. Then utter desolation follows, with the stripping of roofs, demolition of walls, tearing down of statues, and overthrow of altars, and the priests must either keep quiet or die.[39]

This reign of holy terror fell not on Palmyra alone but on most of the cities of the East. Maternus Cynegius was personally involved in the destruction of many pagan temples, at Apamea for example.[40]

The utter insignificance of Palmyra is vividly illustrated in Procopius' account of the buildings of Justinian. The latter restored the defenses of the Euphrates and the irrigation of farmlands at Sura, Callinicum, Resafa/Sergiopolis, Membij/Hierapolis, Zeugma, Europus, Neocaesarea, and Antioch.[41] Almost as an afterthought, at the very end of his Syrian section, Procopius adds:

> There is, too, in Phoenicia, by the side of Lebanon [!] a city named Palmyra, which was built in the desert in ancient times, and which was conveniently placed on the road by which our enemies the Saracens would enter our country. . . . This place, which through lapse of time had become almost entirely deserted, was strongly fortified by Emperor Justinian, who supplied it abundantly with water and filled it with a garrison of soldiers, so as to check the inroads of the Saracens.[42]

The fourth century saw increasing instability in the local institutions of the empire. Central authority was remote, and few could afford the burdens of local office. Brigandage increased; "Poor men, veterans, and particularly farmers who had forfeited their lands to the taxgatherer, supplied the principal recruits."[43] About 359 there dwelt in Syria, near Apamea, the Maratocupreni,

> a fierce race of brigands, dreaded because they roamed about quietly under the guise of honorable traders and soldiers and fell upon rich houses and estates and towns. . . . A united body of these godless men, disguised as the retinue of a state treasurer and one of them as that official himself, in the darkness of evening, preceded by the mournful cry of the herald, entered a city and beset with swords the fine houses of a distinguished citizen, as if he had been proscribed and condemned to death.[44]

The most notable feature of fourth-century Syria is the rise of the holy men, whose importance as charismatic focuses of authority has been so strikingly brought to scholarly attention by the work of Peter Brown.[45] These "athletes of virtue" established themselves in the rocky crevices of the desert, living on bread and water, and sometimes on grass that they reaped with a little sickle. They drew to themselves those who came to wonder at their miracles, to learn holiness, or to obtain political advice.

St. Ephraim, the opponent of Bardaisan and adapter of the tunes of Harmonius,

> ate no food but barley and dry pulse and occasionally vegetables; his drink was water. His body was dried on his bones like a potter's vessel. His clothes were of the many-coloured rags of the dust-heap. He was short in stature. He was sad at all times, and he did not indulge in laughter at all. He was bald and beardless.[46]

Though not strictly a hermit, he lived in a cave; but the literary expression of his spirituality and his learning required too much energy to permit the extraordinary mortifications of his coevals, such as Simeon the Stylite—the most famous of all, noted for 1,244 consecutive prostrations on top of his column before the Lord (as Peter Brown says, the horrifying thing is not the number of prostrations but the thought of the layman who stood there counting them).[47] Through his conspicuous asceticism Simeon became one of the most important political figures in the eastern provinces, offering advice even to emperors.

Though the emperor had managed to become the representative of god on earth in the West, and in the Greek portions of the empire, he never achieved that position in the Syrian East. In Syria religion often took on a gnostic tinge, and the present deity was less in demand. In the West politics became clothed in the trappings of religion, but in the East a man's religious credentials gave him political power—so in Islam religion and law became virtually one, in a development far from alien to the people who later gave their allegiance to Allah.

Not all the holy men were as admired as St. Ephraim or Simeon the Stylite. Some combined the two categories of holy man and brigand. In the late summer unemployed, and unemployable, peasants might gather around a wandering hermit, such as the interesting Alexander the Sleepless. His miracles encompassed both the restoration of fertility to the fields and the extinction of the sons of those who offended God.

> When the saint had passed through all the desert, accompanied by the brothers [of whom there were perhaps four hundred] enthusiastically singing psalms, he came to the city of Solomon, mentioned in the Book of Kings, Palmyra which he built in the desert. The citizens (who are Jews, though by name Christians), spying afar off the multitude of the brothers, shut the gates against them as they came closer, saying to one another: "Who will feed so many men? If they enter the city, we shall all die of starvation." When the saint saw this, he praised God, saying "It is good to trust in the Lord rather than in men [Ps. 118.8]. Be of good cheer, brothers; when you least expect it, God will visit us." The barbarians who were encamped in that region exhibited no ordinary hospitality. When they had passed three days in the desert, God sent, according to the word of the holy men, some cameleers who were four stations distant from the city, and who brought them all their food. They accepted it, thanked God and enjoyed it, and whatever was left over they shared with the city beggars who had been sent out to them.[48]

No doubt Libanius was thinking of hermit-brigands like this when he referred to the "black-robed tribe who eat more than elephants."[49]

Those whom the city could not support, the nomads of the desert nourished. So the life of the desert became the dominant note of the region, while Palmyra shrank and shrank into an Ottoman village (though not a small one—Benjamin of Tudela recorded two thousand

Jews there in the twelfth century).[50] Its latest destruction came at the hands of Tamburlaine.

The Rediscovery of Palmyra

Two centuries later the first European visitors began to appear. William Halifax, who traveled with merchants from Aleppo in 1678, found thirty or forty families dwelling there in wretched huts. He wrote:

> The world itself cannot afford the like mixture of the remains of the greatest state and magnificence together with the extremity of filth and poverty: the nearest parallel I can think of is the Temple of Baal destroyed by Jehu, and converted into a draught house 2 Kin: 10, 25, and if, what is not improbable, this was a temple of Jupiter Belus, the similitude will run upon all four.[51]

Here romantic response to ruin vies with a proper Christian approval of the decline of pagan temples.

The best known visit, that by Wood and Dawkins in 1751, resulted in the erection in many parts of Europe of buildings with details that copied or recalled those of Palmyra. Just as Stuart and Revett's *Antiquities of Athens* had produced Shugborough and other country parks, as well as numerous individual buildings, so Wood and Dawkins spawned such places as Schloss Wörlitz in Germany, by Erdmannsdorff.[52]

Lady Hester Stanhope made the city the scene of a spectacle of magnificence surely unmatched since Zenobia's day.

> Hester Stanhope rode under the great colonnade, the first European woman who had ever set foot in this crumbling capital. The inhabitants had prepared her a reception in the tradition of those which they had once awarded to their empress. On the columns with their projecting consoles, where the mark of cramp irons testified to the former existence of marble statuary, stood the most beautiful girls of the place, with their pointed breasts and slim thighs but faintly concealed by transparent robes and their heads swathed in long white veils. Some carried garlands, while those on the side of the triumphal arch and under the gateway bore palms in their hands. As the caravan advanced, they remained inanimate as if carved in bronze; then, when Lady Hester had passed, they leapt to the ground and joined in a wild dance at her side. Under the triumphal

arch, built by Zenobia to celebrate her Egyptian conquests, the procession came to a halt, and the loveliest of all the living statues bent down from her pedestal to place a wreath on Lady Hester's head, while bearded elders recited odes in her honour and young boys followed in her train playing on Arabian instruments. Fifteen hundred people, the total population of Palmyra, acclaimed her as their *Melika*.[53]

More and more Palmyra seemed to be finding its existence justified as the inspiration or the plaything of the fantasies of its western visitors—though the inhabitants of Palmyra probably welcomed the excitement of this extraordinary carnival.

A surprising note of dissonance from the usual ecstasies over the beauty of the ruins, admired from Wood and Dawkins on, appears in the account of Irby and Mangles in 1823.

Great, however, was our disappointment when, on a minute examination, we found that there was not a single column, pediment, architrave, portal or frieze worthy of any admiration. . . . The plates of Wood and Dawkins are certainly well executed, but they have done more than justice to the originals. . . . We judged Palmyra to be hardly worthy of the time, expense, anxiety, and fatiguing journey which we had undergone to visit it.[54]

Their dismissive attitude is the last shame of Zenobia's realm.

Few present-day travelers would be so unimpressed, and Charles Addison's account of his tour in 1838 strikes a happier note. Perhaps he was more hospitably welcomed. He was

received and accommodated by a finely dressed portly Arab lady, adorned with amber necklaces and bracelets, and having her head surrounded with a band of gold coins strung together. She appeared about six feet high, very stout, and as strong as a lion.[55]

Yes, you have guessed it: he regards this Arab Meg Dods as a second Zenobia.

Perhaps the ghost of the ancient queen still hovers around the ruins, seeking the honor of the Western World. For me, however, she lives on instantiated not in strapping female restaurateurs but in those arrogant yet haunted eyes of the effigied dead, looking beyond the dark that engulfed them, beyond the inevitable end that overtook their brief glory, unblinkingly on the blinding light of the sun. It was from the stones that we began; they are the reason that the story of Palmyra is worth telling and can come alive for us today. It is with the stones that we end. Zenobia's citizens stare out at their Western foes, confident that their way was right and true. Their dignity is not that of noble defeat but that of the creators of something imperishable, a legacy that can enlarge our own perspective.

Appendix: Zenobia in Modern Times

Zenobia's career in Western literature begins with Chaucer. Intriguingly, her chastity gives her her claim to fame.[1] In *The Canterbury Tales*, the poet closely follows the topics of the *Historia Augusta* and anticipates the glowing portrait by Gibbon.

> Cenobia, of Palymerie Queene,
> As writen persiens of hir noblesse,
> So worthy was in armes and so keene,
> That no wight passed hire in hardynesse,
> Ne in lynage, ne in oother gentillesse.[2]

Chaucer's immediate source for all this was Boccaccio's *De claris mulieribus*, in which the author makes Zenobia a model of chastity and valor. Indeed, as Antonia Fraser has recently made clear in her interesting study *Boadicea's Chariot*,[3] there are several polarities common to historians' portrayal of all warrior-queens: They are extremely chaste (Zenobia) or extremely lustful (Boadicea), beautiful but deep-voiced, fair-skinned but given to hunting in youth (for the last, besides Zenobia, also the Latin heroine Camilla, and Indira Gandhi), and so on. One must always be alert to the tendency of portraiture to slide into cliché and distort history in a more subtle way than a fictional retelling can.

The reigns of powerful queens seem to have evoked images of Zenobia. She appears, for example, on an Elizabethan tapestry at Hardwick Hall in Derbyshire. But she is not otherwise much referred to, to my knowledge, in Renaissance England.

The drama of her fate made the theme of a play of the fifteenth-century Italian writer Fulvio Testi, which opens with a long dialogue between Emperor Aurelian and the newly captured Zenobia, in which the emperor exhibits all the chivalry of any hero in Tasso or Ariosto:

> Reina (ed e ben guisto,
> Che senza regno ancora

> Con regio nome il tuo valor s'honori),
> Rasserena la fronte . . .[4]

The theme continues through five acts of rhetorical exchange and even involves the Sibyl of Tivoli. It is rather remarkable that no other dramatist in the next four centuries latched onto her story. One might have expected something from the pen of Nathaniel Lee, whose subjects included such classical and late antique themes as *The Rival Queens* (about Alexander the Great), *Sophonisba, Theodosius,* and *Constantine.* But the only seventeenth-century treatment is a 148-page prose drama by the Abbé d'Aubignac Hédélin, entitled *Zénobie Tragédie, où la vérité de l'histoire est conservée dans l'observation des plus rigoureuses riegles du Poème Dramatique* (1647). A fleeting appearance in Ben Jonson's *Masque of Queenes* (where she was represented by the Dowager Countess of Derby in a "carnation petticoat") hardly qualifies as historical drama. But perhaps the period had already become unfamiliar (except to the erudite Ben Jonson) as a result of the curriculum that concentrated on the early empire and then skipped to the great Christian emperors, whose world seemed continuous with the contemporary Christian states.

Robert Wood's discovery of Palmyra and his great publication of 1751 prompted interest in Zenobia's city at many levels. Architects incorporated motifs in buildings in many parts of Europe. And a scale model of its ruins, inspired by two of the book's plates, was made from such materials as vellum, mica, and mother-of-pearl, by a talented lady's-maid at the country house of Erddig near Wrexham in North Wales.[5] But the queen herself was almost forgotten.

Her name makes the title of several plays of the seventeenth and eighteenth centuries, including Carl Antonio Dondini's *Zenobia e Radamisto* of 1669, the anonymous Portuguese *Zenobia no Oriente* of 1780 (?), and the splendidly titled *Zenobia oder das Muster rechtschaffener ehelichen Liebe* ("Zenobia or the model of properly constituted marital love") by J. Mattheson (Hamburg, 1726). But in all these Zenobia is the name of an Armenian princess married to one Radamistus. The same is true of Metastasio's *Zenobia,* which was translated into English by John Hoole in 1780, and of Arthur Murphy's *Zenobia* of 1768. J. H. Wilkins' play *Zenobia Queen of Palmyra* (1851; revised as *The Egyptian* in 1853) is far from a bad play. But it is somewhat determinedly Shakespearean in its use of comic, lowlife subplot and mechanicals; in the eventual suicide of the queen; and in the nomenclature of its principals, which looks forward to the days of Asterix—the greedy merchant of Palmyra, Hujus, is matched by a character called Bulbus, and even a Roman soldier named Spontaneius. Much less good is W. Marsham Adams' *Zenobia or the Fall of Palmyra* (1870), written in the most intolerable fustian ("Peace, prating dotard, peace," etc.), though its portrait of the villainous bishop Paul has its appeal to lovers of high camp.

Lord Tennyson gives Zenobia a brief mention in *The Princess*, where she appears among a gallery of heroines that are suitable models for noble girls.

> Look, our hall!
> Our statues!—not of those that men desire,
> Sleek odalisques, or oracles of mode,
> Nor stunted squaws of West or East; but she
> That taught the Sabine how to rule, and she
> The foundress of the Babylonian wall,
> The Carian Artemisia strong in war,
> The Rhodope, that built the pyramid,
> Clelia, Cornelia, with the Palmyrene
> That fought Aurelian, and the Roman brows
> Of Agrippina.[6]

Julia Margaret Cameron acquired an interest in Zenobia, perhaps from her conversations with Tennyson. She made one photograph of her maid (her usual model) in the costume she supposed Zenobia might have worn.

The poem of Nicholas Michell quoted in the Introduction is typical of the attitudes of the early Victorian age. William Wright's fine book *Palmyra and Zenobia* (1895) is unashamedly moved by the glamour of the martial queen, but it adds to the literary tradition a new and characteristic element. He visits Palmyra to seek the queen. A near-contemporary writer, Reverend William Ware, was the author of a heroic schoolboy romance entitled *Zenobia* (1889). In this the queen becomes a model of everything most admired in Victorian womanhood—a pious widow, a loving mother, a decorous and intelligent conversationalist, and a good manager of the servants—and she is a charismatic warrior-leader to boot.[7]

Painters occasionally found in Zenobia a telling theme. A painting by G. B. Tiepolo in the National Gallery of Art in Washington is thought to represent Queen Zenobia rallying her troops against Rome. It was probably a companion piece to his *Triumph of Aurelian*, now in the Galleria Sabauda in Turin. Both may have been designed for the palace of the Zenobio family of Venice.[8] A splendid picture of 1888 by Herbert Gustave Schmalz, *Zenobia's Last Look on Palmyra*, is an almost parodic example of the grand and melancholy history painting of the High Victorian period. The gorgeously clad queen, already wearing her golden chains, looks down from a high balcony over a fantasy scene of spreading temples, porticoes, and colonnades, which might be from the hand of John Martin. Noble melancholy suffuses her brow as the sun goes down behind the wheeling desert birds. The picture, overblown as it is, might easily be a stage set for Cecil B. DeMille.

The cinematic possibilities of the larger-than-life Roman Empire recur to mind when reading the most notable production of the present century, Alexander Baron's lurid and raunchy novel *Queen of the East*, whose absurdities do not entitle it to more space here, though its historical research is occasionally acute. Even worse is the only scholarly book in English on Zenobia of this century, *Zenobia of Palmyra* by Agnes Carr Vaughan (1969), which fills out the historical framework with unjustified and generally implausible psychological detail. If one looks for a detailed exposition of the historian's view of Zenobia today, one is constrained to fall back on *Zenobie de Palmyre*, the lengthy and conscientious tome of the commander general of the Syrian armed forces, Moustapha Tlass. This book takes the historical interpretation full circle from the Roman view: Zenobia is a constitutional monarch with full popular support, whose failure is as tragic and significant as the ill-fated epoch of the Latin Crusades against the Arab world. The survival of Zenobia's legend, for Tlass, is a proof of the ultimate justice of the divine. She is such a living heroine of Syria that she even graces the Syrian banknotes.

Zenobia's name does not appear so frequently in modern English writing, though she is something more than a footnote to Boadicea in Antonia Fraser's book. Her alter ego Lady Hester Stanhope did make the headlines in February 1989, when her bones were removed from the grounds of her mountain fastness of Joun in Lebanon as a result of vandalism and reinterred in safety in the grounds of the British Embassy in Beirut. Lady Hester had been rehabilitated by the nation she renounced. Perhaps Zenobia is also due for some rehabilitation.

[1991. The first Iraqi ship attacked under the terms of the UN embargo in August 1990 was called the Zanubiyah.]

Chronology

Date	Roman Emperor	Event	Persian Emperor
64 B.C.		Pompey annexes Syria.	
41 B.C.		Mark Antony at Palmyra.	
A.D. 17		Regio Palmyrena established.	
17–19		Porticoes of Temple of Bel.	
18/19		Germanicus in Syria.	
32		Dedication of Temple of Bel.	
50–70		Palmyrene merchants established at Spasinou Charax.	
58		Inscription of L. Spedius Chrysanthus, publicanus.	
Before 67		First tariff law.	
75		Milestone of Trajan the elder 27 km ENE of Palmyra.	
98	Trajan		
100		Palmyra becomes civitas libera instead of stipendiaria (Seyrig).	
106		Trajan annexes Nabataea.	
108		First reference to Palmyrene merchants at Vologesias.	
114		Palmyra enters empire(?) (Fevrier).	
115		Altar of Temple of Baalshamin.	
116		Trajan forms first Palmyrene units; Trajan's Parthian War.	
117	Hadrian		
129		Hadrian at Palmyra.	
130/1		Dedication of Temple of Baalshamin.	
131		Palmyrene merchants honor Palmyrene satrap of Characene.	
132		First inscription of Soados.	
137	Antoninus Pius	Tariff inscription erected.	
From 150		Roman military posts south of Dura-Europos; temple of imperial cult at Vologesias.	
155–59		Dedications to M. Ulpius Yarhai.	
161	Marcus Aurelius		

Date	Roman Emperor	Event	Persian Emperor
161–69	Lucius Verus		
161–66		War against Persia.	
167		Garrison in Palmyra (ILS 8869).	
180	Commodus		
193	Septimius Severus	Synodiarch Taimarsu; monumental arch and agora built at Palmyra.	
198		Aelius Borra appointed strategos epi tes eirenes.	
199		Dedications to Ogeilo, strategos kata ton nomadon.	
211	Caracalla		
211 or 212		Palmyra becomes colonia with ius italicum.	
214		Birth of Aurelian.	
218	Macrinus	Odenathus I (if he existed) becomes senator (or 235).	
219	Elagabalus		
220		Birth of Odenathus, son of Septimius Hairan.	
222	Severus Alexander		
227		Fall of Arsacids.	
228		Ardashir becomes king of Persia; Persians occupy Mesene.	Ardashir I
230		Persians invade Roman territory.	
232		Severus Alexander's Persian War.	
235	Maximin		
238	Gordian I, II, III		
241		Fall of Hatra.	Shapur I
244	Philip the Arab		
248–50		Jotapian pretender.	
249	Decius		
251	Trebonianus	October: Herodes/Hairan, son of Odenathus, becomes senator.	
252		April: statue of Odenathus, son of Hairan, exarch and ras. Shapur's second campaign.	
253	Valerian		
253/4		Uranius Antoninus pretender; Mareades/Cyriades pretender(?).	
256		Shapur's third campaign; destruction of Dura-Europus; Shapur at Antioch.	
257		Capture of Antioch; birth of Wahballath(?).	

Date	Roman Emperor	Event	Persian Emperor
257/8		Valerian appoints Odenathus governor of Syria-Phoenicia.	
258		Gallic Empire; Odenathus described as lamprotatos, hypatikos, and despotes.	
259	Gallienus	Valerian captured by Shapur.	
260		Edict of tolerance.	
261		Pretenders in Syria (before June): the two Macriani; Callistus/Ballista and his son Quietus; Paul of Samosata becomes bishop of Antioch; Autumn: Odenathus crushes pretenders at Battle of Emesa; Scythians burn Nicomedia.	
262		Odenathus conquers Shapur, becomes dux Romanorum, restitutor totius Orientis; April: Worod referred to as procurator ducenarius; Scythians pillage Ephesus; Gallienus celebrates triumph.	
263		Revolt of Byzantium suppressed; First Council of Antioch condemns Paul of Samosata.	
264		Revolt of Trebellianus in Cilicia.	
265		Worod is argapet.	
266		Worod's cursus honorum inscribed at Palmyra; Odenathus besieges Ctesiphon, conquers Nisibis and Carrhae.	
267		Goths at Thessaloniki; Heruli at Athens; Proclamation of Aureolus; Odenathus and Hairan, on the march against the Goths in Asia Minor, are murdered, before August 29; Wahballath becomes king of Palmyra, with Zenobia as regent; Gallienus mints coins, Oriens Aug(usti) in Asia Minor.	
268	Claudius	Second Council of Antioch condemns Paul of Samosata.	

Date	Roman Emperor	Event	Persian Emperor
269		St. Antony retires to the desert; late in the year (or early 270) Zenobia invades Egypt and Palestine; Tenagino Probus fails to recapture Egypt.	
270	Aurelian	Claudius dies of plague; his coemperor Quintillus reigns briefly and dies; coins of 269/70 at Alexandria and Antioch show year 4 of Wahballath, year 1 of Aurelian; Paul of Samosata expelled from Antioch.	
271		Coins of 270/1 show year 5 of Wahballath, year 2 of Aurelian; coins of Wahballath year 5 and Zenobia Augusta; August: statue of Odenathus King of Kings at Palmyra; late in 271 (early: Drijvers), Aurelian leaves Rome for Palmyra; by end of 271 Probus the future emperor has recaptured Egypt.	
272		Capture of Tyana; Summer: battles of Antioch and Emesa; August: siege and conquest of Palmyra (Drijvers: August 271); no coins of Wahballath from 271/2; revolt of Apsaeus (or early 273; early 272: Drijvers).	
273		Spring: Palmyra razed (August 272: Drijvers); revolt of Firmus crushed (August 272: Drijvers); December: Aurelian conquers Tetricus after a seven-month march from the East; Aurelian returns to Rome.	Hormizd; Vahram I
274		Aurelian celebrates his triumph; Aurelian's reforms at Rome, building of Walls of Rome; birth of Constantine (possibly).	
275	Tacitus	January: Aurelian murdered in Thrace; interregnum.	
276	Probus	Tacitus murdered.	Vahram II
276–82		Probus' victories against Persia.	

Date	Roman Emperor	Event	Persian Emperor
293			Vahram III
293–303		Baths of Diocletian built at Palmyra.	Narses

Note: H. Drijvers redates the chronology of the Palmyrene revolt on the basis of the inscription of Haddudan, arguing that it refers to help given to Aurelian during the second siege of Palmyra, which must therefore be dated back to before the date of that inscription. But after the second sack of Palmyra, there was no city to put it up in!

Notes

Introduction

1. Michell 1854, 277.
2. Cantineau 1930–, 3.5.
3. SHA *Trig. Tyr.* 30.23.
4. SHA *Aur.* 27.2–4.
5. Gibbon 1909, 1:325.
6. SHA *Trig. Tyr.* 30.1.
7. Dawkins and Wood 1753.
8. Wright 1895, 127–28.
9. Millar 1969.
10. SHA *Aur.* 10.1; Syme 1968, 98.
11. Syme 1968, 1971a, 1983. There is a convenient summary of the case in "Controversy Abating and Credulity Curbed"; Syme 1983, 209–23. See also T. D. Barnes 1978.
12. Syme 1968, 113.
13. D. Magie, ed., *SHA* 3:192–93.
14. Syme 1968, 118–25.
15. Syme 1968, 207–8.
16. Woodman 1988.
17. These reflections are prompted by Veyne 1988.
18. Enmann 1884.
19. See David S. Potter 1990.
20. See Jeffreys, Croke, and Scott 1990.
21. A. P. Caussin de Perceval 1847, 26–46, 189–99; Piotrovskii 1970; Philby 1981.
22. Graf 1989c; Parker 1986; Kennedy and Riley 1990.
23. The main collections of inscriptions are Cantineau 1930– and Chabot 1992 (in French). Reference is made to those in other collections (*CISem, OGIS, ILS*) at appropriate places in the text. Many are assembled in English translation in Dodgeon and Lieu 1991.
24. Michalowski 1960–.
25. An important synthesis is *Palmyra* 1987. See also Starcky and Gawlikowski 1985.
26. Browning 1979; Colledge 1976a.
27. Volney 1791, 2–3.

Chapter 1

1. Double 1877, 5.
2. Wright 1895, 59–60.
3. Early in this century salt was the chief source of income for Tadmor; Musil 1928, quoted in Teixidor 1984.
4. "Solomon built Tadmor in the desert" (II Chron. 8.4); cf. II Kings 9.13; cf. Joseph. *AJ* 3.6.1.
5. Malalas *Chron.* 143, 426.
6. Hitti 1957, 312.
7. Wright 1895, 32–36.
8. Michell 1854, 280.
9. Grainger 1990, 28.
10. Weulersse 1946; Grant 1937.
11. Millar 1987b.
12. Amm. Marc. 14.3.3.
13. Is. 21.16; Gen. 25.13; Plin. *HN* 5.12.
14. App. *BC* 5.1.9.
15. Dodwell 1987, 147.
16. Bouchier 1916.
17. Tac. *Hist.* 1.4.2: "Evulgato imperii arcano posse principem alibi quam Romae fieri."
18. Renan 1869, 183.
19. Bouchier 1916, 75.
20. Philostr. *VA* 3.58.
21. Posidonius frag. 62a–b Kidd=Ath. 5. 210–11, 12. 527e; trans. Bevan 1902, 1:224.
22. Gertrude Bell 1907.
23. A. H. M. Jones 1937, 248, 266, 285–86; Libanius *Or.* 11.230 (referring to "large, well-populated villages, more populous than many cities, with χειροτέχναι as in the cities, associating with each other in fairs").
24. See Graf 1989a, 384–85. It has been argued that this was a widespread reaction on the borders of Arabia during the third century, and, more extremely, by Werner Caskel, that this, plus the breakdown of caravan traffic after the fall of Palmyra, contributed to a "Bedouinization" of the area; discussion in Graf 1989a, 392.
25. Weulersse 1946.
26. Harper 1928.
27. For the modern position, Weulersse 1946, 116–17.
28. Libanius *Or.* 47.4.11–13.
29. Libanius *Or.* 47.32.
30. Patlagean 1977, 239–40.
31. Weulersse 1946, 88–89.
32. Cf. Garnsey and Saller 1987 48–49; MacMullen 1974, 30–40 and notes.
33. Libanius *Or.* 50.34.
34. Libanius *Or.* 50, "On Forced Labor."
35. Weber 1976, 408.

36. Homer *Od.* 9.
37. Shaw 1982–83.
38. Briant 1982.
39. Lawrence 1935, 34–35.
40. Quoted in Wilson 1988, 81–82.
41. A common allegation, at least, in Tehran.
42. Mommsen 1908–13, 5:423; see Février 1931a. A. H. M. Jones (1937, 267) agrees with Mommsen. See Gawlikowski 1983; Richmond 1963.
43. Pliny *HN* 5, 88.
44. Will 1985b. Seyrig (1933) sees Palmyra as a subject city early, but with altered status as a *civitas libera* from ca. A.D. 100.
45. Février 1931a.
46. Février 1931a, 27, citing Ulpian Dig. 50.15.1; followed by Starcky and Gawlikowski 1985, 51–52; but cf. Isaac 1990, 144.
47. Isaac 1990.
48. Badian 1968, 11, 33.
49. Gawlikowski 1973, 45.
50. David Kennedy 1981, 193.
51. Richmond 1963.
52. *ILS* 8869.
53. Julian 131D Loeb.
54. Eunap. *Vit. Soph.* 496.
55. Juv. *Sat.* 3.62–65; trans. William Gifford.
56. Ps.-Virgil *Copa* ll. 1–4.
57. Goodhue 1977.
58. C. P. Jones 1978.
59. H. W. Pleket, quoted in Garnsey, Hopkins, and Whittaker 1983, 140.
60. Salvianus *de Gub. dei.* 4.14.

Chapter 2

1. App. *BC* 5.1.9.
2. The references are assembled in Casson 1989, 16; see also Crone 1987.
3. Pliny *HN* 12.54.112.
4. Pliny *HN* 12.54.118.
5. Agatharchides 5 frag. 104 Burstein; cf. Groom 1981, 71, para. 102.
6. Pliny *HN* 12.41.82–88.
7. Varro *Sat. Men.* 2.38; Heurgon 1942, 122–23.
8. Fauré 1987, 246–47.
9. Apicius (Teubner ed., 77); trans. Edwards 1984, 282.
10. Ath. 1.7a–b.
11. Pliny *HN* 12.41.84.
12. The latest discussions are those of Sidebotham (1986, 36–38) and Casson (1989, 17, 38). Sidebotham states that the Romans had no concept of a balance of trade; and it may be observed that Pliny ignores the counterweight of the customs dues that the trade brought into Rome.
13. Tac. *Ann.* 3.53.

14. Miller 1969, 148–52. Miller tends to overestimate the dependence of Rome on the Far East. Many of the products that he regards as Far Eastern could be found in the Arabian region; Crone 1987, 54, 57, 70, 71.
15. Diod. Sic. 19.94.5; cf. 2.48.9 for the importance of the balsam tree to the Nabataeans. In general, see Glueck 1965.
16. Strabo 16.4.21–26.
17. The earliest voyage using the monsoon—by Eudoxus—is placed by Strabo (2.98–99) ca. 116 B.C. The *Periplus Maris Erythraei* 57 says that the monsoon was called Hippalus after its discoverer (no date given). Perhaps he was Eudoxus' steersman (Casson 1989, 224).
18. Pliny *HN* 6.104–6; Casson 1989, app. 3.
19. As argued in a lecture by David Johnson in May 1987; but contrast Groom 1981, 212.
20. *Periplus Maris Erythraei* 19; cf. Strabo 16.4.23; Groom 1981, 207.
21. Strabo 16.4.23.
22. Sidebotham 1986, 71. This assumes that Pliny's information is contemporary.
23. S. Thomas Parker 1986: cf. Bowersock 1983, 70. Control by 24 B.C.; Graf 1978.
24. Dio Cass. 53.29.3–4; cf. Strabo 16.4.24.
25. Strabo 16.4.24; cf. S. Thomas Parker 1986.
26. Strabo 17.1.13.
27. Pliny *HN* 12.32.65.
28. Johnson 1987; Bowersock 1983, 21, 64.
29. Bowersock 1983, 85–87; unknown to Crone, who argues for the decline of Petra (1987, 26). Personal communication from David Graf. Cf. Graf 1987, 319; Graf 1989b.
30. Raschke 1978, 644, n. 821.
31. Al-Ansary 1981.
32. Pliny *HN* 6.26.101.
33. S. Thomas Parker 1986; see further chapter 4.
34. App. *BC* 5.1.9.
35. Amm. Marc. 22.4.5.
36. Liebeschuetz 1972, 78.
37. Gibbon 1909, 4:244–45.
38. For what follows see Leggett 1949.
39. Arist. *Hist. An.* 5.551b.
40. Haussig 1983, 16.
41. See in general Franck and Brownstone 1986; Haussig 1983, esp. 61ff. For holidays on the Silk Road see Bonavia 1988.
42. Leggett 1949, 120. A similar account of this silent trade in Amm. Marc. 23.6.68 may be modeled on Herodotus' description of such trade among the Carthaginians (4.196): one party leaves their goods on the seashore and goes away; the other party then approaches and leaves gold for the goods.
43. Sen. *Ben.* 7.9.5.
44. *Annals of the Han Dynasty,* in Hirth [1885] 1975, 41–42.

45. Tarn 1951, 54–55; Hopkirk 1980, 29.
46. Cable 1942, 62.
47. Exhibits in the Royal Ontario Museum. See Vollmer, Keall, and Nagai-Berthrong 1983.
48. Gibbon 1909, 4:246.
49. Wheeler 1954, 183.
50. Gibbon 1909, 4:246–47.
51. Hirth [1885] 1975, 39, para. 22.
52. Hirth [1885] 1975, 39, para. 20. Kennedy and Northedge 1988, 6–7.
53. Franck and Brownstone 1986, 126–27; Hirth 1885, 165–66.
54. Miller 1969, 136.
55. Miller 1969, 120.
56. Nodelman 1960.
57. Tr. Burkitt 1904, 219.
58. Cantineau 1930, 25, no. 34; Drexhage 1988, 24, no. 3.
59. Drexhage 1988, nos. 8, 9.
60. Drexhage 1988, no. 7.
61. Drexhage 1988, 143.
62. Drexhage 1988, no. 2.
63. Drexhage 1988, no. 1.
64. Raschke 1978, 850n.821.
65. Palmyrene sea-commerce is discussed in Seyrig 1936 and Seyrig 1941b, 252–70.
66. Hirth [1885] 1975, 43, para. 38–39; Franck and Brownstone 1986, 129.
67. Strabo 16.1.27.
68. See in general Nodelman 1960.
69. Drexhage 1988, 29. Rostovtzeff (1932a, 109) suggested that caravans through Palmyra might then go to Petra also—a strange route that would involve two sets of customs duties. This cannot be likely. Sidebotham (1986, 110) suggests that the very high tax rate of 25 percent at these ports may be a survival from Hellenistic administration.
70. On Maes Titianus see Ptol. 1.11.7.
71. Amm. Marc. 14.3.3.
72. Bulliet 1990, 47; most of the following detail derives from this source.
73. Leonard 1894.
74. Moorehead 1963.
75. Bulliet 1990, 19–21.

Chapter 3

1. Ware 1889, 53–54.
2. Polyb. 5.79.
3. Colledge 1976b; on imperial building in general see Mitchell 1987, 333–65.
4. Sherwin-White 1973, 276; J. K. Stark 1971.
5. App. *BC* 5.1.9.
6. Matthews 1984; Will 1983.

7. Inscription of 74 or 75/6.
8. Gawlikowski 1983.
9. Février 1931a, chapter 5.
10. Harper 1928, 105–68.
11. Gawlikowski 1973, chapter 2, pp. 74–80.
12. "ὁ ἐν Παλμυροῖς τεταγμένος"; MacMullen 1963, 92, citing Seyrig 1933, 157; Seyrig 1941a, 155–75.
13. See T. W. Potter 1987, 79.
14. Colledge 1976a, 23.
15. Proem 2.
16. Pliny HN 5.21.88.
17. Mesnil du Buisson 1962, 21, 23; cited in Raschke 1978, 840n.778.
18. Tchalenko 1953–58.
19. Wright 1895, 56.
20. Teixidor 1963, 33–46; Matthews 1984.
21. Mark Sykes, quoted in Lewis 1987, 55.
22. Will (1957) argued that Palmyra's wealth came from agricultural landholding: see Raschke 1978, 840n.779.
23. Lewis 1987, 49. Dio Chrysostomus (35.15–17) remarks on the importance for a city's prosperity of the existence of law courts there, because it draws in crowds. But this comment cannot be easily applied to Palmyra.
24. CISem 2.3.3913; trans. Levick 1985, 89–95. For an important general discussion see Matthews 1984.
25. A. H. M. Jones 1937, 458n.2.
26. Cic. ad Att. 6.1.15; Badian 1968, 36; Teixidor 1984, 67–68.
27. Drexhage 1988, no. 29; cf. Teixidor 1984, conclusion.
28. Rostovtzeff (1932b, 105) describes Macedonian landowners of Dura turning into levantine merchants; cf. Rostovtzeff 1926, 153 on the rich man of the second century: "Money acquired by commerce was increased by lending it out mostly on mortgage."
29. Finley 1973, 76; cf. Ste. Croix 1972, 267n.61.
30. See in general Veyne 1989.
31. Isa. 23.8.
32. Drexhage 1988, no. 17.
33. Drexhage 1988, no. 33.
34. Drexhage 1988, no. 32.
35. Drexhage 1988, no. 31.
36. Drexhage 1988, nos. 36, 37, 39.
37. Drexhage 1988, no. 40.
38. Matthews (by implication—1984) and Drexhage (explicitly—1988, 94, 117) regard these figures as interchangeable. Shalamallath, it is true, is described as chief merchant rather than synodiarch.
39. Will 1957; Gawlikowski 1983; cf. Stein 1941.
40. Burton 1875, 68–69.
41. See Schwartz 1960.
42. For the principle see Wallace-Hadrill 1990, 250: "As property owners draw-

ing rents from the lease of *horrea* and *tabernae*, a substantial portion of the urban elite must have derived at least part of their income from trade, even if they did not actually run businesses"; he cites Garnsey 1976.

43. Quoted in William L. MacDonald 1986, 273.
44. Vitr. 1.7.
45. Ael. Arist. *Or.* 26.101; William L. MacDonald 1986, 4.
46. See Colledge 1976a.
47. SHA *Hadr.* 14.3.
48. Wright 1895, 71.
49. William L. MacDonald 1986, 43.
50. But see chapter 5, nn. 8–55.
51. Graf 1989c.
52. Février 1931a.
53. Février 1931b; Teixidor 1979; Milik 1972.
54. *CIS* 2.3915; A. H. M. Jones 1937, 267.
55. Wright 1895, 78.
56. Wright 1895, 82–83.
57. Starcky 1965.
58. Teixidor 1979, 115–19.
59. E.g., Dan. 2.10; Ps. 72.19.
60. Discussed by Teixidor 1977, 124–28.
61. Bouchier 1916, 248–49.
62. Segal 1970, 48.
63. Joshua the Stylite, quoted in Segal 1970, 106.
64. Joseph. *BJ* 2.146; Qumran Rule 6.3–4.
65. Cf. the relief in Colledge 1976a, pl. 19.
66. MacMullen 1981, 37–38; Gawlikowski (1973, 74–80) indicates the political importance of the symposiarch.
67. Hdt. 1.181–82.
68. Joseph. *AJ* 18.65–80.
69. Wilken 1983, 23.
70. St. Augustine *Ep.* 22.6.
71. Brown 1981, 35.
72. *RSP* 199=Gawlikowski 1973, 100.
73. *CIS* 2.3279.
74. See pp. 77–78 on Odenathus' origins.
75. MacMullen 1981, 80.
76. On Palmyrene dress see Browning 1979, 31.
77. Double 1877, 81–82.
78. Altheim and Stiehl 1965, 256.
79. Rostovtzeff 1926, 425.
80. Chabot 1922, 49.
81. Haddudan: Cantineau 1930–, 9.40; Dodgeon and Lieu 1991, 4.10.1. Ogeilu: Dodgeon and Lieu 1991, 4.1.5.
82. Altheim and Stiehl 1965, 252.
83. Dodgeon and Lieu 1991, 4.1.4, 4.1.5.

84. *CISem* 2.4202=Dodgeon and Lieu 1991, 4.1.3.
85. Graf 1989a, says 222; Altheim and Stiehl 1965, 235; Gawlikowski 1985, 254–59.
86. Cantineau 1930, 23, no. 17.
87. Zonar. 11.23–24; D. Magie, ed., *SHA* 3:104.
88. Fundamental is Gawlikowski 1985.
89. Dodgeon and Lieu 1991, 4.1.4.
90. Dodgeon and Lieu 1991, 4.1.5.
91. SHA *Trig. Tyr.* 16.
92. Cantineau 1930–, 5.4, cf. 3.9.
93. Procop. *B. Pers.* 2.5.
94. *CISem* 2.3946=Dodgeon and Lieu 1991, 4.6.1.
95. Schlumberger 1951, 151, no. 21; cf. Altheim and Stiehl 1965, 2.254.
96. Dodgeon and Lieu 1991, 4.3.2.; including Drexhage 1988, no. 40.
97. SHA *Trig. Tyr.* 16.
98. *IGR* 3.1032=Dodgeon and Lieu 1991, 4.2.6.

Chapter 4

1. Breeze and Dobson 1976; Divine 1969.
2. Chatwin 1989, 216.
3. Graf 1978; S. Thomas Parker 1986; Shahid 1984b.
4. Kennedy and Riley 1990.
5. Isaac 1990.
6. For the following quotes from Plutarch on Crassus' defeat see Plut. *Crassus* 19–33.
7. Plut. *Antony* 45.2.
8. Pliny *HN* 6.18.47.
9. Hor. *Odes* 3.5.5–9.
10. Dubs 1957.
11. Raschke 1978, 679–81.
12. Quoted in Freya Stark 1966, 235.
13. Freya Stark 1966, 104.
14. Braund 1984.
15. Luttwak 1976; note the criticisms of Benjamin Isaac (1990, 372–418).
16. Fronto *Ad Verum Imp.* 2.3.16, Loeb 2:215.
17. Cf. Kennedy and Riley 1990, 122.
18. Luttwak 1976, 108, 111.
19. Chapot 1907, 378.
20. Dio Cass. *Epit. Xiph.* 75.3.2–3.
21. Herodian 4.9; *Acta Alexandrinorum*, ed. Musurillo 18.
22. Herodian 4.10.2–4.
23. Dio Cass. *Epit. Xiph.* 79.1.5.
24. Tabari 1.818.7; Altheim and Stiehl 1965, 268–69.
25. On the Sassanid Empire see Christensen 1936; Frye 1984.
26. Herodian 6.5.3.
27. Heliodorus, *Aethiopica*, trans. Underdowne and Wright, 271–72.

28. Amm. Marc. 25.1.12; See Amm. Marc. 16.10.7–8 for what follows.
29. Trans. Frye 1984, app. 4.
30. Firdausi *Shahnameh* 6.23.2.
31. Lactant. *de Mortibus Persecutorum*, chapter 5; for this and other sources in French translation see Gagé 1964.
32. Gibbon 1909, 1:292.
33. *Chronicle of Sert* 2, in Gagé 1964, 316; see Lieu, "Captives, Refugees and Exiles," in Freeman and Kennedy 1986, 2:475–505.
34. Frye 1984, 372.
35. On Mani see Widengren 1965; Puech 1949; Lieu 1985; Brown 1969; Koenen and Henrichs 1970, 1975, 1978, 1981, 1982; Cameron and Dewey 1979.
36. Drower 1937.
37. *Eis Basilea* 7–14, cited by Alföldy 1974, 94.
38. Oros. 7.22.6.
39. MacMullen 1976; Crawford 1975.
40. MacMullen 1976, 107.
41. MacMullen 1976, 117.
42. Oros. 4.6.3–5.
43. *Epitome de Caesaribus* 28.4; see Bowersock 1983, chapter 9.
44. Gibbon 1909, 1:209.
45. Pohlsander 1980.
46. Gibbon 1909, 1:256.
47. David S. Potter 1990, 248–49; Sullivan 1977.
48. Zos. 1.20.
49. Malalas 12.296; Rostovtzeff 1943; Delbrueck 1948; Baldus 1971.
50. Bowersock 1983, 128.
51. David S. Potter 1990, 48–49, 324–26.
52. Malalas 12.296; Libanius *Or.* 24.38; SHA *Trig. Tyr.*, "Cyriades"; *FHG* 4.292; David S. Potter 1990, 268–72.
53. For the chronology, cf. n. 57.
54. *Orac. Sib.* 13.89–102. The translations are by J. J. Collins.
55. Amm. Marc. 23.5.3.
56. *Orac. Sib.* 13.125–30.
57. I follow the chronology of Drijvers against earlier views putting these events in 253.
58. On Dura-Europos see Rostovtzeff 1938; Perkins 1971; Hopkins 1979; Goodenough 1974.
59. These frescoes are housed in a special courtyard in the Damascus Museum, in a room where dim lighting preserves their brilliant colors.
60. On Vorodes' pro-Persian sympathies see Schlumberger 1972; Seyrig 1950.
61. SHA *Gall.* 3.1–2, *Trig. Tyr.* 14.1, 15.4, 18.1; see David S. Potter 1990, 344–46.
62. Gibbon 1909, 1:293, drawing on Petrus Patricius, *FGrH* 4.F10. On Petrus' sources see David S. Potter 1990, 90.
63. Zonar. 12.23–24, in David S. Potter 1990, 390–93; The translation of ἐπανόρθωτης as restitutor is preferable to Alföldi's corrector. Cantineau 1930, 19–20; Altheim and Stiehl 1965, 253. The titles did not stop Romans, or

Emesenes, from seeing him as essentially a barbarian: Petrus Patricius frag. 167, 168; Alföldi 1938, 84.

64. See Dodgeon and Lieu 1991, 4.3.2. *Lord* is *despotes* (Greek) or *mr* (Palmyrene); see Cantineau 1930–, 3.17; *CISem* 2.3945. Odenathus did not use the title King of Kings; this first appears in Zenobia's inscriptions of 271 (*CISem* 2.3971, 3946=Cantineau 1930–, 3.19).

65. *Orac. Sib.* 13.164ff.

66. Libanius *Ep.* 1006.

67. Cf. *CAH* 12.280. In an earlier century Herod had made use of the private army of the Babylonian Jew Zamaris; Joseph. *AJ* 27.23–31.

68. Festus *Brev.* 23; Oros. 7.22.12.

69. Dodgeon and Lieu 1991, 4.2.5.

70. Zos. 1.39.20.

71. Zonar. 12.24 (*PI* 633). For Alexander, see Arr. *Anab.* 4.13.1–2 etc; Bosworth 1989, 118.

72. SHA *Trig. Tyr.* 17.

73. *FHG* 4.195 (C. Müller); Dodgeon and Lieu 1991, 4.4.1; Gawlikowski 1985; Seyrig 1963.

74. Gawlikowski 1985.

75. John of Antioch frag. 152.2; Dodgeon and Lieu 1991, 4.4.1; *CAH* 12.176.

76. Caussin de Perceval 1847, 196–97.

Chapter 5

1. Chaucer 1966, 192–93, ll. 3442–44, 3493–3500.

2. Tlass 1986.

3. Seyrig 1963, 161.

4. *CISem* 2.3971; see chapter 4 n. 64.

5. Chaucer 1966, 192, ll. 3453–58.

6. SHA *Aur.* 27.6. Unfortunately the author of the *Historia Augusta* inadvertently makes this particular claim dubious when he writes that a letter of hers to Aurelian was dictated by her in Syrian and translated by the sophist Nicomachus into Greek.

7. SHA *Trig. Tyr.* 30.12.

8. Chaucer 1966, 192, ll. 3467–76.

9. Philo *Vit. Mos.* 28; Philo *Spec.* 13.13; Augustine *de Bono Coniugi* 13.15; *CSEL* 41.208.

10. Shaw 1987, 44, n. 185.

11. Segal 1963.

12. Caussin de Perceval 1847, 199.

13. SHA *Trig. Tyr.* 30.12.

14. SHA *Gall.* 13.2–3.

15. See Dodgeon and Lieu 1991, 4.1.5.

16. *IGR* 3.1032; Seyrig 1937a, 1–4; *CAH* 12.274.

17. Tlass 1986, 274.

18. SHA *Aur.* 38.1.

19. A more complex solution (two sons called Hairan) in Seyrig 1963; cf. David S. Potter 1990, 386–88.
20. Dodgeon and Lieu 1991, 4.2.4.
21. Dodgeon and Lieu 1991, 4.2.5.
22. *CIS* 2.3971=*OGIS* 649; Cantineau 1930–, 3.20=*OGIS* 648.
23. Mattingly 1936; Alföldi 1938.
24. *P. Oxy.* 1264; BGU 946; see Dodgeon and Lieu 1991, 4.6.4.
25. *CISem* 2.3971=Dodgeon and Lieu 1991, 4.4.5. *OGIS* 647 gives the Greek text only.
26. See in general Fraser 1988; Macurdy 1937; Abbott 1941.
27. Boccaccio 1964, 6.
28. Is she the same as the Nikaule of Joseph. *AJ* 8.158?
29. Hdt. 2.100.
30. I Kings 10; Qur'an Sura 27. See in general Pritchard 1974; Philby 1981.
31. Groom 1981, 54 n. 31, 241.
32. On these see Abbott 1941.
33. MacAdam and Graf 1989.
34. Amm. Marc. 31.16.4; Shahid 1984a, 1984b.
35. "In the course of pleading her defense, she involved many others on the ground that they had misled her since she was a woman" (Zos. 1.56.2). The "womanliness" of this tactic is emphasized and held up for admiration by Fraser (1988, 124).
36. Bowersock 1969.
37. Rostovtzeff 1932a, 122.
38. *CAH* 12.176–77.
39. Schlumberger 1972.
40. Graf 1989c.
41. SHA *Aur.* 33.
42. The guests of a Hadrami king include representatives of Qršhtn (Quraysh?), Tadmar, Kašd, and Hind. See Crone 1987, 169; Graf 1989c, 147.
43. Cantineau 1930–, 3.18=*IGR* 3.1049 (Dodgeon and Lieu 1991, 4.8.5).
44. Gibbon 1909, 1:327.
45. SHA *Trig. Tyr.* 30.19.
46. SHA *Trig. Tyr.* 30.2.
47. Vergil *Aeneid* 4.622–29, trans. John Dryden.
48. Summarized by Altheim and Stiehl 1965, 256–58.
49. R. Fellmann, in *Palmyra* 1987, 131–36.
50. Ware 1889, 99.
51. Tabari, in Caussin de Perceval 1847, 30.
52. Procop. *Buildings of Justinian* 2.8.
53. Procop. *Buildings of Justinian* 2.8.
54. Tabari, in Caussin de Perceval 1847, 30.
55. Wright 1895, 139.
56. Gawlikowski 1971.

Chapter 6

1. Eunap. *Vit. Soph.* 456 (Loeb); Scott 1815, 339.

2. SHA *Aur.* 30.3.
3. Porph. *Vit. Plot.* 19.
4. Gibbon 1909, chapter 10.
5. Ware 1889, 446–47.
6. Libanius *Ep.* 1078.
7. Lucian *de Mercede Conductis.*
8. Bowersock 1969. On Julia see also Turton 1974. On what follows see in general Millar 1969. I have not seen Bowersock, "The Hellenism of Zenobia," cited in Bowersock 1990, 7–8.
9. Millar 1969; Cameron 1967; Bowersock 1983, 175–76.
10. Menander Rhetor *Treatise* 1; see Bowersock 1983, 135; Graf 1989a, 398.
11. SHA *Aur.* 27.6; Syme 1968, 111.
12. David S. Potter 1990, 71–72.
13. Lamberton 1986, 54–77.
14. Meleager, in *Anth. Pal.* 7.417, trans. A. P. Wright.
15. Dam. *Vit. Isid.*, Asmus 55.
16. Euseb. *HEccl.* 6.39, 7.32.39; Shahid 1989, 209.
17. Libanius *Ep.* 1006.
18. Gibbon 1909, 4:62–81.
19. Lieu 1985, chapter 2; in general, Segal 1970, and Howard's edition of the *Teaching of Addai.*
20. Euseb. *HEccl.* 6.21.3–4; Turton 1974, 184.
21. Pohlsander 1980.
22. Lane Fox 1986, 519–21.
23. Euseb. *HEccl.* 4.30; Drijvers 1966.
24. Bardaisan *Book of the Laws of Countries,* Cureton 27.
25. For St. Ephraim see esp. Ephraim tr. McVey 1989.
26. Tr. Burkitt 1904, 218–23.
27. *Hymn on the Nativity* 27 vv. 16, 21–22: cf. the modern carol referring to the "sun of righteousness."
28. Lucian *de Syria Dea;* Goossens 1943.
29. Hyginus *Poet. Astr.* 2.30; Ovid *Fasti* 2.473–74; See the interesting note in Cumont 1911, 245n.36.
30. Plut. *On Superstition* 170D.
31. MacMullen 1981, 37.
32. Speidel 1978.
33. Augustine *City of God* 2.4–5.
34. Bouchier 1916, 249–50; Amm. Marc. 23.3.2.
35. Cumont 1911, 163–64.
36. Col. 2.8 (the AV's "rudiments of the world" are in fact elemental spirits); cf. Col 2.18.
37. Charbonneaux 1960.
38. Ibn al-Kalbi 14–17; Sura 53.19–20; Hitti 1940, 98–99.
39. Ibn al-Kalbi 14.
40. Ephraim *Hymns on Virginity* 14 v. 7.
41. Artaud 1967, 24–25.
42. Dam. *Vit. Isid.*, Asmus 121–22; Artaud 1967, 25–26.

43. Seyrig 1971.
44. The basic source is Herodian 5.5.3–8.10.
45. Herodian 5.6.5.
46. Turton 1974, 155.
47. SHA *Sev. Alex.* 29.2.
48. Cleanthes SVF I, 112n.499, 114n.510; Hengel 1974, 236, nn. 820, 821.
49. Mara, in *SEG* 7.14.
50. Cic. *Somn. Scipionis* 4.
51. Philo *Spec.* 1.279.
52. Julian *Or.* 138D, 150C, 154A.
53. See also Nilsson 1961, 2.273, 507–19; Nilsson 1952.
54. Joseph. *BJ* 2.128–29.
55. Sura 27.15–44.
56. Renan, *Lettre à Berthelot* (Dialogues et fragments philosophiques, p. 168), cited by Cumont 1956, 184.
57. Burkitt 1904; Lane Fox 1986, 279–80.
58. Browning 1982.
59. A good guide is Chadwick 1967.
60. Lieu 1985, chapter 2.
61. Renan n.d., 115.
62. Celsus *On the True Doctrine.*
63. Abercius, *Vita,* ed. Nissen.
64. Chadwick 1990, 737.
65. Anderson 1986, 209.
66. Euseb. *HEccl.* 7.27–31; Runciman 1955, 19–20.; Stark 1966, chapter 16; Millar 1971. The standard study of Paul of Samosata is still that of Bardy 1929.
67. Euseb. *HEccl.* 7.30.9; Millar 1971, 13.
68. Euseb. *HEccl.* 7.30.13.
69. Athanasius *Hist. Arianorum* 71.1; John Chrysostom *Hom 8 in Joannem;* Filastrius *Diversarum haereseon* 36/64; cf. Theodoret *Haereticarum fabularum compendium* 2.8.
70. Declerck 1984.
71. Euseb. *HEccl.* 30.14.
72. Gregory bar-Hebraeus, cited in *Chronicon Ecclesiast.* sect. 1, Patriarch. Antioch 16. See Bardy 1929, 257 n.2.
73. Millar 1971; David S. Potter 1990, 48.
74. Cumont 1911, 252.
75. *OGIS* 129 = *CIJ* 1449.
76. Bowersock 1984.
77. Phot. *Bibl.* 265; *Patr. Gr.* 104.180b–c.
78. See Graf 1989c.
79. Lane Fox 1986, 570–71, 769nn.
80. Cumont 1911, 252.
81. Childs 1990, 196.
82. Euseb. *HEccl.* 6.21.3–4.
83. Zos. 1.57–8.

Chapter 7

1. Avi-Yonah (1976, 126–7) quotes rabbinic sources describing the imprisonment of rabbis by Odenathus (jTerumot 8, 10–46b) and looking forward to the fall of Palmyra as a release for Palestine (b Yebamot 17a).
2. Harl 1987, 201 n. 87.
3. But see *CAH* 12.180.
4. Caussin de Perceval 1847, 2:29ff; Philby 1981; Piotrovskii 1970; for the queen of Sheba, see Qur'an 27.43.
5. Tabari 745–56; Altheim and Stiehl 1965, 268–69.
6. Bowersock 1983, 132–34.
7. Tabari 760.
8. Caussin de Perceval 1847, 2:34; cf. Tabari 761.
9. Self-mutilation may be in oriental practice a regular act intended to guarantee good faith in a traitor: cf. Pilpay 1987, 198–200.
10. Bowersock 1983, 138–47.
11. Malalas 299.
12. *IGLS* 9107; Seyrig 1941a; S. Thomas Parker 1986, 132.
13. Khouri 1986b, 97.
14. Bowersock 1983, 136; Seyrig 1941a, 46; Dodgeon and Lieu 1991, 4.5.5; B. De Vries "Umm el-Jimal in the First Three Centuries A.D.," in Freeman and Kennedy 1986, 1:227–41.
15. *CIS* 5.663, 1649, 1664–65; Graf 1989c.
16. Cf. Bulliet 1975, 106.
17. Zos. 1.44; see SHA *Claud.* 11.1–2.
18. Parsons 1967, 401. On Zenobia's support in Egypt see J. Schwartz in *Palmyre* 1976.
19. Parsons 1967, 401.
20. Price 1973. Not all agree: J. Schwartz (*Palmyre* 1976) argues for the date of October 22.
21. Zos. 1.50.
22. On the coinage of Zenobia and the chronology see Mattingly 1936, 91, 105; Alföldi 1938; Carson 1978; J. Rea, *P. Oxy.* 11.15–26; Price 1973.
23. SHA *Trig. Tyr.* 30.23.
24. Joseph. *BJ* 2.386.
25. Aur. Vict. 1.6; Bowman 1986, 38; SHA *Sep. Sev.* 8. For criticism of these statistics see Garnsey and Saller 1987, 84–85. See also Rickman 1980, 67–71, 231–35.
26. Tac. *Ann.* 12.43.
27. Pliny *Paneg.* 28.
28. *Orac. Sib.* 13.42–45.
29. Ware 1889, 257–58.
30. Schwartz 1960.
31. SHA *Gall.* 16.1.
32. E.g., MacMullen 1966, 225.
33. MacMullen 1966, viii.
34. Philostr. *Vit. Soph.* 563; Bowman 1986, 42.

35. The only full account of Aurelian's reign is that of Homo (1904), nearly a century old.
36. *CAH* 12.298.
37. Syme 1971a, 209–10.
38. SHA *Aur.* 5.6.
39. Syme 1968, 115.
40. Aur. Victor *Caes.* 35.6; *Epit.* 35.2; Eutropius 9.14.
41. Todd 1978.
42. Homo 1904. Drijvers (1977) argues that Aurelian in fact besieged Palmyra in August 271. But see chronology and note.
43. Isaac 1990, 402.
44. Poidebard 1934; Kennedy and Riley 1990. See map 4.
45. McElderry 1909; Keppie 1984. On II Parthica see Balty 1988, 99–100.
46. Tac. *Ann.* 13.35.
47. Fronto *Ad Verum Imp.* 2.1.19, Loeb 2:148; cf. 2.3.12, Loeb 2:209.
48. MacMullen 1963; Chapot 1907, 151–62.
49. Isaac (1990) suggests this, but with extreme caution since there is no evidence.
50. SHA *Aur.* 22.5.
51. SHA *Aur.* 7.3–4.
52. SHA *Aur.* 24.
53. Vegetius 3.23.
54. Chapot 1907, 172–73, drawing on Vegetius.
55. Joseph. *BJ* 3.86.
56. Isaac 1990, 290–91; cf. SHA *Claud.* 14.2–4.
57. Malalas 12.307; cf. *Notitia Dignitatum* with Matthews 1989, 263, 408.
58. Bell 1907, 320–21.
59. Malalas *Chron.* 234.
60. Zos. 1.50–51.
61. SHA *Aur.* 25.3.
62. Downey 1950.
63. Zos. 1.52.
64. Zos. 1.53.
65. SHA *Aur.* 25.4.
66. Zos. 1.54.2.
67. Bartholomew Plaisted, in Carruthers 1929, 67.
68. Grant 1937, 21–22.
69. SHA *Aur.* 27.5.
70. Zos. 1.54.
71. Amm. Marc. 23.4.
72. Amm. Marc. 23.4.3.
73. Amm. Marc. 23.4.8.
74. Amm. Marc. 23.4.11.
75. Ware 1889, 371–72.
76. SHA *Aur.* 26.
77. Zos. 1.57.
78. Ware 1889, 382.

79. Libanius *Ep.* 21.5; Stein 1923, 456.
80. Zos. 1.56.2.
81. Cantineau 1930–, 9.40 (Dodgeon and Lieu 1991, 4.8.6); Gawlikowski 1971, 420.
82. Zos. 1.56.2–3.
83. Malalas 300.
84. SHA *Aur.* 31.1–10; Zos. 1.59 (Dodgeon and Lieu 1991, 4.8.4); Cantineau 1930–, 3.18 (*IGR* 3.1049; Dodgeon and Lieu 1991, 4.8.5).
85. This assumption is examined by D'Arms (1981).
86. SHA *Firmus,* etc. 3–5.
87. SHA *Firmus* 3.
88. SHA *Firmus* 3.
89. Bowman 1976, 158.
90. Amm. Marc. 22.16.15.
91. SHA *Firmus,* etc. 5.

Chapter 8

1. SHA *Trig. Tyr.* 24.2.
2. SHA *Aur.* 33–34.
3. See in general Payne 1962; Versnel 1970; Künzl 1988.
4. SHA *Aur.* 31.7–9.
5. *ILS* 1210; chapter 3 n. 74–75.
6. Zos. 1.61.2.
7. SHA *Aur.* 28.5, 35.3.
8. MacDonald 1986, 210.
9. Dio Chrys. *Or.* 3.73.
10. Kantorowicz 1963.
11. Herodian 1.14.8.
12. SHA *Gall.* 16.4, 18.2–4.
13. Blois 1976, 159–61.
14. Origen *Contra Celsum* 2.30.
15. Momigliano 1987, 145.
16. Some passages on sun imagery are collected in Harl 1987, 46–47. See also MacMullen 1981, 84–85.
17. Cumont 1956, 199; Halsberghe 1972.
18. Rightly pointed out by Seyrig (1971).
19. On another aspect of this god as Juppiter Consulens see Will 1959 and 1974; Will emphasizes that Juppiter Consulens cannot be identified with Bel.
20. The ritual is described by Macrobius (*Saturnalia* 3.9); see Basanoff 1947.
21. Amm. Marc. 14.6.5; cf. Matthews 1989, 414.
22. This happens to be also the date of the festival of Dushares at Petra.
23. Cf. John Chrysostom *Hom in nat Christi, Patr. Gr.* 49.351–63.
24. C. Wesley, et al., "Hark, the Herald Angels Sing." *English Hymnal no. 24.*
25. Last seen by F. Altheim in 1938: cf. Homo 1904, 184ff.
26. SHA *Trig. Tyr.* 27.2.

27. *CIL* 6.1516; Baldini 1978.
28. Seller 1705, 134. This is presumably the inscription mentioned above, which was published only in 1876.
29. Job 6.18–21.
30. This could also have happened under Diocletian; Graf 1978, 1–26. Aurelian seems to have strengthened the Arabian garrisons with two further cohorts—III Alpinorum and VIII Voluntariorum—and with four units of equites Illyriani; see Graf 1978, 278.
31. Franck and Brownstone 1986, 153.
32. Stein 1941, 299–316.
33. Theodoret *Lives* 1.11.
34. Amm. Marc. 25.9.
35. Tac. *Agr.* 30.
36. A controversial view holds that this period saw a "Bedouinization" of the Arabs, and that as a result they acquired the name the Arabs bore for another thousand years, the Saracens, which is first used by Ammianus Marcellinus (e.g., 23.6.13); see Caskel 1954, 36–46.
37. Bowersock 1983, 140.
38. Gassowska 1982, 107–23.
39. Libanius *Or.* 30.8.
40. Keay 1988, 198; Matthews 1975, 110–11, 142–44.
41. Procop. *Buildings of Justinian* 2.9–11.
42. Procop. *Buildings of Justinian* 2.11.10–12. But Malalas 18.2 makes this event the very first of Justinian's reign.
43. MacMullen 1963, 51.
44. Amm. Marc. 28.2.11–13; MacMullen 1963, 52.
45. Brown 1971.
46. Segal 1970, 18.
47. Brown 1978, 13–14.
48. *Life of Alexander Akoimetes,* in *Patrol. Orient.,* ed. J. de Stoop, 6:659–701.
49. Libanius *Or.* 30.8.
50. Benjamin of Tudela 1907, 31.
51. Halifax [1695] 1890.
52. Watkin and Mellinghoff 1987, 30–32.
53. Haslip 1934, 133.
54. Irby and Mangles 1823, 82.
55. Addison 1838, esp. 329.

Appendix

1. See chapter 5.
2. Chaucer 1966, 192, ll. 3437–41.
3. Fraser 1988.
4. Testi 1659, act 1, scene 1.
5. See Waterson 1990, 44–45.
6. Tennyson, *The Princess* 2.62–72.

7. Ware may have known Wilkins' play, since he, like the earlier author, provides Zenobia with an unhistorical daughter named Julia. In Wilkins she is betrothed to the Persian prince Hormisdas, while General Zabdas pines for her love. In Ware the Roman Piso, the narrator of the novel, is her admirer.
8. Shapley 1974.

Bibliography

Ancient Sources

No edition is noted where there is a readily available text, for example, in the Loeb Library.

Abercius, S. *Vita*. Ed. T. Nissen. London, 1912.
Addai, Teaching of. Ed. G. Phillips. London, 1876. Ed. G. Howard. London, 1981.
Aetheria or Egeria. *Egeria's Travels to the Holy Land*. Tr. John Wilkinson. London, 1971, 1981.
Agatharchides.
Alexander the Sleepless. *Vita*. In *Patrol Orient*, ed. J. de Stoop, 6:659–701.
Ammianus Marcellinus.
Apicius. Ed. M. E. Milham. Leipzig and Stuttgart (Teubner), 1969. Tr. J. Edwards, *The Roman Cookery of Apicius*. London, 1984.
Aurelius Victor.
Bardaisan. *Book of the Laws of Countries*. Tr. W. Cureton. N.p., n.d.
Celsus. *On the True Doctrine*. Tr. J. Hoffman. New York, 1987.
Commodian.
Damascius. *Vita Isidori*. Ed. R. Asmus. Leipzig, 1911.
Dexippus. *FGrH* 100, vol. 2. 456–60.
Dio Cassius.
Dio Chrysostomus.
Ephraim the Syrian. Tr. K. E. McVey. New York, 1989.
Eutropius.
Festus. *Breviarium*.
Firdausi. *Shahnameh*. Vol. 6. Tr. A. G. Warner and E. Warner. London, 1912.
Fragmenta Historicorum Graecorum. Ed. C. Müller. 5 vols. Paris, 1841–70.
Fronto. *Ad Verum Imperatorem*.
Heliodorus. *Aethiopica*. Tr. T. Underdowne and F. A. Wright. London, 1923.
Herodian.
Ibn al-Kalbi. *Book of the Idols*. Tr. N. Arnim Faris. Princeton, 1952.
Isidore of Charax. The *Parthian Stations*. Ed. W. H. Schoff. Philadelphia, 1914. *GGM* 1.
Jacob of Serugh. *Homily: Fall of the Idols*. Ed. P. Martin. *ZDMG* 29 (1875): 107–47.
Jerome. *Life of Malchus*.
Josephus. *Antiquitates Judaicae; Bellum Judaicum*.

Julian. *Hymn to the Sun.*
Juvenal. *Satires.*
Libanius. *Orationes; Epistulae.*
Lucian. *de Syria Dea.*
Macrobius. *Saturnalia.*
Malalas, John. *Chronicle.* Tr. E. Jeffreys, M. Jeffreys, and R. Scott. Melbourne, 1986.
Melito of Sardis. In *Spicilegium Syriacum,* by W. Cureton (London, 1855), 41–100.
Oracula Sibyllina. In ed. J. H. Charlesworth *The Old Testament Pseudepigrapha,* vol. 1, London, 1983. For book 13, see David S. Potter 1990.
Orosius. *Historiae adversus paganos.*
Patrologia Graeca.
Periplus Maris Erythraei. Ed. L. Casson. Princeton, 1989.
Petrus Patricius.
Procopius. *On the Buildings of Justinian.*
Ps.-Virgil. *Copa.*
Ptolemy. *Geographia.*
Qur'an.
Scriptores Historiae Augustae. *Historia Augusta.* 3 vols. Ed. and tr. D. Magie. Cambridge, Mass., 1922–32.
Seneca. *De Beneficiis.*
Tabari. *The History of al-Tabari.* Vol. 4. Tr. and ann. Moshe Perlmann. Albany, 1987.
Tabula Peutingeriana. Ed. A. Levi and M. Levi. Rome, 1978.
Theodoret of Cyrrhus. *A History of the Monks of Syria.* Tr. R. M. Price. Kalamazoo, 1985.
Vegetius.
Vitruvius.
Zonaras.
Zosimus. *New History.* Tr. R. T. Ridley. Sydney, 1982.

Secondary Works

Abbott, Nadia. 1941. "Pre-Islamic Arab Queens." *American Journal of Semitic Languages and Literature* 58:1–22.
Al-Ansary, A. 1981. *Qaryat al-Fau.* Beckenham.
Alföldi, A. 1938. "Die römische Münzprägung und die historischen Ereignisse im Osten zwischen 260 und 270 n. Chr." *Berytus* 5.1: 47–92. In *Studien zur Geschichte der Weltkrise des 3. Jahrhunderts nach Christus.* Darmstadt, 1967.
Alföldy, G. 1974. "The Crisis of the Third Century as Seen by Contemporaries." *GRBS* 15:98–102.
Altheim, F., and R. Stiehl. 1965. *Die Araber in der alten Welt* II. Berlin.
Anderson, Graham, 1986. *Philostratus.* Beckenham.
Artaud, Antonin. 1967. *Héliogabale ou l'anarchiste couronné* in *Oeuvres complètes.* Vol. 7. Paris.

Avi-Yonah, M. 1954. *The Madaba Mosaic Map.* Jerusalem.
———. 1976. *The Jews of Palestine.* Oxford.
Badian, E. 1968. *Roman Imperialism in the Late Republic.* Ithaca, N.Y.
Baldini, A. 1975. "Il ruolo di Paolo di Samosata nella politica culturale di Zenobia e la decisione di Aureliano ad Antiochia." *Riv. Stor. dell'Antichità* 5:59–78.
———. 1978. "Discendenti a Roma di Zenobia?" *ZPE* 30:145–49.
Baldus, H. R. 1971. *Uranius Antoninus.* Bonn.
Balty J. C. 1977. "Apamée de Syrie." *ANRW* 2:8.
———. 1981a. "L'oracle d'Apamée." *AntClass* 50:5–14.
———. 1981b. *Guide d'Apamée.* Brussels.
———. 1988. "Apamea in Syria in the Second and Third Centuries A.D." *JRS* 78:91–104.
Bardy, J. 1929. *Paul de Samosate.* 2d ed. Louvain.
Barnes, T. D. 1978. *The Sources of the Historia Augusta.* Brussels.
Basanoff, V. 1947. *Evocatio.* Paris.
Baynes, N. H. 1926. *The Historia Augusta: Its Date and Purpose.* Oxford.
Benabou, M. 1976. *La résistance africaine à la romanisation.* Paris.
Bevan, E. R. 1902. *The House of Seleucus.* London.
Blois, L. de. 1976. *The Policy of the Emperor Gallienus.* Leiden.
Bolin, S. 1958. *State and Currency in the Roman Empire to 300 A.D.* Stockholm.
Bosworth, A. B. 1989. *Conquest and Empire: The Reign of Alexander the Great.* Cambridge.
Bouchier, E. S. 1916. *Syria as a Roman Province.* Oxford.
———. 1921. *A Short History of Antioch.* Oxford.
Boulnois, L. 1963. *La route de la soie.* Paris. English trans., *The Silk Road.* London, 1966.
Bowersock, G. 1969. *Greek Sophists in the Roman Empire.* Oxford.
———. 1971. "A report on Arabia Provincia." *JRS* 61:219.
———. 1983. *Roman Arabia.* Cambridge, Mass.
———. 1984. "The Miracle of Memnon." *BASP* 21:21–32.
———. 1987. "The Hellenism of Zenobia." In *Greek Connections*, ed. J. T. A. Koumoulides, 19–27. Notre Dame.
———. 1990. *Hellenism in Late Antiquity.* Cambridge.
Bowersock, G. W., et al. 1977. *Edward Gibbon and the Decline and Fall of the Roman Empire.* Cambridge, Mass.
Bowman, A. K. 1976. "Papyri and Imperial History, 1960–1975." *JRS* 66:153–73.
———. 1986. *Egypt after the Pharaohs.* London.
Brauer, George C. 1975. *The Age of the Soldier Emperors.* Park Ridge, N.J.
Braund, D. C. 1984. *Rome and the Friendly King.* Beckenham.
Breeze, D. J., and Brian Dobson. 1976. *Hadrian's Wall.* Harmondsworth.
Briant, P. 1982. *Etat et pasteurs dans le moyen-orient ancien.* Cambridge and Paris.
Broughton, T. R. S. 1929. *The Romanisation of Africa Proconsularis.* Baltimore.
Brown, Peter. 1969. "The Diffusion of Manichaeanism in the Late Roman Empire." *JRS* 59:92–103.

———. 1971. "The Rise and Function of the Holy Man in Late Antiquity." *JRS* 61:80–101. In *Society and the Holy in Late Antiquity*, 103–52. London, 1982.

———. 1978. *The Making of Late Antiquity*. Cambridge, Mass.

———. 1981. *The Cult of the Saints*. London.

Browning, Iain. 1977. *Petra*. London.

———. 1979. *Palmyra*. London.

———. 1982. *Jerash and the Decapolis*. London.

Bulliet, Richard W. 1990. *The Camel and the Wheel*. Cambridge, Mass.

Burkitt, F. C. 1904. *Early Eastern Christianity*. London.

Cable, Mildred. 1942. *The Gobi Desert*. London.

The Cambridge Ancient History. 1939. Vol. 12, *The Imperial Crisis and Recovery A.D. 193–324*, ed. S. A. Cook, F. E. Adcock, M. P. Charlesworth, and N. H. Baynes. Cambridge.

Cameron, Alan. 1967. "The Date of Porphyry's κατα χριστιανων." *CQ* 17: 382–84.

Cameron, R., and A. Dewey. 1979. *The Cologne Mani-Codex*. Chico, Calif.

Campbell, J. B. 1984. *The Emperor and the Roman Army*. Oxford.

Cantineau, J. 1930. *Inscriptions palmyréniennes*. Damascus.

———. 1930–. *Inventaire des inscriptions de Palmyre*. 11 vols. Beirut.

———. 1934. *Le dialecte arabe de Palmyre*. Vols. 1–2. Damascus. (not seen.)

———. 1935. *Grammaire du palmyrénien épigraphique*. (not seen.)

Carson, R. A. G. 1978. "Antoniniani of Zenobia." *Numismatica e antichità classiche* 7:221–28.

Casey, John. 1991. *The Legions in the Later Roman Empire*. The fourth annual Caerleon lecture. Caerleon.

Caskel, Werner. 1954. "The Bedouinization of Arabia." In *Studies in Islamic Cultural History*, ed. G. E. von Grunebaum, 36–46.

Casson, Lionel. 1989. *The Periplus Maris Erythraei: Text with Introduction, Translation and Commentary*. Princeton.

Caussin de Perceval, A. P. 1847. 2 vols. *Essai sur l'histoire des arabes avant l'islamisme*. Paris.

Chabot, J. B. 1922. *Choix d'inscriptions de Palmyre*. Paris.

Chad, C. 1972. *Les Dynastes d'Emèse*. Beirut.

Chadwick, Henry. 1966. *Early Christian Thought and the Classical Tradition*. Oxford.

———. 1967. *The Early Church*. Harmondsworth.

———. 1990. "A Thoroughly Unecumenical Scene." *TLS*, July 6.

Champdor, Albert. 1953. *Les Ruines de Palmyre*. Paris.

Chapot, Victor. 1907. *La Frontiere de l'Euphrate de Pompée à la conquête arabe*. Paris.

Charbonneaux, J. 1960. "Aion et Philippe l'Arabe." *MEFR* 72:253–72.

Chatwin, Bruce. 1989. *What Am I Doing Here*. London.

Chitty, Derwas. 1977. *The Desert a City*. Crestwood, N.Y.

Christensen, A. 1936. *Iran sous les Sassanides*. Copenhagen.

Collart, P., and J. Vicari. 1969. *Le Sanctuaire de Baalshamin à Palmyre*. Vols. 1–2. Rome.

Colledge, Malcom A. R. 1976a. *The Art of Palmyra*. London.

————. 1976b. "Le temple de Bel: Qui l'a fait, et pourquoi?" In *Palmyre: Bilan et perspectives*, 45–52. Strasbourg.

————. 1987. "Parthian Cultural Elements at Roman Palmyra." *Mesopotamia* 22:19–28.

Crawford, M. H. 1975. "Finance Coinage and Money from the Severans to Constantine." *ANRW* 2.2: 560–93.

Crone, Patricia. 1987. *Meccan Trade and the Rise of Islam*. Oxford.

Cumont, Franz. 1911. *Oriental religions in Roman Paganism*. New York. Originally published in French, 1906.

————. 1912. *Astrology and Religion among the Greeks and Romans*. New York.

————. 1917. *Etudes syriennes*. Paris.

————. 1922–23. *Fouilles de Doura-Europos I–II*. Paris.

————. 1956. *The Mysteries of Mithras*. New York. Originally published as *Les Mystères de Mithras*. (Paris, 1902).

Cureton, W. 1855. *Spicilegium Syriacum*. London.

D'Arms, J. H. 1981. *Commerce and Social Standing in Ancient Rome*. Cambridge, Mass.

Declerck, J. H. 1984. "Deux nouveaux fragments attribuées à Paul de Samosate." *Byzantion* 54:116–40.

Delbrueck, R. 1948. "Uranius of Emesa." *NumChron* 8:11–29.

Dihle, Albrecht. 1984. "Serer und Chinesen." In his *Antike und Orient: Gesammelte Aufsätze*, 201–15. Heidelberg.

Divine, David. 1969. *The Northwest Frontier of Rome*. London.

Dodgeon, Michael, and S. N. C. Lieu. 1991. *The Roman Eastern Frontier and the Persian Wars A.D. 226–323*. London.

Dodwell, Christina. 1987. *A Traveller on Horseback*. London.

Double, L. 1877. *Les Césars de Palmyre*. Paris.

Downey, G. 1950. "Aurelian's Victory over Zenobia at Immae." *TAPA* 81:57–68.

————. 1961. *A History of Antioch in Syria*. Princeton.

Drexhage, Raphaela. 1988. *Studien zum römischen Osthandel*. Bonn.

Drijvers, H. J. W. 1966. *Bardaisan of Edessa*. Assen.

————. 1976. *The Religion of Palmyra*. Leiden.

————. 1977. "Hatra Palmyra and Edessa." *ANRW* 2.8: 799–906.

————. 1984. *East of Antioch: Studies in Early Syriac Christianity*. Leiden.

Drower, E. S. 1937. *The Mandaeans of Iraq and Iran*. Oxford.

Dubs, Homer H. 1957. *A Roman City in Ancient China*. London.

Dunant, C. 1971. *Le Sanctuaire de Baalshamin à Palmyre*. Vol. 3. Rome.

Dussaud, R. 1955. *La pénétration des Arabes en Syrie avant l'Islam*. Paris.

Enmann, Alex. 1884. "Eine verlorene Geschichte der römischen Kaiser." *Philologus*, suppl. 4:335–501.

Ensslin, W. 1949. *Zu den Kriegen des Sassaniden Schapur I*. Munich.

Fauré, Paul. 1987. *Parfums et aromatiques de l'antiquité*. Paris.

Fellmann, R. 1970. *Le Sanctuaire de Baalshamin à Palmyre*. Vol. 5. Rome.

Fellmann, R., and C. Dunant. 1975. *Le Sanctuaire de Baalshamin à Palmyre*. Vol. 6. Rome.

Fentress, E. W. B. 1979. *Numidia and the Roman Army*. Oxford.

Ferguson, John. 1970. *Religions of the Roman Empire*. London.

———. 1978. "China and Rome." *ANRW* 2.9.2: 581–603.

Ferrill, Arthur. 1986. *The Fall of Rome: The Military Explanation*. London.

Février, J. G. 1931a. *Essai sur l'histoire politique et économique de Palmyre*. Paris.

———. 1931b. *La réligion des Palmyréniens*. Paris.

Finley, M. I. 1973. *The Ancient Economy*. London.

Franck, Irene, and David Brownstone. 1986. *The Silk Road*. New York.

Frank, Tenney. 1933–40. *An Economic Survey of Ancient Rome*. Baltimore.

Fraser, Antonia. 1988. *Boadicea's Chariot: The Warrior Queens*. London.

Freeman, P., and D. Kennedy, eds. 1986. *The Defence of the Roman and Byzantine East*. 2. vols. Oxford.

Frézouls, E. 1976. "Questions d'urbanisme palmyrenien." In *Palmyre: Bilan et perspectives*, 191–207. Strasbourg.

———, ed. 1987. *Sociétés urbaines, sociétés rurales dans l'Asie mineure et la Syrie hellénistiques et romaines*. Strasbourg.

Frye, R. N. 1984. *The History of Ancient Iran*. Munich.

Fustel de Coulanges, N. D. 1980. *The Ancient City*. Baltimore. Originally published as *La cité antique* (Paris, 1873).

Gagé, J. 1964. *La montée des Sassanides et l'heure de Palmyre*. Paris.

Garnsey, P., 1976. "Urban Property Investment." In *Studies in Roman Property*, ed. M. I. Finley, 123–36. Cambridge.

Garnsey, P., K. Hopkins, and R. Whittaker. 1983. *Trade in the Ancient Economy*. Cambridge.

Garnsey, P., and R. Saller. 1987. *The Roman Empire*. London.

Gassowska, B. 1982. "Maternus Cynegius, praef.praet. Orientis, and the destruction of the Allat temple in Palmyra." *Archaeologia* 33:107–23.

Gawlikowski, M. 1970. *Monuments funeraires de Palmyre*. Warsaw.

———. 1971. "Inscriptions de Palmyre." *Syria* 48:407–26.

———. 1973. *Palmyre VI: Le temple Palmyrenien*. Warsaw.

———. 1983. "Palmyre et l'Euphrate." *Syria* 60:53–68.

———. 1985. "Les Princes de Palmyre." *Syria* 62:251–61.

———. 1987a. "The Roman Frontier on the Euphrates." *Mesopotamia* 22:71–80.

———. 1987b. "Some Directions and Perspectives of Research: Graeco-Roman Syria." *Mesopotamia* 22:11–17.

———. 1988. "Le commerce de Palmyre sur terre et sur eau." In *L'Arabie et ses mers bordieres*, vol. 1, ed. J. F. Salles, 163–72. Lyon.

Gibbon, Edward. 1909. *The Decline and Fall of the Roman Empire*. 2d ed., ed. J. B. Bury. 7 vols. London.

Glueck, Nelson. 1965. *Deities and Dolphins*. London.

Goodenough, E. R. 1974. *Jewish Symbols in the Greco-Roman Period*. Vol. 11. New Haven, Conn.

Goodhue, Nicholas. 1977. *The Lucus Furrinae and the Sanctuary of the Syrian Gods*. Amsterdam.

Goossens, G. 1943. *Hiérapolis de Syrie*. Louvain.

Graf, David F. 1978. "The Saracens and the Defense of the Arabian Frontier." *BASOR* 229:1–26.

———. 1987. "The Roman Road System of Arabia Petraea," *AJA* 91:389.

———. 1988. "Qura 'Arabiyya and Provincia Arabia." In *Géographie Historique au Proche-Orient*, 171–211. Paris.

———. 1989a. "Rome and the Saracens." In *L'Arabie préislamique et son environnement historique et culturel*, ed. T. Fahd, 341–400. Leiden.

———. 1989b. "Les routes romaines d'Arabie Petrée." *Le Monde de la Bible* 59:54–56.

———. 1989c. "Zenobia and the Arabs." In *The Eastern Frontier of the Roman Empire*, ed. D. H. French and C. S. Lightfoot, 1:143–67. Oxford.

Grainger, J. D. 1990. *The Cities of Seleukid Syria*. Oxford.

Grant, C. P. 1937. *The Syrian Desert*. London.

Groom, Nigel. 1981. *Frankincense and Myrrh*. London.

Halsberghe, G. 1972. *Sol Invictus*. Leiden.

Harl, Kenneth. 1987. *Civic Coins and Civic Politics in the Roman East A.D. 180–275*. Berkeley and Los Angeles.

Harper, George M. 1928. "Village Administration in the Roman Province of Syria." *YCS* 1: 105–168.

Haussig, H. W. 1983. *Die Geschichte Zentralasiens und der Seidenstrasse in vorislamischer Zeit*. Darmstadt.

Hengel, Martin. 1974. *Judaism and Hellenism*. London.

———. 1980. *Jews, Greeks and Barbarians*. London.

Heurgon, J. 1942. *Etude sur les inscriptions osques de Capoue dites iuvilas*. Paris.

Hirth, F. [1885] 1975. *China and the Roman Orient*. Shanghai and Hong Kong. Reprint. Chicago.

Hitti, P. K. 1940. *History of the Arabs*. London.

———. 1957. *History of Syria*. London.

Homo, Leon. 1904. *Essai sur le regne de l'empereur Aurelien*. Paris.

Hopkins, Clark. 1979. *The Discovery of Dura-Europus*. New Haven, Conn.

Hopkirk, Peter. 1980. *Foreign Devils on the Silk Road*. Oxford.

Ingholt, Harald, H. Seyrig, and J. Starcky. 1955. *Recueil des tesseres de Palmyre*. Paris.

Isaac, Benjamin. 1984. "Bandits in Judaea and Arabia." *HSCP* 88: 171–204.

———. 1990. *The Limits of Empire: The Roman Army in the East*. Oxford.

Jamme, A. 1963. *The Al-'Uqlah Texts*. Documentation sud-Arabe 3. Washington.

Jeffreys, E., B. Croke, and R. Scott. 1990. *Studies in John Malalas*. Sydney.

Jones, A. H. M. 1937. *Cities of the Eastern Roman Provinces*. Oxford.

———. 1940. *The Greek City from Alexander to Justinian*. Oxford.

Jones, C. P. 1978. "A Syrian in Lyon." *AJP* 99:336–53.

Kantorowicz, E. 1963. "Oriens Augusti—Lever du Roi." *DOP* 17:119–77.

Keay, S. 1988. *Roman Spain*. London.

Kennedy, David. 1981. "Auxilia and Numeri Raised in the Roman Province of Syria." Ph.D. diss., Oxford.

Kennedy, David, and A. Northedge. 1988. *Excavations at 'Ana*. Chichester.

Kennedy, David, and Derrick Riley. 1990. *Rome's Desert Frontier from the Air*. London.

Kennedy, Hugh, 1985. "From Polis to Madina: Urban Change in Late Antique and Early Islamic Syria." *Past and Present* 106-9:3-27.

Keppie, Lawrence. 1984. *The Making of the Roman Army: From Republic to Empire*. London.

Khouri, Rami. 1986a. *Jerash: A Frontier City of the Roman East*. London.

———. 1986b. *Petra. A Guide to the Capital of the Nabataeans*. London.

Klengel, Horst. 1987. *Syrien zwischen Alexander und Mohammed*. Berlin.

Koenen, L., and A. Henrichs. 1970. "Ein griechischer Mani-Kodex." *ZPE* 5:97-216.

———. 1975. "Der Kölner Mani-Kodex." *ZPE* 19:1-85.

———. 1978. "Der Kölner Mani-Kodex." *ZPE* 32:87-199.

———. 1981. "Der Kölner Mani-Kodex." *ZPE* 44:201-318.

———. 1982. "Der Kölner Mani-Kodex." *ZPE* 48:1-59.

Krencker, D., and W. Zschietzschmann. 1938. *Römische Tempel in Syrien*. Berlin.

Künzl, E. 1988. *Der Römische Triumph: Siegesfeiern im antiken Rom*. Munich.

Lamberton, Robert. 1986. *Homer the Theologian*. Berkeley and Los Angeles.

Lane Fox, R. 1986. *Pagans and Christians*. London.

Lauffray, J. 1983. *Halabiyya-Zenobia*. Paris.

Lawrence, T. E. 1935. *Seven Pillars of Wisdom*. London.

Leggett, W. F. 1949. *The Story of Silk*. London.

Leonard, A. G. 1894. *The Camel: Its Uses and Management*. London.

Lepper, F. 1948. *Trajan's Parthian War*. Oxford.

Levick, B. M. 1985. *The Government of the Roman Empire*. Beckenham.

Lewis, Norman N. 1987. *Nomads and Settlers in Syria and Jordan, 1880-1980*. Cambridge.

Liebeschuetz, J. H. W. G. 1972. *Antioch: City and Imperial Administration in the Later Roman Empire*. Oxford.

Lieu, S. N. C. 1985. *Manichaeism in the Later Roman Empire and Mediaeval China*. Manchester.

Littman, Enno. 1904. *Semitic Inscriptions*. Part 4 of the publications of an American Archaeological Expedition to Syria in 1899-1900. New York.

Luttwak, Edward N. 1976. *The Grand Strategy of the Roman Empire*. Baltimore.

McAdam, H. I., and D. F. Graf. 1989. "Inscriptions from the Southern Hawran Survey 1985." *ADAJ* 33:177-97.

McCullough, W. Stewart. 1982. *A Short History of Syriac Christianity to the Rise of Islam*. Chico, Calif.

McDermot, B. C. 1954. "Roman Emperors in the Sassanian Reliefs." *JRS* 44:76-80.

MacDonald, David. 1986. "Dating the Fall of Dura-Europus." *Historia* 35: 45-68.

MacDonald, William L. 1986. *The Architecture of the Roman Empire*. Vol. 2. New Haven, Conn.

McElderry, R. K. 1909. "The Legions of the Euphrates Frontier." *CQ* 3:44–53.

MacMullen, Ramsay. 1963. *Soldier and Civilian in the Later Roman Empire.* Cambridge, Mass.

——. 1966. *Enemies of the Roman Order.* Cambridge, Mass.

——. 1974. *Roman Social relations.* New Haven, Conn.

——. 1976. *The Roman Government's Response to Crisis 235–337.* New Haven, Conn.

——. 1981. *Paganism in the Roman Empire.* New Haven, Conn.

——. 1984. *Christianizing the Roman Empire.* New Haven, Conn.

Macurdy, Grace H. 1937. *Vassal Queens of the Roman Empire.* Baltimore.

Maricq, A. 1958. "Classica et Orientalia 5: *Res Gestae divi Saporis.*" *Syria* 5:295–360.

Matthews, J. F. 1973. "Symmachus and the Oriental Cults." *JRS* 63:175–95.

——. 1975. *Western Aristocracies and Imperial Court.* Oxford.

——. 1984. "The Tax Law of Palmyra: Evidence for Economic History in a City of the Roman East." *JRS* 74:157–180.

——. 1989. *The Roman Empire of Ammianus.* London.

Mattingly, H. 1936. "The Palmyrene Princes." *NumChron* 5:91, 105.

Meeks, W. A., and R. L. Wilken. 1978. *Jews and Christians in Antioch in the First Four Centuries of the Common Era.* Missoula.

Mesnil du Buisson, Comte du. 1962. *Les tessères et les monnaies de Palmyre.* Paris.

Michalowski, Kazimierz. 1960–. *Palmyra.* London.

Milik, J. T. 1972. *Dedicaces faites par des dieux (Palmyre, Hatra, Tyr) et des thiases semitiques à l'époque romaine.* Paris.

Millar, F. G. B. 1969. "P. Herennius Dexippus: The Greek World and the Third-Century Invasions." *JRS* 59:12–29.

——. 1971. "Paul of Samosata, Zenobia and Aurelian: The Church, Local Culture and Political Allegiance in Third-Century Syria." *JRS* 61:1–17.

——. 1982. "Emperors, Frontiers and Foreign Relations 31 B.C.–A.D. 378." *Britannia* 13:1–23.

——. 1987a. "Empire, Community and Culture in the Roman Near East: Greeks, Syrians, Jews and Arabs." *JJS* 38:143–64.

——. 1987b. "The Problem of Hellenistic Syria." In *Hellenism in the East*, ed. A. Kuhrt and S. Sherwin-White, 110–33. London.

Miller, J. Innes. 1969. *The Spice Trade of the Roman Empire.* Oxford.

Mitchell, S. 1987. "Imperial Building in the Eastern Roman Provinces." *HSCP* 91:333–65.

Momigliano, Arnaldo. 1987. *On Pagans, Jews and Christians.* Middletown, Conn.

Mommsen, Theodor. 1908–13. *History of Rome.* London.

——. 1909. *The Provinces of the Roman Empire from Caesar to Diocletian.* Tr. W. P. Dickson. 2 vols. London.

Moorehead, Alan. 1963. *Cooper's Creek.* London.

Musil, Alois. 1928. *Palmyrena: A Topographical Itinerary.* New York.

Nilsson, Martin. 1952. *Opuscula selecta.* 2:462–504. Lund.

——. 1961. *Geschichte der griechischen Religion.* Vol. 2. 2d ed. Munich.

Nodelman, S. A. 1960. "A Preliminary History of Characene." *Berytus* 13:83–121.

Oden, R. A. 1977. *Studies in Lucian's De Syria Dea*. Missoula.

Olmstead, A. T. 1942. "The Mid-third Century of the Christian Era." *ClPhil* 37:241–62, 398–420.

Palmyre: Fouilles polonaises I–VIII. 1959–84. Vols. 1–6, ed. Kazimierz Michalowski; vol. 7, ed. Anna Sadurska; vol. 8, ed. Michael Gawlikowski. Warsaw, The Hague, and Paris.

Palmyra: Geschichte, Kunst und Kultur der syrischen Oasenstadt. 1987. Exhibition catalogue. Linz.

Palmyre: Bilan et Perspectives. 1976. Strasbourg.

Parker, H. M. D. 1958. *The Roman Legions*. Cambridge.

Parker, S. Thomas. 1986. *Romans and Saracens: A History of the Arabian Frontier*. Winona Lake, Ind.

Parsons, P. J. 1967. "A Proclamation of Vaballathus?" *ChrEg* 84:397–401.

Patlagean, Evelyne. 1977. *Pauvreté économique et pauvreté sociale à Byzance: 4e–7e siècle*. Paris and The Hague.

Payne, Robert. 1962. *The Roman Triumph*. London.

Perkins, Ann. 1971. *The Art of Dura-Europos*. Oxford.

Peters, F. E. 1978. "Romans and Bedouin in Southern Syria." *JNES* 37:315–26.

Philby, H. St. J. 1981. *The Queen of Sheba*. London.

Pilpay 1987. *Fables*. London.

Piotrovskii, M. 1970. "Arabskaya Versiya Istorii Tsaritsy Zenobii (Az-Zabby)." *Palestinskii Sbornik* 21:170–83.

Pohlsander, H. A. 1980. "Philip the Arab and Christianity." *Historia* 29:463–73.

Poidebard, A. 1934. *La Trace de Rome dans le désert de Syrie*. Paris.

Potter, David S. 1990. *Prophecy and History in the Crisis of the Roman Empire: A Historical Commentary on the Thirteenth Sibylline Oracle*. Oxford.

Potter, T. W. 1987. *Roman Italy*. London.

Prentice, W. K. 1908. *Greek and Latin Inscriptions*. Part 3 of Publications of an American Archaeological Expedition to Syria 1899–1900. New York.

Price, M. J. 1973. "The Lost Year: Greek Light on a Problem of Roman Chronology." *NumChron*, ser. 7, 13:75–86.

Pritchard, J. B. 1974. *Solomon and Sheba*. London.

Puech, H. C. 1949. *Le manichéisme, son fondateur, sa doctrine*. Paris.

Ragette, F. 1980. *Baalbek*. London.

Rajak, Tessa. 1983. *Josephus*. London.

Rashke, M. G. 1978. "New Studies in Roman Commerce with the East." *ANRW* 2.9.2: 604–1378.

Rea, J. R. 1967. "A Letter of Severus Alexander?" *ChrEg* 84:391–96.

———. 1972. *P.Oxy.* 11.15–26.

Renan, Ernest. 1869. *The Apostles*. London. Originally published as *Les Apôtres* (Paris, 1866).

———. n.d. *Marcus Aurelius and the End of the Ancient World*. Tr. W. G. Hutchinson. London.

Reville, J. 1886. *La réligion à Rome sous les Sévères*. Paris.

Rey-Coquais, J. P. 1978. "Syrie romaine de Poppée à Diocletien." *JRS* 68:44–73.
Richmond, I. A. 1963. "Palmyra under the Aegis of Rome." *JRS* 53:43–54.
Rickman, Geoffrey. 1980. *The Corn Supply of Ancient Rome.* Oxford.
Riedmatten, H. de, 1952. *Les actes du procès de Paul de Samosate.* Fribourg.
Rosenthal, F. 1936. *Die Sprache der palmyrenischen Inschriften.* Leipzig.
Rostovtzeff, Michael. 1932a. *Caravan Cities.* Oxford.
———. 1932b. "The Caravan Gods of Palmyra." *JRS* 22:107–16.
———. 1933. "Hadad and Atargatis at Palmyra." *AJA* 37:58–63, pl. 9.
———. 1938. *Dura-Europos and its Art.* Oxford.
———. 1943. "Res gestae divi Saporis and Dura." *Berytus* 8:17–60.
———. 1957. *The Social and Economic History of the Roman Empire.* 2d ed. Oxford.
Runciman, Steven. 1955. *The Medieval Manichee.* Cambridge.
Ste. Croix, G. E. M. de. 1972. *The Origins of the Peloponnesian War.* London.
Sallet, A. von. 1866. *Die Fürsten von Palmyra.* Berlin.
Schlumberger, D. 1951. *La Palmyrène du nord-ouest.* Paris.
———. 1972. "Vorod l'agoranome." *Syria* 48:339–41.
Schmitthenner, W. 1979. "Rome and India: Aspects of Universal History during the Principate." *JRS* 69:90–106.
Schober, Joseph. 1930. *Silk and Silk Industry.* London.
Schwartz, Jacques. 1960. "L'empire romain et le commerce oriental." *Annales* (Jan–Feb): 18–44.
———. 1976. "Palmyre et l'opposition à Rome en Egypte." In *Palmyre: Bilan et Perspectives,* 139–51. Strasbourg.
———. 1986. "L'Histoire Auguste et Palmyre." In *Bonner Historia Augusta Colloquium 1964/5,* 185–95. Bonn.
Segal, J. B. 1963. "The Sabian Mysteries: The Planet Cult of Ancient Harran." In *Vanished Civilisations,* ed. E. Bacon, 201–20.
———. 1970. *Edessa: The Blessed City.* Oxford.
Seller, Abednego. 1705. *The Antiquities of Palmyra, alias Tadmor.* 2d ed. London.
Seyrig, Henri. 1933. "Nouveaux monuments palmyréniens des cultes de Bêl et de Baalshamin." *Syria* 14:253–82.
———. 1936. "Inscription relative au commerce maritime de Palmyre." In *Mélanges Cumont,* vol. 1, 397–402. Paris.
———. 1937a. "Note sur Hérodien, prince de Palmyre." *Syria* 18:1–4.
———. 1937b. "Armes et costumes Iraniennes de Palmyre." *Syria* 18:4–31.
———. 1941a. "Les inscriptions de Bostra." *Syria* 22:44–48.
———. 1941b. "Inscriptions grecques de l'agora de Palmyre." *Syria* 22:223–70.
———. 1950. "Palmyra and the East." *JRS* 40:1–7.
———. 1963. "Les fils du roi Odainat." *AAS* 13:171–72. In his *Scripta Varia,* 265–78. Paris, 1985.
———. 1971. "Le Culte du soleil en Syrie à l'époque romaine." *Syria* 48: 337–73.
Seyrig, Henri, et al. 1975. *Le Temple de Bêl à Palmyre.* BAH 83. Paris.
Shahid, Irfan. 1984a. *Byzantium and the Arabs in the Fourth Century.* Washington, D.C.

———. 1984b. *Rome and the Arabs.* Washington, D.C.

———. 1989. *Byzantium and the Arabs in the Fifth Century.* Washington, D.C.

Shapley, F. R. 1974. "Tiepolo's Zenobia Cycle." In *Hortus Imaginum: Essays in Western Art,* ed. R. Enggass and M. Stokstad, 193–98. Lawrence, Kans.

Shaw, Brent. 1982–83. "'Eaters of Flesh, Drinkers of Milk': The Ancient Mediterranean Ideology of the Pastoral Nomad." *Ancient Society* 13/14:5–31.

———. 1987. "The Family in Late Antiquity: The Experience of Augustine." *Past & Present* 115:3–51.

Sherwin-White, A. N. 1973. *The Roman Citizenship.* Oxford.

———. 1984. *Roman Foreign Policy in the East.* London.

Sidebotham, Steven. E. 1986. *Roman Economic Policy in the Erythra Thalassa: 30 B.C.–A.D. 217. Mnemosyne,* suppl. 91.

Speidel, M. P. 1978. *The Religion of Jupiter Dolichenus in the Roman Army.* Leiden.

———. 1984. "Palmyrenian Irregulars at Koptos." *BASP* 21:22–24.

Starcky, J. 1952. *Palmyre.* Paris.

———. 1965. "Nouvelles stèles funéraires à Petra." *ADAJ* 10:43–49.

Starcky, J., and M. Gawlikowski. 1985. *Palmyre.* Rev. ed. Paris.

Starcky, J., and S. Munajjed. 1948. *Palmyre.* Damascus.

Stark, Freya. 1966. *Rome on the Euphrates.* London.

Stark, J. K. 1971. *Personal Names in Palmyrene Inscriptions.* Oxford.

Stein, A. 1923. "Kallinikos von Petra." *Hermes* 58:448–56.

———. 1941. "The Ancient Trade Route Past Hatra and Its Roman Posts." *JRAS* 299–316.

Sullivan, R. D. 1977. "The Dynasty of Emesa." *ANRW* 2.8: 198–219.

Syme, Ronald. 1939. *The Roman Revolution.* Oxford.

———. 1968. *Ammianus and the Historia Augusta.* Oxford.

———. 1971a. *Emperors and Biography.* Oxford.

———. 1971b. *The Historia Augusta: A Call for Clarity.* Bonn.

———. 1983. *Historia Augusta Papers.* Oxford.

Tarn, W. W. 1951. *The Greeks in Bactria and India.* Cambridge.

Tchalenko, G. 1953–58. *Villages antiques de la Syrie du nord.* Vols. 1–3. Paris.

Teggart, F. J. 1939. *Rome and China.* Berkeley and Los Angeles.

Teixidor, J. 1963. "Deux Inscriptions Palmyréniennes du Musée de Bagdad. *Syria* 40:33–46.

———. 1977. *The Pagan God.* Princeton.

———. 1979. *The Pantheon of Palmyra.* Leiden.

———. 1984. *Un port romain du désert, Palmyre.* Semitica 34. Paris.

Tlass, Mustafa. 1986. *Zénobie de Palmyre.* Damascus.

Todd, Malcolm. 1978. *The Walls of Rome.* London.

Turcan, R. 1978. *Le culte impérial au IIIe siecle.* Paris.

———. 1989. *Les Cultes orientaux dans le monde romain.* Paris.

Turton, Godfrey. 1974. *The Syrian Princesses.* London.

Vaughan, Agnes Carr. 1967. *Zenobia of Palmyra.* New York.

Versnel, H. 1970. *Triumphus.* Leiden.

Veyne, Paul. 1988. *Did the Greeks Believe in Their Myths?* Chicago. Originally published as *Les Grecs ont-ils crus à leurs mythes?* (Paris, 1983).

―――. 1989. *Bread and Circuses*. London.

Vööbus, A. 1958-60. *History of Asceticism in the Syrian Orient*. Vols. 1-2. Louvain.

Vollmer, John E., E. J. Keall, and E. Nagai-Berthrong. 1983. *Silk Roads—China Ships*. Exhibition catalog. Toronto.

Walden, J. H. W. 1912. *The Universities of Ancient Greece*. New York.

Wallace-Hadrill, Andrew, and John Rich. 1990. *City and Country in the Ancient World*. London.

Ware, William. 1889. *Zenobia, Queen of Palmyra*. London.

Warmington, E. H. 1928. *The Commerce between the Roman Empire and the East*. Cambridge.

Waterson, Merlin. 1990. *The Servants' Hall: The Domestic History of a Country House*. London.

Watkin, D. and T. Mellinghoff. 1987. *German Architecture and the Classical Ideal 1740-1840*. London.

Weber, Max. 1976. *The Agrarian Sociology of Ancient Civilizations*. London.

Webster, Graham. 1985. *The Roman Imperial Army*. 3d ed. London.

Weiss, Harvey, ed. 1985. *Ebla to Damascus: Art and Archaeology of Ancient Syria*. Exhibition catalog. Washington, D.C.

Wells, C. M. 1982. *Roman Africa*. Ottawa.

Weulersse, J. 1946. *Paysans de Syrie et Proche-Orient*. N.p.

Wheeler, Mortimer. 1954. *Rome beyond the Imperial Frontiers*. Harmondsworth.

Widengren, Geo. 1965. *Mani and Manichaeism*. London. Originally published in German, 1960.

Wiegand, Th. 1932. *Palmyra: Ergebnisse der Expeditionen von 1902-1917*. Berlin.

Wilken, R. L. 1983. *John Chrysostom and the Jews*. Berkeley and Los Angeles.

Will, E. 1949. "La tour funéraire de Palmyre." *Syria* 26:87-116.

―――. 1957. "Marchands et chefs de caravanes à Palmyre." *Syria* 34:262-77.

―――. 1959. "Une figure du culte solaire d'Aurélien: Juppiter consul vel consulens." *Syria* 36:193-205.

―――. 1974. "Juppiter Consul ou un Bêl fantomatique." *Syria* 51:226-29.

―――. 1983. "Le développement urbain de Palmyre: Temoignages épigraphiques anciens et nouveaux." *Syria* 60:69-81.

―――. 1985a. "La déesse au chien de Palmyre." *Syria* 62:149-55.

―――. 1985b. "Pline l'ancien et Palmyre: un problème d'histoire ou d'histoire littéraire?" *Syria* 62:263-69.

Williams, Stephen. 1985. *Diocletian and the Roman Recovery*. London.

Wilson, A. N. 1988. *Tolstoy*. London.

Winkworth, C. 1924. "On heathen deities in the doctrine of Addai." *JThS* 25:402-3.

Winter, Engelbert. 1988. *Die sassanidisch-römischen Friedensverträge des 3. Jahrhunderts n. Chr.* Frankfurt.

Wissmann, H. von. 1976. "Die Geschichte des Sabäerreiches und der Feldzug des Aelius Gallus." *ANRW* 2.9: 1. Berlin.

Woodman, A. J. 1988. *Rhetoric in Classical Historiography*. London and Portland, Oreg.

Wright, William. 1894. *A Short History of Syriac Literature*. London.
———. 1895. *Palmyra and Zenobia*. London.
Zaehner, R. C. 1961. *The Dawn and Twilight of Zoroastrianism*. London.

Selected Travel and Literary Works Relevant to Zenobia and Palmyra

Addison, Charles G. 1838. *Damascus and Palmyra: A Journey to the East*. London.
Baron, Alexander. 1956. *Queen of the East*. Novel. London.
Beaufort, Emily A. 1861–62. *Egyptian Sepulchres and Syrian Shrines*. London.
Belgiojoso, Cristina Princess Barbiano di. 1858. *Asie Mineure et Syrie*. Paris.
Bell, Gertrude. 1907. *The Desert and the Sown*. London.
Benjamin of Tudela. 1907. *Itinerary*. Ed. M. N. Adler. London.
Boccaccio, Giovanni. 1964. *De claris mulieribus*. Trans. G. A. Guarino. London.
Bonavia, Judy. 1988. *Collins Illustrated Guide to the Silk Road*. London.
Burckhardt, John Lewis. 1822. *Travels in Syria*. London.
Burton, Isabel. 1875. *The Inner Life of Syria, Palestine and the Holy Land*. London.
Carruthers, Douglas. 1929. *The Desert Route to India*. Contains the diaries of Bartholomew Plaisted, Gaylard Roberts and son, John Carmichael, and William Beawes, and also an extensive bibliography of travelers. Hakluyt Society publ. ser. 2, no. 63. London.
Cassas, L. F. 1799. *Voyage pittoresque de la Syrie*. Paris.
Chaucer, Geoffrey. 1966. *Works*. Ed. F. N. Robinson. Oxford.
Childs, Virginia. 1990. *Lady Hester Stanhope*. London.
Dawkins, James, and Robert Wood, 1753. *The Ruins of Palmyra*. London.
Halifax, William. [1695] 1890. *A Relation of a Voyage to Tadmor begun ye 29th Sep 1691*. Reprint. Ed. C. R. Cowder. London.
Haslip, Joan. 1934. *Lady Hester Stanhope: A Biography*. London.
Irby, C. L., and J. Mangles. 1823. *Travels in Egypt, Nubia, Syria, Asia Minor 1817–1818*. London.
Jenner, Michael. 1986. *Syria in View*. Photographic essay. London.
Jonson, Ben. *The Masque of Queenes*.
Meryon, Dr. Charles. 1846. *Travels of Lady Hester Stanhope*. London.
Michell, Nicholas. 1854. *Ruins of Many Lands*. 4th ed. Poems. London.
Odenthal, Johannes. 1983. *Syrien. DuMont Kunst-Reiseführer*. Cologne.
Scott, Sir Walter. 1815. *Guy Mannering*. Edinburgh.
Skene, F. M. 1864. *Rambles in the Deserts of Syria*. London.
Testi, Fulvio. 1659. *L'Arsinda, ovvero La Discendenza dei Ser[enissi]mi prencipi d'Este*. Play. Venice.
Thubron, Colin. 1967. *Mirror to Damascus*. London.
Volney, C. F. C. Comte de. 1787. *Voyage en Syrie et en Egypte*. Paris.
———. 1791. *The Ruins; or, Meditations on the Revolutions of Empires*. London.

Index

Abercius, St., 147-48
Abgar (king of Edessa), 20, 22, 134, 136
Abraham, 22, 48, 114, 140, 145
Adams, W. Marsham, 162, 199
Adda-Guppi, Queen, 119
Addai, 134
Addison, Charles, 194
Aelana, 35
Agriculture, 19, 24; at Palmyra, 54-57
Agrippa, Marcus, 21
Alexander the Great, 23, 32, 40, 46-47, 82, 87, 108, 123, 145, 168, 169
Alexander of Palmyra, 5
Alexander Severus, 77, 91, 98, 145, 162
Alexander the Sleepless, 192
Alexandria, 2, 59, 89, 131, 164, 179
Amelius, 132
Ammianus Marcellinus, 38, 47; quoted, 92, 103; on siege weapons, 173-74
'Amr ibn 'Adi, 157, 189
Annals of the Han Dynasty, 41
Antioch, 2, 18, 19, 20, 22-23, 25, 43, 66, 93, 94, 102-3, 117, 127, 144, 147, 148, 150-51, 164, 165, 166-67, 168-69, 177, 190; battle of, 169-70
Antiochus (Zenobia's successor), 127, 178
Antiochus IV Epiphanes, 2, 22, 112, 118
Antipater of Gadara, 21
Antipater of Sidon, 132

Antoninus, Marcus, Emperor, 42, 44, 60
Antony, Mark, 4, 20, 53, 84, 118
Antony, St., 3, 148, 155
Apamea, 20, 66, 88, 93, 132, 148, 166, 190, 191
Aphaca, 72, 153, 176
Apicius, 9, 33-34
Apollonius of Tyana, 22, 131, 145, 146, 167-68, 177
Appian, quoted, 31, 38, 53
Apsaeus, Septimius, 122, 178
Arabia (Arabs), 1, 48, 75, 83, 101; as "happy" country, 33; kings of southern, 122; queens of, 118-21; Zenobia attacks, 158
Ardashir, 90, 156
Armenia, 19, 21, 83, 85-87, 88, 119, 166
Artaud, Antonin, 141-43, 144
Assyria, 26, 83
Astrology, 135-36, 141, 146, 148, 152-53
Athens, 2, 22, 51, 131-33
Augustine, St., 8, 74, 96, 114; quoted, 140
Augustus, Caesar, 31, 36, 43, 81, 87, 132, 160
Aurelian, Emperor, 1, 2, 3, 4, 5, 10, 17, 39, 108, 117, 118, 121, 129, 132, 150, 162; accession, 159; attacks Palmyra, 165-77, 179; coinage, 99-100; devotion to sun, 183-87; general account of, 163-65; triumph of, 181-83; walls, 165
Aurelius, Marcus, Emperor, 41, 134, 162

Auxiliaries, 27–28, 99, 167
Avidius Cassius, 162

Babylon, 45, 64, 73, 119, 146
Bactra, 40, 43
Ballista (pretender), 105–6
Baqqa, 156–57
Barbalissus, 93, 104
Barbarian invasions, 97–98, 155, 165
Bardaisan of Edessa, 134–36, 146, 148, 191
Baron, Alexander, 4, 118, 123, 200; fantasizes about prostitutes, 59; on Paul of Samosata, 149–50; romance of Aurelian and Zenobia, 162
Batnae: fair at, 19, 48; conquered by Shapur, 93
Bedouin, 20, 26, 60, 74, 106, 127, 173; legends of Palmyra, 17
Bedouinization, 208N.24
Bell, Gertrude, quoted, 23, 169
Benjamin of Tudela, 192–93
Berenice (port), 37
Berytus, 20; law school and black magic at, 21
Beth She'arim, 122, 152
Bishapur, 94, 95
Black Stones, 141–43
Boccaccio, Giovanni, 119
Bosporan kingdom, 85, 88
Bostra, 35, 38, 66, 100, 145, 158
Brigands (bandits), 24, 38, 43, 81, 100, 173, 191
Burton, Isabel, 62
Burton, Sir Richard, 69

Callinicum, 125, 177, 190
Callinicus of Petra, 131, 177
Camels, 15, 24, 51, 70, 168; importance of 48–49; not suicidal, 48
Canatha (Qanawat), 30, 68
Caracalla, 28, 53, 82, 89–90, 99, 143, 162, 184
Carrhae (Harran), 22, 72, 84, 90, 91, 93–94, 105, 106, 114, 140, 162
Cataphracts, 91–92

Charax, Characene. See Spasinou Charax
Chaucer, Geoffrey, 111, 112–13, 197
China (Chinese), 34, 39–47
Christianity (christians), 3, 73, 94, 131, 134–35, 136–40, 185, 190; acknowledged by Aurelian, 151; cause fall of Rome?, 8; on chastity, 114; criticised in Historia Augusta?, 9; at Dura-Europos, 104; heresies, 147; persecution, 187; of Philip the Arab, 101; in Syria, 146–51
Cicero, 58, 132, 145
Circesium, 47, 93, 173
Cities, 24–25, 28–29
Claudius, Emperor, 2, 155, 159, 163
Cleanthes, 145
Cleopatra, 4, 5, 18, 112, 118, 123, 124, 131, 185
Coinage, 99–100; debased in Rome, 164; of Zenobia and Wahballath, 159–60
Commodian, 97
Constantine, Emperor, 4, 172, 186
Coptos, 36, 37, 60
Corbulo, 21, 28, 68, 87, 166
Crassus, Marcus, 2; defeat at Carrhae, 22, 83–85, 140, 171
Creticus Silanus, 2, 17, 53
Crispinus (prefect), 77
Ctesiphon, 2, 21, 44, 87, 88, 89, 96, 107, 108, 188
Cyriades. See Mareades

Damascius (Life of Isidore), 133; quoted, 142–43
Damascus, 19, 47, 62; museum, 66, 105
Daphne (suburb of Antioch), 23, 148, 169; battle at, 170–71
David: at Dura, 104; kills Goliath at Palmyra, 17; psalms of, 136
Dexippus, 8
Dictys the Cretan, 9
Dido, 120, 123

Dio, Cassius, 10, 108; quoted, 36, 89
Diocletian, Emperor, 4, 5, 24, 186, 188; baths at Palmyra, 67, 124, 190; camp of Palmyra, 124; price edict, 33
Double, L., quoted, 15
Dura-Europos, 3, 19, 20, 48, 66, 91, 93, 125, 139, 140, 151, 165, 167, 190; general description, 104-5

Ebla, 65, 119
Ecbatana, 44, 119
Edessa, 20, 22, 72, 90, 94, 148
Efqa (spring), 52, 71, 72
Egypt, 155, 158-59, 160-61, 165, 178-79
Elagabalus, Emperor, 18, 22, 39, 98, 141, 143-45, 162, 184, 186
Emesa, 19, 22, 28, 53, 77, 101, 105, 130, 133, 141, 142, 144-45, 153, 155, 168, 170-72, 177, 186
Ephorus, 8
Ephraim, St., 136, 138, 141, 191-92
Epiphania, 19
Epiphanius, 130
Euergetism, 63
Eunapius, 29, 130
Eusebius, 134, 135, 149-50
Eutropius, 10

Firdausi, Shahnameh, 94
Firmicus Maternus, 146
Firmus (of Egypt), 113, 178-79
Fish, sacred, 22, 139
Friendly kings, 28, 85
Frontier, roman eastern, 81-82, 87

Gadara, 20, 21, 38, 131-32
Gallienus, Emperor, 2, 3, 78, 97, 101, 105-6, 108, 155, 161, 185, 186
Gallus, Aelius, 36
Gaul (Gallic Empire), 160, 163-64
Gaza, 35
Genethlius of Petra, 131
Gennaes (merchant post), 61

Gerasa (Jerash), 20, 21, 38, 70, 146
Germanicus, 52, 58
Gibbon, Edward, 5, 11, 13, 25, 134; on Elagabalus, 144; on Longinus, 113, 130; on luxury, 31; on Odenathus, 106-7; on Philip's Secular Games, 100; on Shapur, 94; on silk, 39; on silk road, 43
Gnosticism, 136, 147
Gods: Aglibol, 65, 72, 73-75; Allah, 65, 141; Allat, 65, 71, 74, 75, 141; anonymous, 70, 71, 152; Apollo, 153, 172, 176; Arsu and Azizu, 48, 68, 71, 75; Artemis-Azzanathkona, 104, 139; Astarte, 70, 139, 144, 153; Atargatis, 68, 71, 135, 139; Baal of Heliopolis, 29; Baal of Tyre, 70; Baalshamin, 71, 73, 139; Bel, 27, 62, 64, 71, 73, 77, 139, 177; Bol, 71; Christ, 75, 95, 187; Derceto, 119, 139; Djennaye, 75; Du-rahlun, 71; Elagabal, 22, 29, 141-44, 171, 183; Elqonera, 73; Gadde, 75, 139; Jupiter Dolichenus, 75, 104, 140, 148; Malakbel, 65, 72, 73-75; Melqart, 70: Mithras, 75, 104, 139, 140, 185; Nebo, 65, 119; Sams, 74, Selene, 123-24; Semitic triads, 70; Sin, 22, 140; Syrian Goddess, 22, 29, 140; Yahweh, 71; Yarhibol, 71, 74, 75, 143, 153; Yarhibol of Dura, 104, 139; Yarhibol of Palmyra, 70-75, 104, 139; Yarhibol of Syria, 29, 135. *See also* Sun; Temples
Golden Fleece, 40
Gordian emperors, 93, 98, 100, 164
Grand Strategy, 87-88
Gregory the wonder-worker, 134

Haddudan, Septimius, 77, 127, 177
Haddudan Hadda, Maqqai, 78
Hadrian, Emperor, 8, 28, 38, 53, 54, 60, 65, 98; Hadrian's Wall, 81, 127

Hairan(es), Septimius, 77, 78, 111–12
Halifax, William, 193
Hama. *See* Epiphania
Harmonius, 136, 191
Harran. *See* Carrhae
Hatra, 68, 91, 188
Hedelin, Abbe, 162, 198
Heliodorus, 133; quoted, 91–92
Heliopolis (Baalbek), 17, 20, 22, 143
Herennianus (son of Zenobia), 6, 114–15
Herodes (Hairan), 78, 79, 108, 114
Herodian, quoted, 89–90, 91
Herodianus (? son of Zenobia), 114–15
Herodotus, 25, 119
Hierapolis (Membij), 22, 72, 93, 103, 119, 126, 139, 142, 190
Historia Augusta, 6, 8–9, 90, 97–98, 106, 130, 158, 173; on angel of Antioch, 170; on Apollonius of Tyana, 167; on Aurelian, 163–64, 181–82; on Firmus, 178–79; on Herodes, 79; on letters of Aurelian and Zenobia, 175–76; on Mareades, 102; on Severus Alexander, 145; on Zenobia, 112, 114, 121–22, 160
Hit, 19, 47
Holy men, 191–92
Homs. *See* Emesa
Hymn of the Soul, 45, 136–38

Iamblichus: novelist, 133; philosopher, 146
Immae, Battle of, 8, 170
Imru, l-Qais, 124, 157, 190
India, 35, 38, 96
Inflation, 98–100
Irby and Mangles, 194
Isidore of Charax, 43, 87

Jadhima, king of Tanukh, 156–58, 189
Jerusalem, 17, 20, 22, 88; Palmyrene bishops of, 133

Jesus, 22, 73
Jews, 3, 30, 72, 139, 148, 152
John Chrysostom, 150
Josephus, 72, 73, 146, 160, 168
Joshua the Stylite, quoted, 72
Jotapian, 101
Judaea, 20, 21, 85, 88, 94, 122
Judaism, 18, 71, 134, 146, 151–53
Julia Domna, 65, 121, 131–32, 143, 162
Julia Mamaea, 134, 153
Julian, Emperor, 29, 89, 172, 131, 145, 187
Julianus (two merchants named), 30
Justinian, Emperor, 126, 190
Juvenal, 29, 144
Jzh-jzh, 84

al-Kalbi, ibn, 141
Kan Ying, 43–45
Karter (chief mobedh), 96
Khaldun, ibn, 25
Kushans, 43, 46–47, 91

Laodicea, 20, 28
Lawrence, T.E., 4; quoted, 25
Legions, 127; Bostra, 158; locations in east, 88, 148, 166; make emperors, 21, 162; pay, 99; religion of, 140; slackness of eastern, 166–67; tactics, 84–85; in villages, 25
Leuke Kome, 35, 36, 59
Libanius, 24; on Odenathus, 107, 133; on hermit-brigands, 192
Longinus, Cassius, 3, 6, 113, 121, 129–31, 133, 177
Lucian, 22, 131, 132, 140, 148
Luxury, 31, 38–39

Macrianus, 105–6
Macrinus, Emperor, 90, 98, 143, 162
Maeonius, 108
Maes Titianus, 47
Malalas, John, 11, 17, 101, 158, 177
Male Agrippa, 53, 65
Mandaeans, 95, 141

Mani, 95–97, 135, 139
Manichaeanism, 152–53
Maps, 165–66
Mara bar Serapion, 134
Marcion, 134, 147, 148
Mareades, 102–3, 105
Maternus Cynegius (praetorian prefect of the East), 190
Mavia (queen of Tanukh), 120, 158
Mecca, 62, 158
Meleager of Gadara, 21, 132
Melito of Sardis, 134
Merv, 43, 45, 60, 84, 91
Mesene, 45
Mesopotamia, 19, 21, 44, 83, 87, 91, 189
Michell, Nicholas, quoted, 1, 17, 199
Monks, 190–91
Monsoon, discovery of, 35, 44
Mosaics, syrian, 66–67
Musil, Alois, 12
Myos Hormos (? = Abu Sha'ar), 36

Nabataea(ns), 11, 21, 27, 34, 36–38, 46, 87, 139
Nasor, Vaballath, 77
Nehardea, sacked by Odenathus, 115
Neoplatonism, 132, 145–46
Nero, Emperor, 33
Nicomachus, 131, 167; of Trebizond, 132
Nisibis (Nusaybin), 52, 90, 91, 102, 106, 166, 188–89; James of, 189
Nitocris, 18, 199–20
Nobata, ibn, 114
Nomads, 19, 23, 25–28, 38, 52, 61, 88, 161, 192
Numenius of Apamea, 132

Odenathus, Septimius, 2, 3, 6, 10, 67, 74–75, 76–79, 90, 103, 105–9, 111–12, 115, 118–19, 122–23, 127, 131, 132, 156, 163–64, 167, 179
Odenathus the philosopher, 133
Odenathus the rhetor, 133
Odes of Solomon, 136, 138

Ogeilas, T. Aelius, 61
Ogeilo, 77
Ogeilu, 77, 78, 127
Ogelos, 61
Orientalism, 4, 48
Origen, 134, 150, 153, 185
Orosius, 8, 107; quoted, 97
Ostriches, 9, 144, 172, 178

Palmyra, 3, 91, 105, 115, 151; annexation, date of, 27; architecture, 54, 63, 64–67; art, 3, 13, 66–67; Aurelian's campaigns against, 165–77, 179; climate, 130; clothing, 75–76; dedicatory inscriptions, 59–64, 76; excavations at, 12–13; growth of, 51–76; income of, 56–57; institutions, 53–54, 77; language, 2, 11–12; legends of, 17; location, 18; merchants, 31, 38, 45, 59–63, 161; and nomads, 27; population, 53, 68, 77; portraits, 69–70; rediscovery, 193–95; religion, 29, 140; in ruins, 188–93; tariff inscription, 52, 56, 57–59; tombs, 52, 68; trade and trade routes, 19, 38, 47, 82; trades at, 54; tribes, 52, 67–68; troops, 27, 28, 171
Pan Ch'ao, 43
Parthia (Parthians), 19, 43–44, 68, 82, 83–87, 88, 89–90, 104, 136, 166
Pastoralism, 19
Patronage, 24
Paul of Samosata, 66, 147, 148–51
Paul, St., 9, 71, 95, 141
Peasants, 23–25
Periplus Maris Erythraei, 37
Persia (Persians), 1, 28, 100, 126, 188; archers, 173; army, 91–92, 102–3, 106–7; Aurelian in, 164; empire, 19, 82, 90–95, 98; hunting, 113; Sassanid dynasty, 79, 90
Persian Gulf, 44
Pertinax, Emperor, 162
Pescennius Niger, 162

Petra, 21, 35, 37, 158
Philadelphia (Amman), 38
Philippopolis (Shahba), 100, 141
Philippus Arabus, Emperor, 93,
  100–101, 141, 162
Philo of Alexandria, 114, 145
Philo of Byblos, 133
Philodemus of Gadara, 21, 132
Philostratus, 131
Phoenicians, 18
Plato, 129, 130
Pliny the Elder, 39, 87; on date of
  annexation of Palmyra, 27; on
  luxury, 31; on Palmyra's fertility,
  56; on spice trade (quoted), 37
Plotinus, 130
Polis, 20, 21, 53
Polybius (quoted), 64
Pompey the Great, 20
Poppaea, 33
Porphyry, 130, 133
Posidonius of Apamea, 22, 139, 145
Postumus (Gallic Emperor), 107,
  160, 164
Probus, Emperor, 159, 165, 188
Probus, Tenagino, 2, 158–59
Procopius, 2, 78; on city of Zeno-
  bia, 125–26; on ruins of Palmyra,
  190
Property, 24

Qaleh-e-Yazdegerd, 43
Qaryat al-Fau, 38
Qaryatein, 17
Qasir, 157
Qasr al-Hair al-Gharbi, 17, 53
Qasr al-Hair ash-Sharqi, 17
Queens, Arab. See Arabia (Arabs)
Queens, Greek, 120
Queens, Israelite, 120
Quietus, 105
Qur'an, 65, 146

Rabbula, bishop of Edessa, 136
Raphia, battle of, 52
Raqqa, 47
Ras Shamra. See Ugarit

Ras tadmor, 78, 117
Red Sea, 35, 44, 47
Renan, Ernest, 22, 146, 148
Rivers: Danube, 81, 87, 98, 155,
  163–64; Euphrates, 19, 24, 44,
  45–46, 52, 53, 76, 81–82, 84, 87,
  88, 89, 103, 106, 112, 119, 139,
  156, 172, 177; Ganges, 46; Indus,
  45–46; Nile, 152; Orontes, 19,
  170, 171; Rhine, 81, 87, 98;
  Tigris, 88, 91, 95, 152, 188–89
Roads, roman, 27, 47, 66, 82, 87,
  89, 166
Roman Empire, 1, 81, 90; third-century crisis of, 97–100
Rome, 1, 100, 129, 130, 143–45,
  150, 161, 162, 181–83; sun-cult at,
  183–87
Rufinus, Q. Aradaius or Cocceius,
  108

Sabians, 114, 141
Sabinus, Aurelius (of Porolissus), 30
Saints, stylite, 120
Sallust, 31
Salvian, 30
Samosata, 57, 88, 127, 148, 166
Sampsigeramus of Emesa, 20, 101
Sandarion, 177–78
Seleuceia, 45, 47, 60, 93, 148,
  176
Seleucus Nicator, 20
Seller, Abednego, 7, 11–12
Semiramis, 1, 5, 18, 119, 121, 139
Seneca, 9, 40
Septimius Severus, Emperor, 53, 65,
  89, 98, 121, 143, 161, 162
Shalamallath, Julius Aurelius, 61
Shapur I (Persian emperor), 76, 101,
  102, 106, 107, 166, 185; con-
  quests, 93; at Dura, 104–5;
  inscription at Naqsh-e-Rustam, 93,
  95; policy, 95
Shapur II, 189
Sheba, queen of, 17, 32, 120, 147,
  156, 157
Shipping insurance, 63

Shushtar, 94
Sibylline Oracles, 10, 97, 106, 132, 161; quoted, 102–3
Siege warfare, 92, 168, 173–75
Silk and silk route, 39–47
Simeon Stylites (Saint), 120, 191–92
Soados, 60–61
Solomon, King, 17, 64, 104, 192
Spasinou Charax, 45, 52, 61
Spedius Chrysanthus, L., 58
Spice trade, 26, 31–38
Stanhope, Lady Hester, 7, 120, 153, 193–94, 200
Stone Tower, 40, 42
Strabo, 35; quoted, 37, 46
Suetonius, 8
Sun, religion of, 4, 71, 74–75, 101, 131, 138, 140, 152; and Aurelian, 183–87; and Elagabalus, 143–45; in general, 145–46; temple at Rome, 177, 184
Sura, 27, 190
Sykes, Mark (quoted), 56
Symposiarchs, 53, 73, 77
Synodiarchs, 61–63
Syria: emperors from, 162; literature of, 132–38; merchants, 30, 60; modern, 18; Persian conquest of, 93, 102–3; power-broker of Empire, 106; religion in, 138–43, 192; Roman conceptions of, 29–30, 101, 155; Roman province, 18–26, 53

al-Tabari, 11, 90, 156, 189–90
Tacitus, 8, 21, 160–61
Tadmor, 1, 15, 66
Taimarsu, 61
Takht-e-Suleiman, 17
Tanukh, 90, 156–58, 161, 173, 189
Tatian, 138, 148
Tavernier, Jean-Baptiste, 7
Taxation, 20, 23–24, 98–99; of carts and camels, 49; of silk trade, 46; of spice trade, 37–38; at Palmyra, 57
Tax-farming, 58

Temples of Palmyra: Aglibol and Malakbel, 68; Allat, 65, 190; Arsu, 68; Atargatis, 68; Baal-shamin, 52, 63, 65, 68; Bel, 27, 52, 53, 64, 65, 146, 183–84, 189; funerary, 67; Garden of the Gods, 68; Nebo, 65
Tetricus (Gallic emperor), 164, 181–82, 187
Theodosius, 9
Tiberius, Emperor, 27–28, 52
Timagenes, 122, 158
Timolaus (son of Zenobia), 6, 113, 114–15, 121
Tolstoy, Leo (quoted), 26
Toparchies, 23
Trade, 30, 31–50, 59–63, 87, 178
Trading aristocracies, 59–60
Trajan, Emperor, 21, 27, 38, 47, 82, 87–88, 98, 161, 184
Trajan the Elder, 27, 66, 87
Tyana, 102, 167–68
Tyre, 20, 28, 60, 70, 107, 114, 132

Ugarit, 18, 65, 119
Umayyads, 17
Umm el-Jimal (Thainatha), 156, 158
Uranius Antoninus, 101–2
Urbanization, 19, 24. *See also* Polis; Cities

Vaballathus. *See* Wahballath
Vahram I (Persian emperor), 96–7
Valerian, Emperor, 93–94, 97, 98, 101, 102, 105, 107, 141
Valle, Pietro della, 7
Varro, 33
Vegetius, 165, 168
Vergil, quoted, 123
Verus, L., Emperor, 28, 104, 166
Vespasian, 21, 27, 28, 87, 146, 162
Victoria (Gallic empress), 121, 160–61, 164, 181
Victoria (queen of England), 6
Villages, 23–24
Vitruvius, 54, 64
Volney, Count C.F.C. de, 13

Vologesias, 45, 60, 61
Vopiscus, Flavius (bogus historian), 9
Vorodes, Septimius (Worod), 62, 77, 78–79, 105, 117, 122

Wahballath, 2, 75, 108, 112, 114–15, 117–18, 121, 124, 159, 165
Ware, William, 51, 123, 131, 161, 199; quoted, 124, 174–75
"weak periphery," 85
Weber, Max, 25
Wood, Robert, 7, 193–94, 198
Worod. See Vorodes
Wright, William, 14, 127, 199; quoted, 7, 15, 56, 66, 69

Yaddai, 61

Zabbai (general), 118, 122
Zabda(s) (general), 118, 122, 155, 158, 170, 177
Zabdas (bishop of Jerusalem), 133
Zabdibel, 52
Zabdilas. See Zenobios, Julius Aurelius
Zalabiye, 125–26

Zebba (= Zenobia), 114, 156–58
Zebeida, Julius Aurelius, 61
Zenobia (queen of Palmyra), 1, 7, 8, 51, 75, 107–9; account of, 111–27; aims, 160–63; Arab legends, 11, 156–58; army, 127; in Asia Minor, 159; and Aurelian, 4; buildings, 125; campaigns, 158–60; court, 121–23, 129, 132, 133; Greek descent, 27, 112; Judaizing?, 71, 114, 150, 151–52; letters to Aurelian, 10, 132, 175–76; modern reception of, 197–200; palace of, 67, 124, 125; parentage, 2; at Rome, 181, 183; sons, 78, 114–15; at Tibur, 187–89
Zenobia, city of (Halabiye), 11, 125–27
Zenobios, Julius Aurelius, 2, 77; others, 133
Zeugma, 57, 83, 88, 126, 166, 190
Zonaras, 10, 108
Zoroastrianism, 96, 139
Zosimus, 8, 121, 153, 171, 172, 176, 183–84; quoted, 158–59, 169–70

PLATES

1. Palmyra, general view from Qala'at ibn Ma'an

2. Tetrapylon, Palmyra

3. The Theater, Palmyra

4. Shops lining the main street. Qala'at ibn Ma'an is in the distance.

5. The temple of Bel from the Meridien Hotel

6. Zodiac ceiling from the Temple of Bel (from Dawkins and Wood, *The Ruins of Palmyra*)

7. Scale model of the Temple of Bel, Palmyra Museum

8. The Monumental Arch from the east

9. The Monumental Arch and Colonnaded Street from the west
   (from Dawkins and Wood, *The Ruins of Palmyra*)

10. The Temple of Baalshamin

11. The Temple of Baalshamin (from Dawkins and Wood, *The Ruins of Palmyra*)

12. Allat as Tyche of Palmyra, Yale University Art Gallery

13. The great gods of Palmyra, Baalshamin flanked by Moon and Sun, Musée du Louvre AO. (Photo © R.M.N.)

14. The god Arsu mounted on a camel, Yale University Art Gallery

15. Sacrifice to the Palmyrene gods, from the Temple of the Palmyrene Gods, Dura-Europus. (Dura Europos collection, Yale University Art Gallery)

16. Palmyrenes with camel, Palmyra Museum

17. Palmyrene merchant with ship, Palmyra Museum

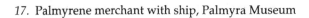

18. One of the tomb towers of Palmyra

19. Palmyrene luxury. Note the brocaded garments. Palmyra Museum

20. (*Above left*) Funerary portrait,
    Palmyra, Royal Ontario Museum

21. (*Above right*) Funerary portrait,
    Palmyra, Palmyra Museum

22. Funerary relief. Instead of a
    portrait, the dead person is veiled.
    Palmyra Museum

23. Zenobia on the Euphrates, fortification walls (dating from the reign of Justinian)

24. Zenobia on the Euphrates, view from the river to the west

a

b

c

25 a–c. Coin Portraits: Zenobia,
Wahballath, and Aurelian

25 d. Zenobia on the currency of modern Syria

26. Zenobia addressing her
troops, by Giambattista
Tiepolo, National Gallery of
Art, Washington, D.C.

27. Zenobia's last look on
Palmyra, by Herbert
Schmalz, Art Gallery of
South Australia, Adelaide

Printed and bound by CPI Group (UK) Ltd, Croydon, CR0 4YY

09/06/2025

14686147-0001